MARK TWAIN
and
WEST POINT

"*Mark Twain and West Point* admirably explores Twain's encounters with West Point, its personnel, and its students. The book is a welcome addition to our knowledge of Twain" (James S. Leonard, editor, *Mark Twain Circular*).

"Whether discussing Mark Twain's unfinished work 'Which Was the Dream?' using the academy as an analytical framework or picturing West Point as Twain saw it, Leon provides fresh, provocative images. This will be a useful addition to libraries of students of West Point's history and students of Twain's work" (Brig. Gen. [Ret.] Harold W. Nelson, former Chief, United States Army Military History).

"Leon's meticulous study of Mark Twain's surprisingly sustained and extensive association with West Point has resulted in a fascinating book that will be extremely useful to literature and history students interested in the crosscurrents of nineteenth-century American culture" (Col. Joseph T. Cox, professor of English, United States Military Academy).

Announcement of Mark Twain's lecture
in the Cadet Mess Hall, 30 April 1887.
SOURCE: USMA Archives

MARK TWAIN
and
WEST POINT

Philip W. Leon

ECW PRESS

CANADIAN CATALOGUING IN PUBLICATION DATA

Leon, Philip W.
Mark Twain and West Point

Includes bibliographical references and index.
ISBN 1-55022-277-5

1. Twain, Mark, 1835–1910 — Homes and haunts —
New York (State) — West Point.   2. Twain, Mark,
1835–1910 — Criticism and interpretation.
3. United States Military Academy (West Point, N.Y.).
4. United States Military Academy
(West Point, N.Y.) in literature.   1. Title.

PS1334.L46 1996 818'.409 C96-930145-6

This book was made possible by a grant
from The Citadel Development Foundation.

Set in Caslon by ECW Type & Art, Oakville, Ontario.
Printed by Imprimerie Gagné Ltée, Louiseville, Québec.

Distributed in Canada by General Distribution Services,
30 Lesmill Road, Don Mills, Ontario M3B 2T6.

Distributed in the United States by Login Publishers Consortium,
1436 West Randolph Street, Chicago, Illinois, U.S.A. 60607.

Distributed in the United Kingdom by Cardiff Academic Press,
St. Fagans Road, Fairwater, Cardiff CF5 3AE.

Published by ECW PRESS,
2120 Queen Street East, Suite 200,
Toronto, Ontario M4E 1E2.

All I know about military matters
I got from the gentlemen at West Point,
and to them belongs the credit.

Mark Twain

MARK TWAIN, 8 June 1881

This book is dedicated to my son

BRADLEY GRANT LEON

in the happy memory of his years at West Point

And to our other West Point "sons"

CHARLES KRUMWIEDE (Class of 1991)
HAROLD ASKINS (Class of 1992)
JASON SMITH (Class of 1992)

CONTENTS

ILLUSTRATIONS

Preface

Will we ever feel that we have explored or at least located all levels, closets, airshafts, and trapdoors of Mark Twain's personality? "We" know that he visited West Point several times during the 1880s and that somehow the best edition of *[Date, 1601.] Conversation, as it was by the Social Fireside, in the Time of the Tudors* got printed there — whether inappropriately we're not sure. But his coming biographers will have to cope with the fact that, as the wife of one of its superintendents said, Twain was "fascinated" with West Point, visiting it — as Philip W. Leon establishes — ten times from 1876 to 1890. If the Clemens family had not moved abroad, he surely would have gone there still again, because both guest and hosts had completely enjoyed each other.

Actually, "visit" is too flat to cover what happened. Twain usually gave a free performance, stayed two or three days, watched drills and parades avidly, and yarned informally with or, rather, at the cadets. Though Joseph H. Twichell, his minister-crony who had served as a chaplain during the Civil War, reinforced him two or three times, Twain was the chief mover; once he tried to recruit William Dean Howells — who had a Quaker-pacifist back-ground — to come along. We will now read differently some passages in his works. For example, I cannot assume anymore that irony controlled a concluding paragraph in *The Adventures of*

Tom Sawyer: "Judge Thatcher hoped to see Tom a great lawyer or a great soldier some day. He said he meant to look to it that Tom should be admitted to the National military academy and afterwards trained in the best law school in the country, in order that he might be ready for either career or both" (chap. 35). Far more important, how do we match Twain's admiring fascination against the consensus that *Adventures of Huckleberry Finn*, completed right in the middle of that series of jaunts to the United States Military Academy, expressed the deepest, purest essence of Mark Twain: his resistance to any kind of regimentation, his delight in slouching spontaneity, his leveling irreverence?

Because Leon has strong ties to the academy (and to The Citadel), not only could he develop this subject empathetically but he knew exactly where to search; and he got, if needed, special effort from archivists. He has recovered basic letters and reminiscences, some hard to find and others yet unpublished. A literary scholar himself, he aims ultimately toward helping us read Twain. Most obviously, he adds weight to Hank Morgan's founding of his own West Point in *A Connecticut Yankee in King Arthur's Court* and especially to the competitive examinations for cadetship, a live issue — we learn — for the late nineteenth century also. For "Which Was the Dream?" Leon draws many factual parallels between its main character and the military figures with whom Twain interacted over the years. Though Henry James imagined a more sedate observer, Twain qualifies for his person "on whom nothing is lost."

Leon heaps up materiel for foragers from many camps. The literary historian will find useful details on Twain's whereabouts and, more interestingly, on another platoon of acquaintances. Here the standout, on the basis of the entire life story, is not even General Oliver Otis Howard but Charles Erskine Scott Wood, who arranged for the West Point printing of *1601* while improving some minor touches. Once more we can watch how easily or else hungrily Twain made friends among all sectors of society. Still, beneath the solid facts, we start grasping harder for his personhood. Accepting, maybe admiring, him as unfit for military discipline, we have forgiven him for quitting the Marion Rangers in 1861; we shudder to imagine what private disasters he would have inevitably caused himself as a soldier; we grin when Leon judges that he "probably would not have been a proficient cadet." Nevertheless, however combatively informal, Twain found no fault with the ideals or conduct of the people at the academy. More positively, as Leon points out, the first reference to it in his notebooks praises not just the "plenty of ceremony" but the "fortitude taught there." Twenty-three years later, while conceding that the hazing of plebes at West Point could quickly turn cruel, he argued that a fistfight if "conducted in a spirit of fairness, . . . makes boys manly." Overall, Leon convinces me, the culture transacted there appealed to one of Twain's vital selves and fitted somehow into his arsenal of emotions and values.

The most poignant insight here comes from realizing what friendships as well as loyalties Twain had to override when he attacked the behavior of the United States army during the campaign to crush the Filipino nationalists; some of the "boys" who had lionized him at the academy were leading those troops. Psychobiographers will probe into less demonstrable patterns and perhaps unanswerable questions. Just what was the basis of his vicarious pleasure in the conformity that the routine at the academy minutely demanded? Or in its parades, when hundreds of human beings functioned as a unit, displaying their machine-like character that *What Is Man?* later expounded wryly? Were Twain's outings to West Point another kind of escape to late boyhood? Or merely a weekend pass to bachelorhood, a quickie furlough from the predominantly female household in Hartford (except for the one time that wife Olivia went too)?

Leon leaves us plenty to think about or simply to remember. Most vivid if disturbing somehow is the picture of Twain putting on General William Tecumseh Sherman's "uniform coat and hat" to make "incomprehensible" speeches at whistle-stops on the train from Hartford to West Point. Most dominant is the highly characteristic tableau, as drawn in his listeners' reminiscences, of him in the cadets' quarters yarning away, chair tipped back, until or, Twain-like, even past "lights out."

LOUIS J. BUDD

ACKNOWLEDGMENTS

I have profited from the advice and suggestions of many friends and colleagues in the preparation of this book. Thomas A. Tenney, author of *Mark Twain: A Reference Guide* (1977) and editor of the *Mark Twain Journal*, read my manuscript, gave me access to his large personal library of Twainiana, and provided guidance and advice from start to finish. I am indebted to Mark Twain scholar Louis J. Budd of Duke University for writing the preface to this study. Others who read my manuscript and offered valuable suggestions were James S. Leonard, editor of the *Mark Twain Circular* and coeditor with Tenney of *Satire or Evasion? Black Perspectives on Huckleberry Finn* (1992); Lieutenant General Dave R. Palmer, former superintendent at the academy and author of *The River and the Rock* (1969), the seminal history of fortress West Point during the colonial and Revolutionary War era; Brigadier General Harold W. Nelson, formerly the United States Army chief of military history; Colonel Peter L. Stromberg, head of the English department at West Point; and Colonels John A. Calabro and Joseph T. Cox, professors of English.

Jim Zwick, editor of *Mark Twain's Weapons of Satire* (1992), clarified Mark Twain's relationship with the military during the Spanish-American War. Kevin J. Bochynski, a dedicated Mark Twain scholar, provided information derived from a Mark Twain database to which he is a principal contributor. His ability to extract information from electronic texts was indispensable to this study.

At the Mark Twain Project, the vast repository of material at The Bancroft Library, University of California, Berkeley, I wish to thank general editor Robert H. Hirst, associate editor Victor

Fischer, and administrative assistant Brenda J. Bailey for their responses to requests for a variety of materials: photographs, letters, and other archival documents.

At West Point I am grateful to a number of people who directly assisted with my research. Joseph E. Dineen, author of *The Illustrated History of Sports at West Point* (1988) and a friend for many years, provided valuable photographic support. At the West Point Library, Alan C. Aimone, chief of special collections, led me to important eyewitness accounts of Mark Twain's visits by cadets and others. Judith A. Sibley, West Point manuscript librarian, guided me through the manuscripts, especially official orders announcing Twain's visits. At the West Point Archives, James V.T. McEnery, Dorothy Rapp, and Alicia Mauldin, library technicians in the special collections division, helped me to obtain photographs of superintendents, faculty, staff, and cadets whom Mark Twain knew at the academy. Major David Eubanks, one of my best former students and currently an instructor in the Department of English at West Point, researched and found items vital to this study. In the Academy Relations office, Colonel James N. Hawthorne, Colonel Bruce K. Bell, Andrea R. Hamburger, and Nikki Farelli-Barnes facilitated access to many of the resources at West Point. I also want to thank Colonel Pierce A. Rushton Jr., formerly the director of admissions, who gave me the opportunity to live and work where Mark Twain visited a century earlier.

For items concerning a special discussion of Mark Twain's relationship with Cadet Oberlin M. Carter (USMA 1880), I wish to thank Sharen E.-L.S. Wixon, reference librarian, CEL Regional Library, in Savannah, Georgia; Colonel Gordon B. Smith, attorney at law; and Joseph Page, technical librarian of the Savannah District Corps of Engineers.

Two Mark Twain scholars, Barbara Schmidt of Tarleton State University and Kevin MacDonnell, owner of MacDonnell Rare Books, Austin, Texas, were instrumental in my gaining further insight into the famous writer's attempts to exploit his political connections to obtain a cadetship for his nephew.

At The Citadel Debbe Causey of the Daniel Library obtained dozens of books and articles on interlibrary loan and located sources in rare-book rooms and special collections at other libraries. In the English department Robert A. White and Libby Walker offered steadfast encouragement. I am deeply grateful to Vice President for Academic Affairs and Dean of the College R. Clifton Poole and The Citadel Development Foundation for their generous financial support of my research trips to West Point and other sites.

P. W. L.

INTRODUCTION

Mark Twain and West Point are American cultural icons. Best known by unofficial names, "Mark Twain" was the public persona of Samuel Langhorne Clemens (1835–1910), and "West Point" is the popular name for the United States Military Academy, established in 1802 to produce army officers. Some scholars prefer to distinguish between Mark Twain the public figure and Samuel Clemens the private person; likewise, West Point is a military post, one of whose tenant organizations is the United States Military Academy. In the interest of brevity and consistency, I will use the popular names in this study.

In 1876 Mark Twain, already widely known and loved, began his first of at least ten visits to West Point, where he delighted the cadets with stories, jokes, and speeches. On these visits to the academy from his home in Hartford, Connecticut, he met with the cadets in small groups; he also addressed the entire corps, the faculty and staff, and their guests. He was fascinated with West Point and enjoyed the company of the young men and their officers. His stays at the post, sometimes for as long as four days, were, in the eyes of the cadets, as impressive as those of any president, king, or general officer. Cadet diaries, memoirs, and letters home to family attest to his popularity.

Mark Twain's many lecture tours and books such as *The Innocents Abroad* (1869), *Roughing It* (1872), *The Gilded Age* (1873), *Sketches New and Old* (1875), and *The Adventures of Tom Sawyer* (1876) had established his name. During the years 1876–90, when he appeared at West Point, he published works such as *A Tramp Abroad* (1880), *The Prince and the Pauper* (1882), and *Life on the Mississippi* (1883). In 1885 his classic *Adventures of Huckleberry*

Finn cemented his place in American letters. Showing the direct influence of his visits to West Point, *A Connecticut Yankee in King Arthur's Court* appeared in 1889.

While the cadets felt honored to have the famous author and humorist visit them, for his part Mark Twain was impressed with West Point's reputation for producing leaders. During the Civil War, generals such as Ulysses S. Grant, William T. Sherman, Philip H. Sheridan, George C. Meade, Robert E. Lee, Thomas J. "Stonewall" Jackson, Albert Sidney Johnston, Braxton Bragg, and James Longstreet — all West Pointers — led forces as the most important commanders on both sides. The president of the Confederacy, Jefferson Davis, graduated from West Point. Following the Civil War, West Pointers such as Wesley Merritt, Oliver O. Howard, and particularly the flamboyant George Armstrong Custer gained fame in the Plains Indian campaigns. All of these officers were Mark Twain's contemporaries. Another generation would produce John J. Pershing and Peyton C. March, cadets during the years that the humorist was associated with the academy; both of them later became chief of staff of the army.

Drawing upon archival sources — letters, memoirs, diaries, and contemporary newspaper accounts — this book acquaints the general reader with the mutual affection between America's favorite storyteller and the cadets of the nation's premier military academy.

CHAPTER I

"Develop Rapidly into a Manly Man": West Point in the 1880s

I

When Mark Twain began his visits, the academy, in the eight decades since its founding, had become a symbol of the national consciousness and had graduated leaders of distinction, many of whom he knew personally. After his first visit to the beautiful army post on the bluffs high above the Hudson River, Mark Twain took advantage of every opportunity to return. What was the West Point mystique that prompted him to visit there so often and to entertain without charge? When one considers that his books most familiar to a general audience depict energetic boys maturing into a knowledge of the world, and that as a young man his own yearning for adventure took him to the still-untamed West and around the world, and that many of the officers he met at West Point had served dutifully and bravely in the Civil War and in the Plains Indian campaigns, it becomes clear that this institution teaching manly behavior in an atmosphere of academic and physical regimentation would hold vast appeal for Mark Twain.

West Point symbolizes success in chapter 35, the final chapter of *The Adventures of Tom Sawyer* (1876), completed at the time of Mark Twain's first visits to the academy. Judge Thatcher "hoped to see Tom a great lawyer or a great soldier some day. He said he meant to look to it that Tom should be admitted to the National military academy and afterwards trained in the best law school in the country in order that he might be ready for either career or both" (233).

Mark Twain thrived in a masculine world, and visited West Point a century before women gained admission in 1976. In their relatively short tenure, women have distinguished themselves as cadet leaders. Kristin Baker of Virginia was the top-ranking cadet, or first captain, in her class of 1990, and Rebecca E. Marier of Louisiana graduated first in her class academically in 1995. Women now serve at West Point at all levels — cadet, faculty, staff, and tactical officer.

In addition to the all-male student population, a significant difference in West Point in Mark Twain's day was the size of the corps of cadets. The West Point that the writer visited was small by today's standard, three hundred to four hundred cadets then in contrast to four thousand in 1996. By law each congressional district and territory and the District of Columbia could have one cadetship at West Point. Although the admissions process differs significantly today, then, as now, the system assured that the corps of cadets would represent a national cross-section. At that time applicants sent letters directly to the secretary of war at the request of the member of Congress or a delegate. In addition to the ten appointments the president distributed as political favors, a number of "at-large" cadetships drew qualified students from the enlisted ranks and from other colleges.

Mark Twain personally discovered the statutory rigidity of the admissions process at the service academies through his unsuccessful efforts in 1874 to obtain an appointment to the United

States Naval Academy at Annapolis (where students were also called cadets) for his nephew Samuel "Sammy" Erasmus Moffett, son of his sister Pamela. In 1865, when Sammy was five years old, his father died, and Mark Twain assumed an active role in assisting his sister and her two children, relocating them from Missouri to Fredonia, New York. He attempted to gain political favor, widely perceived as the only path to a cadetship. In a letter to his mother and sister in 1874, he says, "I saw Gov. [Marshall] Jewell [of Connecticut] today and he said he was still moving in the matter of Sammy's appointment [to Annapolis] and would stick to it till he got a result of a positive nature one way or the other, but thus far he did not know whether to expect success or defeat" (*Mark Twain's Letters* [ed. Paine] 2: 245). Mark Twain revealed his admiration for the efficacious aspects of a military-academy experience when he told Pamela, "Sammy will develop rapidly into a manly man as soon as he is cast loose from your apron strings. You don't teach him to push ahead and do and dare things for himself, but you do just the reverse" (*Mark Twain's Letters* [ed. Paine] 2: 326). Governor Jewell might have been able to exert political influence on others with the power of appointment, but, as Mark Twain discovered, he could not appoint anyone from his own state of Connecticut and certainly not from the neighboring state of New York.

In August and September of 1874, Mark Twain intensified his efforts on Sammy's behalf by writing three letters to Secretary of War William W. Belknap, asking him to obtain an "at-large" appointment from Secretary of the Navy George M. Robeson, one of the most corrupt officials in the Grant administration (Albion 369). He amassed a fortune in the hundreds of thousands of dollars during his tenure by selling navy contracts (Morison and Commager 70). Mark Twain assured Belknap in a letter on 28 August 1874 that Sammy, though he was not yet fourteen years old, possessed the intelligence to pass the "Naval Examination." When Belknap and Robeson urged Mark Twain to enroll Sammy in a preparatory school to allow for further maturation and to establish a more intensive academic foundation than Sammy had been able to obtain, he agreed to this course of action. Although Sammy never won the appointment, he followed his uncle's path as a newspaperman, acquiring a national reputation writing for the San Francisco *Post*, San Francisco *Examiner*, New York *Journal*, as well as *Collier's Weekly* and other magazines.

Albert Bigelow Paine, Mark Twain's biographer, erred in thinking that the humorist wanted Sammy to go to West Point (*Mark Twain's Letters* 2: 245), an oft-repeated misperception. The letters at the Mark Twain Project clearly state that Annapolis alone was the goal. Mark Twain wrote to Belknap on 5 September 1874 saying that he had written to Secretary of the Navy Robeson seeking a cadetship for Sammy at Annapolis. In another letter to Belknap, on 24 September 1874, he thanked him for his efforts "towards the appointment of my nephew to the Naval School." He himself added to the confusion in 1909 when he inscribed a marginal note about Sammy, who had died less than a year before, in his copy of Charles Eliot Norton's two-volume *Letters of James Russell Lowell* (1893), currently in the possession of rare-book dealer Kevin MacDonnell of Austin, Texas. On 25 March 1870, Lowell wrote to Leslie Stephen, a member of the Pre-Raphaelite Brotherhood in England, that he could not afford to visit Stephen. He lamented, "If I only had a few cadetships to sell!" (Lowell 2: 57). Mark Twain underlined these words, and added the marginalia "Does that explain why the (afterwards disgraced) Belknap, Secretary of War, wouldn't give me a West Point cadetship (of the ten at large) for my nephew Sam Moffett? I never could understand it before" (qtd. in MacDonnell). His memory clouded and his spirits depressed, he had forgotten that his efforts on Sammy's behalf thirty-five years earlier were aimed at a cadetship at Annapolis, not West Point.

Lowell's phrase reflects an editorial, "The Sale of Cadetships," in the *New York Times*, 23 February 1870, a month before his letter to Stephen, one of a series of editorials and news articles charging that "the traffic in West Point cadetships has grown into a settled system" among congressional representatives. The editorial declared that "expulsion from Congress is the only adequate penalty" for those representatives who sold cadetships to finance their election campaigns. The next day, Benjamin Franklin Whittemore, a native of Massachusetts, then a carpetbagger representative from South Carolina, resigned from the House because he was under investigation for his conduct regarding his appointments to West Point and Annapolis (*Biographical Directory* 2045). On 16 March 1870, just about one week before Lowell's letter to Stephen, the House censured Roderick Randum Butler, a representative from Tennessee, who had fought in the Union army as a lieutenant colonel, for corruption in his appointments to West Point (*Biographical Directory* 718–19).

Mark Twain deplored the corruption of congressmen who sold cadetships. In *The Gilded Age* (1873), Colonel Mulberry Sellers satirically educates Washington Hawkins on how Congress "polices" itself: "Next they will try each other for various smaller irregularities, like the sale of appointments to West Point cadetships, and that sort of thing — mere trifling pocket-money enterprises that might better be passed over in silence, perhaps; but then one of our Congresses can never rest easy till it has thoroughly purified itself of all blemishes — that is a thing to be applauded" (202).

In a letter on 27 February 1877 to Belknap's successor as secretary of war, George Washington McCrary (1835–90), Mark Twain expressed outrage over political corruption, but he made no mention of a cadetship for Sammy; that plan had been abandoned by then.

While Mark Twain felt confident in Sammy's ability to pass the entrance examination, as late as 1887 those appointed directly by a congressman did not have to submit to competitive examinations for admission to the service academies ("West Point Cadets"). West Point records reveal that the graduation rate for those selected through competitive examination exceeded that for those who received direct appointments, some of which were clearly tainted by politicization. In the years of Mark Twain's association with West Point, forty-seven percent of those appointed by competitive examinations graduated, while only twenty-five percent of those who received direct appointment completed the course ("West Point Cadets"). Whether or not the great humorist knew about these figures, he would implicitly dramatize the fact that those selected competitively succeeded at a higher rate than the sons of those with wealth and influence in his novel *A Connecticut Yankee in King Arthur's Court* (1889), which we explore more fully in chapter 3.

II

Once a young man gained entrance, he soon discovered that West Point instilled in cadets discipline and a willingness to set aside personal freedoms to promote the good of the corps. The overriding principle of obedience permeated daily life at West Point. The theory held that in learning obedience to one's superiors, one learns how to require and receive it from one's subordinates. This belief manifested itself in a system of swift and sure punishment for various offenses and rewards for deeds performed well.

Punishable offenses could occur in both the military and academic spheres. Most of the professors were also military officers, so the strict system extended into the classroom. Cadets demonstrated their preparation by a daily "recitation," presenting orally the concepts of the lesson, or by solving at the blackboard the math and engineering problems assigned for homework. One of the first superintendents at West Point, Sylvanus Thayer, introduced the recitation method still in practice when Mark Twain visited the classrooms. Impressed with the thoroughness of their preparation, he enjoyed watching the cadets stand before their classmates and professors and, in a confident, clear voice, recite the daily lesson.

The cadets found academic life at West Point demanding. Fourth classmen, or "plebes," studied mathematics, French, history, geography, and ethics for the first half of the year. All plebes studied French during the second half of the year because it was still the primary international language, though English was beginning to supplant it as the language of trade and diplomacy. Third classmen continued the study of mathematics, French, and drawing, while second classmen pursued natural philosophy (which today we call physics), chemistry, mineralogy, geology, and drawing. The first classmen, or seniors, studied civil and military engineering; Spanish; international, constitutional, and military law; and history.

Mark Twain revealed his knowledge of the West Point curriculum in several of his writings. In his story "A Horse's Tale" (1906), Brigadier General Tom Alison receives a letter from his sister-in-law Mercedes: "Please let me write again in Spanish, I cannot trust my English, and I am aware, from what your brother used to say, that army officers educated at the Military Academy of the United States are taught our tongue" (*Complete Short Stories* 526). And in chapter 28 of *Life on the Mississippi* (1874), he reinforces West Point's reputation as an engineering school when he has Uncle Mumford speak of efforts to control the mighty Mississippi River:

> The West Point engineers have not their superiors anywhere; they know all that can be known of their abstruse science; and so, since they conceive they can fetter and handcuff that river and boss him, it is but wisdom for the unscientific man to keep still, lie low, and wait till they do it. . . . Four years at West Point and plenty of books and schooling, will learn a man a good deal, I reckon, but it won't learn him the river. (234–36)

The cadets, of course, spent much more time in the barracks than in the classes. There tactical officers kept constant watch on the young men, who might, from time to time, commit genuinely serious military offenses such as gross breaching of military respect, being absent without leave, being intoxicated, or hazing a plebe. In such cases punishment could include confinement, extra tours (hours marching alone with a rifle), suspension, dismissal, or even a court-martial with imprisonment. Because the rules were so clearly defined, part of a cadet's amusement consisted of devoting some of his energy to bending or breaking them without being caught. When he met with small groups of cadets, Mark Twain encouraged them to recount their escapades and practical jokes at the expense of faculty.

Mark Twain learned from his many stays at the academy that, in a typical day, reveille would be sounded at 6:00 a.m., with attendance required. In a footnote in chapter 5 of "A Horse's Tale," he says, "At West Point the bugle is supposed to be saying:

'I can't get 'em up,
I can't get 'em up,
I can't get 'em up in the morning!'
(*Complete Short Stories* 543).

Those late to morning formation received one demerit; those absent received more depending upon the circumstances. At 6:15 the cadets had "police call" to clean their rooms, followed five minutes later by an inspection in which still more demerits might be distributed.

Following room inspection the corps marched to breakfast at the mess hall. This simple act was fraught with danger for the inattentive cadet; he might be late to breakfast formation — another demerit. At 8:00 a.m. half the corps went to class, and the other half returned to the barracks for study and another room inspection. At the time of Twain's visits, only four companies comprised the corps of cadets, each with its own tactical officer who performed a detailed inspection of the rooms.

Cadets had to be present for these inspections. A cadet officer of the day would enter each room and ask, "All right?" The cadets would signal that they were prepared for inspection by answering briskly, "All right, sir." Those cadets who were absent from morning inspection because they were in class would account for themselves by posting cards on their doors listing their hours of recitation.

The midday meal carried the same dangers as breakfast. After lunch the two halves of the corps would switch, one going to recitation, the other to the barracks for study and room inspection. At 4:00 p.m. the battalion (all four companies) drilled for an hour and then conducted a dress parade, which Mark Twain enjoyed immensely when he visited. At the parades the cadets were expected to present themselves in particularly crisp fashion because visitors often attended.

Following the dress parade cadets went to supper in the mess hall with similar possibilities for demerits as at breakfast and dinner. Returning to the barracks cadets were expected to study and to maintain their military equipment. Both cadet and tactical officers inspected to make sure cadets made no unauthorized visits to others' rooms.

At 10:00 p.m., when a bugler sounded taps, all cadets were supposed to be abed, resting from their day's labors. The tactical officer made still another inspection, going from room to room in his company with a lantern, called a "bull's eye," making sure that all cadets were in. Occasionally a cadet would fabricate a dummy, place it in his bunk to deceive the inspector, and "run it" to Highland Falls, perhaps to the legendary Benny Haven's tavern, for a few drinks. Such foolhardy cadets subjected themselves to severe punishment, because tactical officers often made sweeps of the local establishments looking for uncloistered cadets.

Each cadet was required to submit a written explanation for each offense within twenty-four hours. If his explanation contained any misspellings or grammatical errors, he received still further demerits followed by still more written explanations. An accumulation of demerits resulted in "confinement." When not

WALKING AN EXTRA.

Figure 1. "Walking an Extra."
SOURCE: *Harper's New Monthly Magazine* (July 1887)

otherwise engaged in official tasks, a confined cadet was expected to be in his room; tactical officers maintained rosters of confined cadets and conducted daily checks. Those who violated their confinement might be placed under "arrest," literally under lock and key, released only for official duties.

Mark Twain observed cadets serving the most frequently imposed form of punishment: walking "extra tours of duty." On Saturday afternoon, when his friends who had managed not to get caught had some free time, the hapless cadet with demerits equipped himself with cartridge box, bayonet, and rifle and

SUNDAY MORNING INSPECTION.

Figure 2. "Sunday Morning Inspection."
SOURCE: *Harper's New Monthly Magazine* (July 1887)

"walked an extra" back and forth over the paved area at the barracks (see fig. 1). Two hours of continuous walking constituted one tour. Even while completing this punishment, the cadet was scrutinized by cadet and tactical officers who might assign him demerits for "loitering while walking extra tours of duty," "not walking on space assigned to him," or "talking on tour" (Breter 2). Nor did cadets escape inspections on Sunday. Officers would inspect the rooms before the cadets marched to mandatory religious services (see fig. 2). If the rooms passed inspections, the cadets could finally enjoy the privilege of a few hours of leisure on Sunday afternoon.

Rarely was a cadet dismissed for excessive demerits unless he was simply determined to leave the academy. A credit system reduced the number of demerits so that many cadets completed an academic year without a single demerit recorded against them.

III

Military training involved more than simply "close order drill" and marching. Cadets became familiar with pistols, carbines, Gatling guns, and various types of artillery weapons. Mark Twain enjoyed these drills, and, through correspondence with the incumbent superintendent, he ensured that he would be able to observe the cadets performing them when he visited. The superintendents, who had enjoyed Mark Twain's visits, happily granted his wish. Cadets practiced cavalry drills, charging with drawn sabres in centuries-old fashion. While the cavalry charge seems a quaint relic from an earlier time, in the late 1800s the cavalry was the principal show of force in the western territories and states where Indians occasionally mounted an uprising and escaped from their confinement to reservations. The sight of a cavalry troop charging with swords flashing in the sun psychologically deterred an enemy, often obviating the lethal use of small arms or artillery. A young graduate of West Point, newly commissioned as a second lieutenant, might find himself, within weeks of graduation, leading a platoon of cavalry in hostile territory. Dime novels romanticizing military service in the Wild West notwithstanding, a young officer's death was sometimes unheroic; one of the former cadets who met Mark Twain, Lieutenant Allan R. Jordan (USMA 1879), plagued from his cadet days at West Point with sleepwalking, wandered out of his post one night at Camp Verde, Arizona, in 1882. He was found three days later, killed by Indians (Abbott 48).

Although his masterpiece *Adventures of Huckleberry Finn* (1885), published during the time of his visits to West Point, concludes with Tom Sawyer saying that he and Huck and Jim should "go for howling adventures amongst the Injuns" (404), Mark Twain knew that soldiering out West was no boy's game. Shortly after completing *Huckleberry Finn*, he began "Huck Finn and Tom Sawyer among the Indians," a dramatic story involving a trusting group of whites massacred by Indians, who also kidnap and presumably rape a white girl. But he failed to find an appropriate conceptual and thematic focus for this disturbing work, and never completed it.

Mark Twain knew the American West well, having worked as a reporter in Nevada Territory and having traveled in Nebraska Territory in July 1861 (described in chapters 4–7 of *Roughing It*), where much of "Huck Finn and Tom Sawyer among the Indians" takes place. At West Point Mark Twain associated with officers who had served in the West and in the Civil War, and with bright young cadets who would soon serve in dangerous assignments in the territories, and in Mexico, Cuba, and the Philippines.

Although a realist, Mark Twain saw in West Point an institution surfeited with the romance of youthful energy where young men prepared for the assumption of responsibility and duty. In a letter to Henry Ward Beecher on 11 September 1885, after he had visited West Point frequently, he said, "Regular army men have no concealments about each other; and yet they make their awful statements without shade or color or malice — with a frankness and a child-like naïvety, indeed, which is enchanting — and stupefying. West Point seems to teach them that, among other priceless things not to be got in any other college in this world" (*Mark Twain's Letters* [ed. Paine] 2:459). While Mark Twain admired the discipline and regimentation he saw at West Point, he probably would not have been a proficient cadet. Like author Edgar Allan Poe and artist James McNeill Whistler, former cadets who did not complete their courses of study at West Point, he contributed to American culture through his individual works of creativity, not through a willingness to follow orders in a restricted military setting.

Because of the rigid daily schedule, West Point offered virtually no opportunities for entertainment during the week. Only the dances on Saturday night or the appearances of a famous general or touring head of state of a foreign country interrupted the tedious regimentation. Thus, when Mark Twain made his appearances at West Point, the young men greeted him, as we shall see, warmly and enthusiastically. He could not have hoped for a more receptive and appreciative audience, and, according to the recollections of cadets, he reciprocated by imbuing his performances with verve and an inimitable delivery.

CHAPTER II

"I Do Want to See the Boys at West Point": Mark Twain at West Point

I

"Smoking and Just Rambling Along"

A s early as 1878 Mark Twain had expressed affection for the military academy in his journal: "Institutions to be proud of — West Point & Annapolis — plenty of ceremony — fortitude taught there as in Heidelberg dueling — my enthusiasm & desires are dying out, but I do want to see the boys at West Point. I remember yet how they impressed me at the Centennial [in Philadelphia in 1876]" (*Mark Twain's Notebooks and Journals* 2: 126).

Oberlin M. Carter (USMA 1880; see fig. 3), a brilliant cadet appointed to West Point by President Ulysses S. Grant in 1876, provides the first documentation of Mark Twain's visits. Carter said he met Mark Twain in the late 1870s at West Point and visited

Figure 3. Cadet Oberlin M. Carter (USMA 1880) said
Mark Twain visited West Point at least three times
between 1876 and 1880. Carter, who finished first in his
class, later served five years in federal prison for fraud.
SOURCE: USMA Archives

him at his home in Hartford, Connecticut. In a 1940 article in the *Twainian*, published by the Mark Twain Society of Chicago, Carter said that the humorist visited West Point "at least three times during the period 1876 to 1880" (qtd. in Brownell 2).

Carter said that Mark Twain made no formal speeches on these visits, and no newspaper accounts or other records have been found to contradict him. The cadets in Carter's day knew Mark Twain well. When the class of 1879 published its history in 1884, accounting for its activities during the cadet years and in the five years subsequent to graduation, two members of the class quoted an identical passage by Mark Twain. Writing from Fort Maginnis, Montana Territory, Samuel C. Robertson expressed dismay that his life on the frontier had been dull: "It has, I fancy, pretty much the sameness of Mark Twain's life in his diary on board ship — 'got up, washed, and went to bed, for the first day, and for the rest of the week ditto.'" Curtis M. Townsend, stationed in Petersburg, Virginia, was more apologetic: "The calm and even tenor of my way has not produced anything to write about. It is Mark Twain's diary over again, 'Got up, washed, and went to bed'" (qtd. in Abbott 179, 201). Both former cadets quoted from Mark Twain's efforts as a young boy to keep a journal (*Innocents Abroad* 391), but Robertson incorrectly attributes this record to his shipboard journal.

The fact that two members of the same class would use the same reference to Mark Twain indicates that his writings were known at West Point, and that they likely saw him personally during their cadet years. His writings were not required reading at West Point; indeed, the small amount of literature studied at all could only be found in modern-language classes or in a few courses in the classics. The curriculum emphasized engineering, mathematics, and military tactics.

Oberlin Carter's friend Andrew G. "Beaut" Hammond (USMA 1881) was a neighbor and friend of Mark Twain's. ("Beaut" or "Beauty" was West Point slang for the ugliest man in the class, though in this case the cadets used the term ironically, for

Hammond was a handsome young man; see fig. 4.) Hammond worshipped at the Asylum Hill Congregational Church in Hartford, where Mark Twain's friend and spiritual advisor Joseph Hopkins Twichell (1838–1918) was pastor. Twichell participated with Thomas K. Beecher in the marriage ceremony of Mark Twain and Olivia Langdon Clemens, as well as in the christenings of their children.

Because of his friendship with Hammond, Carter was privileged to see Mark Twain at his home in Hartford. Cadets Carter and Hammond accompanied Mrs. Hammond on a somewhat formal social call to the writer's home. Up to his usual mischief, Mark Twain proposed that the two cadets join him privately in his study away from the conversation of Mrs. Hammond and Mrs. Clemens, but, said Carter, Olivia Clemens squelched the idea by her "stony silence" (qtd. in Brownell 1), imprisoning Mark Twain and the cadets in the parlor for the remainder of the visit.

Mark Twain revelled in the company of cadets, and made it a standing practice to join the young men in the barracks away from their officers. For hours into the night, he would hold forth with jokes and stories, the cadets roaring with laughter. On these occasions the tactical officers obligingly overlooked violations of "lights out" and infractions of noise regulations. At least half or more of a senior class could crowd into an upperclassman's room to hear him because the corps was still quite small. The class of 1881, with whom he became particularly close, had only fifty-three members. Some other senior classes that he visited, 1886 and 1888, graduated seventy-seven and forty-four cadets respectively.

Carter's description of these intimate barracks sessions provides an appropriate beginning to establish the warm tone of Mark Twain's time with the cadets:

He had a sharp eye that seemed to look right through you. We were so young that not many of us were aware that he was a great author and speaker. He cocked his feet on one

Figure 4. Cadet Andrew G. "Beaut" Hammond (USMA 1881),
a neighbor of Mark Twain's in Hartford and a member of the
Rev. Joseph Twichell's congregation, arranged Mark Twain's
appearance at One Hundredth Night festivities in 1881.
SOURCE: USMA Archives

chair and slumped down in the one he sat in, smoking and just rambling along, in a conversational tone. Often his eyes were closed, or half-closed and there would be long pauses in which he seemed to be thinking. The first time we gathered, we thought we were going to hear a rip-roaring orator and were sort of disappointed when he just sat down among us and began to ask us questions about ourselves. Then something that was said would start him off on a story — and from then on we just listened. The stories were good, but no other person I've ever known could tell them as Mr. Clemens did. Only a few of us could sit down, the rest just stood, solid-packed, in that small room. Nobody dared cough or make a sound. Everybody was afraid he might miss a word of those stories that drawled along until, suddenly, like a whip cracking, he would come to the point of his story and we would laugh — real laughter that shakes you in the middle.

Yes, he did use some profanity, but it seemed to come in natural. His stories were all clean fun that concerned people he had met somewhere in this country or abroad. I think he enjoyed talking to us boys as much as we enjoyed having him. He impressed me as being a man's man and we were flattered by having him treat us as men. He certainly did not talk down to us as did many of our officers. No man can talk down to anybody, sitting with his coat off on the edge of a tilted-back chair and drawling what he says as if he were totally unaware of his audience. (qtd. in Brownell 2)

These earliest visits of Mark Twain to West Point formed the basis for a pattern that would continue for thirteen years. He would arrive at the post to great fanfare, usually welcomed personally by the superintendent. Then he would be included in some formal social event such as a parade, a "hop" or dance, or a less formal activity such as billiards with the officers in their dayroom. If he delivered an address, typically in the evening in the cadet mess hall, or dining room, he might share the dais with several speakers such as general officers or politicians. Later that night, after the duty day and all the oratory ended, Mark Twain would find his way to the barracks to hold court in the large room of a senior cadet where, enthroned in a "tilted-back chair," he would regale his loyal subjects with jokes and stories.

II

A One Hundredth Night Celebration

28 February 1881

While no records of Mark Twain's first three visits have been found in West Point's official orders, Oberlin Carter's memory places him at the military academy for informal visits between 1876 and 1880. The first formal visit occurred on 28 February 1881, at the urging of Mark Twain's friend Joseph Twichell on behalf of Cadet Andrew Hammond, president of West Point's literary society that year. Twichell noted in his diary that on this visit Mark Twain "read to them, in the course of the evening, as much as an hour and a half, and produced extreme delight" (Smith and Gibson 1: 356–57).

Fortunately we have the record of Cadet Hammond's efforts to bring Mark Twain to West Point; a series of letters to Mark Twain and Twichell gives us a valuable glimpse into the past and an appreciation of the bond between the writer and West Point (see appendix 3). On 9 January 1881, Hammond told Mark Twain that the cadets "and guests would all be delighted, and consider ourselves most highly favored to listen to remarks from you, so I will simply pray that no circumstances will prevent your being our honored guest and chief deliverer on the evening of Saturday Feb. 19th, and that you will find it in the kindness of your heart to do so."

Following the Civil War, cadet theatricals and entertainments, which had been sporadic since at least 1837, became increasingly elaborate affairs organized by the Dialectic Society. This particular event celebrated the happy fact that only one hundred days remained until graduation, a date for which all first classmen yearned. They would soon receive their commissions as second lieutenants and serve in exotic assignments in the army. The second classmen could look forward to becoming seniors with the attendant privileges of that status. Third classmen eagerly awaited summer furloughs following the end of the academic year. And of course the plebes, fourth classmen, could look forward to being "recognized" and finally accorded some reasonably humane treatment at West Point. The tradition of One Hundredth Night remains strong today, with lavish cadet productions of music, skits, and satires of the ranking officers of the academy.

The plans for the appearance of 19 February having gone awry, Cadet Hammond again wrote to Mark Twain, on 28 January, saying that the change of superintendents from John Schofield to Oliver O. Howard delayed his getting final approval of a fixed date for One Hundredth Night. Even so famous a visitor as Mark Twain had to accommodate himself to the inflexible West Point routine described to him by Cadet Hammond:

> Saturday is our regular meeting day, and Saturday evening is ordinarily our only "off" night, and so I would have to get a special "dispensation" in order to have it any other than Saturday. The 21st — Monday — is exactly one hundred days from June and as the next day will probably be a holiday, Gen. Howard says that we can have the meeting on that day — (21st), and as this is, I believe, usually a minister's "play day," I thought that this would be just about the thing for Mr. Twichell, and sincerely trust it will suit you.

Hammond held out for a day when Twichell would be available, knowing that Mark Twain would more likely come if Twichell could accompany him. He asked the humorist if he thought Twichell could find a substitute for his pulpit: "I am sure we would export our Chaplain, and be glad to do it, tho' we might feel slightly conscience stricken for imposing him on the people of Hartford."

Hammond's persistence paid off. In a letter to Twichell on 16 February 1881, he discussed the final plans for Mark Twain's appearance, telling him that it was "all right for the 28th unless some unforeseen obstacle intervenes, and I sincerely hope that there will not." With typical West Point efficiency, Hammond attended to details of their journey: "If you leave Hartford in the morning you can leave New York about 2 or 3 P.M. (I am not sure of the exact time) and we will meet you at the Dock if possible & I guess Genl. Howard will give us the desired permission." Mark Twain looked forward to this visit, and shared his anticipation with his friend William Dean Howells on 27 February 1881, saying, "I go to West Point with Twichell tomorrow, but shall be back Tuesday or Wednesday" (Smith and Gibson 1: 355).

Mark Twain formed a close association with the class of 1881. One of its members, Cadet Williston Fish (see fig. 6), who finished seventh out of fifty-three, kept extensive notes of his cadet days. The typescript of his "Memories of West Point, 1877–1881," housed in the West Point Archives, confirms that Mark Twain was the featured speaker at the One Hundredth Night celebration in 1881, but when Fish wrote a letter to him in 1900 thanking him for the memory, he mistakenly said, "In the spring of 1880 [sic] you came to West Point, and aided the celebration of our One Hundred Nights to June" (see appendix 3). Fish was confused about the date, as other documents, including his own account, confirm. Parts of Fish's memory correspond with that of Captain Carter, who, of course, having graduated in 1880, would not have been present for Mark Twain's appearance at One Hundredth Night in 1881, and, as we have seen, Carter clearly recalled that Mark Twain offered no formal speeches during Carter's time at West Point.

Figure 5. The old Cadet Mess Hall.
SOURCE: USMA Archives

Figure 6.
Cadet Williston Fish
(USMA 1881) wrote
lengthy letters home
describing Mark
Twain's appearance
at West Point.
SOURCE: USMA Archives

The Cadet Mess Hall (see fig. 5) took on a festive appearance on 28 February 1881, with many flags decorating the platform at the north end. Fish remembered one of the stories that becomes increasingly farcical, about identical twin brothers, Clarence and Eugene. Mark Twain declared that he was Eugene. One day one of the boys tripped and fell into a cistern. Fish quotes Mark Twain: "The other twin screamed, and people came running, and tried to rescue the boy, but they were too late. Somebody exclaimed, 'Poor Clarence!' and everybody took it up and exclaimed, 'Poor Clarence!' But it was all a dreadful mistake. It was Eugene. I was the one that fell in the cistern" ("Memories" 65).

Cadet Hiram Chittenden (USMA 1884) wrote to his mother on 6 March 1881 telling of the success of Mark Twain's reading:

> I think I wrote in my last letter that Mark Twain was expected to give a reading here. Well the reading came off last Mon. night and I wish you could have heard him. The whole audience were kept in a continual uproar of laughter, and all by the quaint and colloquial manner in which Mr. Clemens read.
>
> The next day, Mr. Clemens, Gen. Howard, Rev. Dr. Twichies [sic], and Prof. Bass were in our section room during recitation. (21)

For Cadet Fish and others, the most important part of the humorist's visit occurred the next day when Mark Twain met with some of the first classmen late in the afternoon in Beaut Hammond's room. Fish, like Carter, recalled that Mark Twain's chair was "tilted back against the wall" (66).

Fish said that Mark Twain told the cadets the story "How I Escaped Being Killed in a Duel" from his *Roughing It* lecture of 1871–72, ten years before his visit to the class of 1881. The central character, a newspaper editor, finds himself involved in a duel with a rival editor in Virginia City, Nevada, a rough-and-ready mining town. To practice for the duel, he "borrowed a barn door from a

45

ON "FLIRTATION."

Figure 7. Cadets would stroll along
"Flirtation Walk" with their dates.
SOURCE: *Harper's New Monthly Magazine* (July 1887)

man who was absent" (66). The cadets, having spent considerable time on the rifle and pistol range in marksmanship training, howled with laughter at the idea of someone who could not hit the door of a barn engaging in a duel.

Another story Mark Twain told that evening was about a young man who was "cured" of stammering. Like the dueling story, "Cure for Stammering" is from the *Roughing It* lecture. In his *Autobiography* he says the story of the cure for stammering was

one which I have told some hundreds of times on the platform, and which I was always very fond of, because it worked the audience so hard. It was a stammering man's account of how he got cured of his infirmity — which was accomplished by introducing a whistle into the midst of every word which he found himself unable to finish on account of the obstruction of the stammering. And so his whole account was an absurd mixture of stammering and whistling — which was irresistible to an audience properly keyed up for laughter. (46–47)

Having become acquainted with the social life at West Point, Mark Twain selected "Cure for Stammering," as he did all his stories, to fit his audience. He had seen the cadets flirting with girls at the "hops," or dances, and had seen couples strolling toward "Flirtation Walk," off limits to all but cadets and their dates (see fig. 7). He knew the cadets teased each other with their slang expression "spooney-man," indicating those cadets with reputations for success at wooing young women. And he knew the cadets would enjoy this sketch about an unfortunate stammerer attempting to propose to a beautiful girl.

Fish says that

after Mark's visits we were all trying to tell stories with his drawl and his delays and his inflections. Usually, we tried in vain. But Jim Waters did very well.

47

Mark was a genius as a story teller, and there is something in the telling of a story which is a different thing from the story itself, and additional to it. Mark wrote a short essay on the Art of Telling a Story. He spoke particularly of the *pause* which must be neither too *long* nor too *short*. But how long and how short? There are no mechanical rules and no semesters of study which can turn a man into a genius.

I had read in Mark's books the story of borrowing the barn door of the man who was absent; and I knew the story of the stutterer and the story of the twins. Or I thought I knew them, and found that I did not know them at all. (68–69)

Fish told his family Mark Twain's story as he remembered it. His version, while faithful to the events of the story in appendix 1, does not capture the humorist's delivery:

This young man was very desirous of being cured of stammering because he was in love with a beautiful girl. He felt that his position in society, his wealth and even his personal appearance and general endowments were such as to allow him to indulge in hope. But he stuttered badly, and he feared that with this handicap he could not win the prize. He did not stutter always, but only when he talked.

He heard of a professor who would engage to cure stammering perfectly and radically in 12 lessons. In 12 weekly lessons, from 3 to 4 on Wednesday afternoons. This sounded so definite and business-like and reasonable, that the young man immediately matriculated in the course.

The theory of the professor was that stuttering is the baneful effect of excessive mental concentration on the wish to articulate clearly and consecutively. To relieve this excess of concentration from which all stammerers suffered, the pupils were directed to divert their attention to something else — preferably to *whistling*. With a short release from the excessive concentration on articulation, the nerves, and thereby the muscles would be relaxed, and the stammerer would be enabled to continue his discourse with ease and fluency.

The young man, with the greatest diligence, pursued and completed the entire course, so that he won the unqualified commendation of the professor, and graduated *cum laude*, like a character in an old-fashioned story.

With his parchment in his pocket, to give him confidence, and if need should arise, to exhibit as a certificate of his complete cure, he hastened to the young lady, and addressed to her a discourse he had prepared for the occasion. It is true that in this composition he had avoided those sounds which are the most treacherous and elusive, but much is to be pardoned to a lover.

In this discourse our hero offered the young lady his heart and hand, and revealed to her that it was because of his passion that he had undertaken the course of lessons which had resulted in a complete triumph over his infirmity, and he exhibited his certificate with pride and satisfaction.

In our hero's address to the lady, as repeated by Mark, the youth was constantly interrupted by a threatened lapse into stammering, but at each interruption he took refuge in a long and thoughtful whistle, and in due time continued the address. He spoke and whistled intermittently, so that his action was somewhat like that of a hydraulic pump or of Old Faithful.

The young lady listened to the address courteously and kindly, but at the end she said that although she had the greatest regard for the young man and the most sisterly feeling toward him, and although she had the greatest admiration for his courage, and the highest appreciation of the compliment he had paid, and although she had complete confidence in the certificate and although. . . .

While the girl was talking like this, approaching a refusal, the young man, in alarm, interjected arguments and petitions and expostulations, and in his haste and precipitation lapsed oftener into stuttering and took refuge oftener in whistling, and he even resorted to acrimony — and whistling — and they finally ended their ensemble of two voices and a whistle by the damsel saying: "I cannot answer your arguments logically, but of one thing I am sure: I am never going to marry a wheelbarrow." (66–68)

Mark Twain's "How to Tell a Story," mentioned by Cadet Fish, was not published in its entirety until 1895, so the West Point cadets whom Mark Twain visited would not have known of it, though he had used parts of it in earlier appearances. And it contains two stories that might have offended a West Point audience. First, "The Wounded Soldier," telling of a soldier decapitated in battle, would probably have had little humor for the cadets and their officers, in particular, many of whom had served in combat. Second, "The Golden Arm," a ghost story of a woman with a gold artificial arm, would have been an unforgivably insensitive gaffe because the superintendent, General Howard, had lost an arm in the battle of Fair Oaks during the Civil War.

Years later Mark Twain would be reminded of this 1881 visit when he met an academy graduate in Milan, Italy. In a hotel courtyard, thinking himself finally able to relax in a quiet place where he knew no one, he was approached by a young man: "You won't remember me, Mr. Clemens, but I remember you very well. I was a cadet at West Point when you and Rev. Joseph H. Twichell came there some years ago and talked to us on a Hundredth Night" (qtd. in Twain, *Literary Essays* 145). They spent the next two days in friendly reminiscence as they strolled about Milan.

III

"June Week" Festivities

9–11 June 1881

Mark Twain's fifth visit to West Point occurred three months later, in June 1881. On 8 June, at the twelfth annual reunion of the Society of the Army of the Potomac in Hartford, Mark Twain made a speech using West Point as his central motif. Following the Civil War, fraternal organizations such as this society became popular in both the North and the South. Veterans would gather to relive old times, swap stories, honor their heroes, and see and hear famous orators.

These were the days when audiences would sit for hours hearing speaker after speaker. Veterans' gatherings had several purposes: to entertain, to educate, to foster patriotism, and to increase political and social awareness. Often, as was the case on 8 June 1881, the speeches were in response to various traditional toasts such as to "The United States," to "The Army and Navy," to the city and state where the event was taking place, and inevitably to "The Ladies," for these were the days when veterans' organizations were all male, and the evening's entertainment, accompanied by much cigar smoking and brandy drinking, could lean toward the bawdy without fear of female censure.

Mark Twain responded to a toast, "The Benefits of Judicious Training" (see appendix 1), saying he had visited West Point to discover what a civilian should know about telling a soldier how to fight a war, for "the only wise and true way is for the soldier to fight the battle and the unprejudiced civilian to tell him how to do it. . . ." He continued: ". . . I feel proud to state that in the advice which I am about to give you, as soldiers, I am backed up by the highest military authority in the land, yes, in the world, if an American does say it — West Point!" He sprinkled this humorous speech with advice such as "throw out stragglers to right and left to hold your lines of communication against surprise"; "When you leave a battlefield, always leave it in good order. Remove the wreck and rubbish and tidy up the place"; and "take along plenty of camp followers — the more the better."

Mark Twain's mirthful tribute to West Point was one of two major speeches of the evening. The other, General Sherman's, stood in sharp contrast to that of the humorist. Sherman criticized Jefferson Davis, former president of the Confederacy and an 1828 graduate of West Point, who had recently published *The Rise and Fall of the Confederate Government* (1881), in which he bitterly attacks Sherman's order to set fire to Atlanta. Davis says,

> The history of war records no instance of such barbarous cruelty as that which this order designed to perpetuate. It involved the immediate expulsion from their homes and only means of subsistence of thousands of unoffending women and children, whose husbands and fathers were either in the army, in Northern prisons, or had died in battle. In vain did the Mayor and corporate authorities of Atlanta appeal to Sherman to revoke or modify this inhuman order. (2: 564)

Davis similarly attacks Sherman for the burning of Columbia, South Carolina, a depot for Confederate supplies and equipment: "In infamous disregard not only of the established rules of war, but of the common dictates of humanity, the defenseless city was burned to the ground, after the dwelling-houses had been robbed of everything of value, and their helpless inmates subjected to outrage and insult of a character too base to be described" (2: 627).

In his rebuttal, Sherman derided Davis's memory of the events of the sieges of Atlanta and Columbia: "It was not expected that he would feel kindly to those who awakened him so rudely from his dream of empire; but surely in stating facts beyond the reach of his vision or understanding, he ought to have approximated the truth even as to his enemies" (qtd. in "Army of the Potomac" 945).

He cited documents supporting his contention that his forces escorted hundreds of Atlanta's civilians to safety, generously furnishing five days of rations to the hungry populace. He adamantly denied the torching of Columbia by federal troops: "I saw with my own eyes burning cotton bales which had been set on fire by the Confederate cavalry" (qtd. in "Army of the Potomac" 946).

Juxtaposed with Sherman's speech of verbal charge and countercharge, and with an audience whose feelings about the Civil War could reasonably be expected still to run high, Mark Twain's speech must have been a welcome interlude, alleviating some of the acrimony on both sides.

The next day, 9 June 1881, Mark Twain, Joseph Twichell, General Sherman, Secretary of War Robert Lincoln, son of Abraham Lincoln, and a dozen others left by train for West Point and graduation festivities, known traditionally as June Week.

Apparently the intense emotion of the previous night had abated considerably, and General Sherman and the others in the party of distinguished travelers enjoyed high spirits from the start of the journey. In those days the local citizenry routinely met trains stopping in their small town. Everyone knew when the trains were due, and those not otherwise engaged would gather at the station to see what famous people might be aboard. If well-known travelers were on the train, they would often speak to the crowd from the rear platform. Politicians especially took advantage of being seen by relatively large numbers of people spread over wide geographic areas. The practice, of course, became known as "whistle-stop campaigning."

In a good mood following his lengthy attack on Davis, and on his way to a festive weekend at West Point, Sherman playfully insisted that Mark Twain "work his way" on the free ride to the academy. Mark Twain put on Sherman's uniform coat and hat and launched into an incomprehensible speech at stops along the way. At first the crowds showed uncertainty, but then someone would recognize the humorist, the joke would be revealed, and all would join in the humor. Sherman would speak after Mark Twain had "warmed up" the crowds, who enjoyed having the joke played on them; time permitting, Robert Lincoln occasionally made a speech also.

When the party arrived at West Point, they joined in a whirl of activities on that graduation weekend. First classmen had concluded their final examinations three days before, and were ready to let off steam. On 6 June they were examined in law, gunnery, and optical instruments. Later that day a battalion-skirmish drill delighted the many visitors who had been arriving for several days. That night a "hop" at the West Point Hotel lasted until 10:30 p.m., when the cadets had to return to barracks.

On 8 June, the day Mark Twain spoke in Hartford to the Society of the Army of the Potomac, there had been considerable activity at West Point. Largely to show off their skills, but also to entertain family and other visitors, the cadets conducted a pontoon drill under the direction of Captain Raymond. This exercise started late because the members of the board of visitors, called "planks" by the cadets, were delayed twenty minutes. More spectators arrived, and by 5:10 p.m. some five hundred had gathered to watch the cadets' light-artillery drill. The *Army and Navy Journal* of 11 June 1881 reported that the drill "was very exciting; rapid movements of batteries, horses and men all at the sound of the bugle; quick firing of pieces in the charge and retreat, etc." ("Military Academy"). Later, at 7:45 that night, the mortar practice and bomb firing occurred at the north end of the academy grounds at the siege battery. Shells were thrown from the mortars over Crow's Nest, the highest point overlooking the academy.

The next morning featured an infantry-battalion drill at 8:00 a.m., and in the afternoon a cavalry-battalion drill during which one cadet's horse caused pandemonium by dashing into the crowd, running into a fence, and knocking itself senseless. Its rider, Cadet Emery, was unharmed.

The train carrying Mark Twain and the others arrived at 6:00 that evening at Dutchess Junction on the Hudson River above West Point. From there a special steamer brought them downriver to the academy's South Dock, where General Oliver O. Howard and his staff welcomed them. As the highest-ranking dignitary, Secretary of War Lincoln was personally entertained by Superintendent Howard. General Sherman was attended to by Captain Charles H. Hoyt, and other staff officers saw to the needs of Mark Twain, General and Mrs. Nelson A. Miles, General Stewart Van Vliet (USMA 1840), General J. Tidball, General Horace Porter (USMA 1860), General McMahon, Governor Hobart B. Bigelow, and ex-Governors Marshall Jewell and Richard D. Hubbard of Connecticut.

That night, the alumni dinner took place in Schofield Hall, with sixty-one graduates present, including two ex-Confederate generals, the colorful "Fighting Joe" Wheeler (USMA 1859) and Milo T. Polk (USMA 1852).

When the graduation exercises took place on Friday, 10 June 1881, Mark Twain occupied a seat on the dais with the other dignitaries, including Dr. S.S. Laws, president of the University of Missouri. General Christopher C. Augur delivered the official graduation address, but he was overshadowed by other speakers.

As reported in the *Army and Navy Journal* of 18 June 1881, Secretary of War Lincoln told the graduates that among their many duties "none will be more important than the great task of bringing together the two great frontiers of our country, now advancing from the East and West." And General Sherman, in a quick, nervous manner with clipped speech, reminded the graduates that they should "feel grateful to the nation for educating you and for maintaining you while doing your duty" (qtd. in "Military Academy"). Mark Twain did not deliver a formal speech at the graduation exercises, but, according to this account, he "listened [to the other speakers] with all ears, and at the close gave expression to the general sentiment in his compliment to the readiness and quickness of thought of the speaker" ("Military Academy").

Mark Twain felt particularly close to the class of 1881. He had visited with them informally in the late 1870s, had entertained them at their One Hundredth Night celebration, had spent several days with them in their June Week jubilation, and had shared in their final moments together as a class at their graduation.

IV

A Secret Visit to West Point

February 1882

The sixth visit, a personal trip to see his friend Lieutenant Charles Erskine Scott Wood (USMA 1874), took place in 1882 on an uncertain date in February. Making no speeches, not even calling upon the superintendent, Mark Twain clandestinely made the trip over to West Point from Hartford specifically to enlist Wood as a co-conspirator for the secret printing of his salty Elizabethan burlesque *[Date, 1601.] Conversation, as it was by the Social Fireside, in the Time of the Tudors*, hereafter referred to as *1601*. The scatological language shocks some readers when they first learn about this most unusual tale.

As post adjutant from 28 February to 8 September 1881, Wood grew close to Mark Twain through his duties of arranging for his visits during that time. From 1 July 1881 to 30 August 1882, Wood also served as the librarian for the academy, with the additional duty of supervising the post printing press. Having already earned Mark Twain's trust, Wood readily complied when the writer asked him to do a great favor by printing a piece that, because of its risqué nature, he dared not send to a commercial printer.

The West Point edition was not the first time that *1601* had been printed. Mark Twain wrote the story in 1876 and circulated it among his closest friends. In 1880 Alexander Gunn printed four copies in Cleveland, one of which Mark Twain sent to Wood (MacDonnell). Also, Dean Sage printed a dozen copies in Brooklyn. Pirated editions had appeared sporadically in England and

Japan (Turner 11). But the first "authorized" edition of this racy tale, ironically, is associated with West Point, long considered a center of honorable and courtly behavior.

A series of letters between Wood and Mark Twain reveals their increasingly warm regard for each other, and traces the events leading to the printing of *1601*. (The complete texts of these letters are reprinted in appendix 3.) Wood wrote to Mark Twain on 3 February 1882 inviting him and Twichell to West Point on 22 February. Wood's wife had gone to Baltimore to stay through April, and Wood wanted to gather Mark Twain, Twichell, and some other gentlemen friends, among them a "reconstructed" Kentuckian, Mr. Blackburn; Mr. A.W. Drake, art editor for *Century* magazine; and Mr. Jones, "a young artist lately from Russian & Parisian wilds." Wood told Mark Twain that he planned an elaborate evening of feasting on diamondback terrapins sent by a friend from Norfolk, playing whist, and using up "that Scotch Whiskey you left here."

Mark Twain had to decline the invitation. On 11 February Wood wrote a letter to him expressing his disappointment and telling him that he had "anticipated some medieval rambles with you; for until Prince & Pauper I had no idea you were a student of dead days. Let us hope that our pleasures are only postponed and that all will end well." Wood's comment on "medieval rambles" apparently led Mark Twain to consider approaching Wood about printing *1601*.

Mark Twain's response to Wood of 21 February mentions *1601* specifically: "We bear your proffered hospitality in mind, and propose to take advantage of it as early as we can. Speaking of dead days: Have you seen my *1601*? Did not Gen. Sherman and Gen. Van Vliet have it when I was at the Point? It's [sic] circulation is quietly enlarging: A copy of it has just gone to Japan. I shall get into trouble with it yet before I die."

Mark Twain's letter paved the way for his and Twichell's visit to inspect the West Point printing press and to discuss the project (*1601* 16). By agreeing to become part of this venture, Lieutenant

YESTERNIGHT toke her maieftie ẏ queene a fan
tafie fuch as fhee fometimes hath, & hadde to her
clofet certaine ẏ doe write playes, bookes, & fvch
like, thefe beeing my lord Bacon, his worfhip Sr.
Walter Ralegh, Mr. Ben Jonfon, & ẏ childe Francis Beaumonte, wch beeing but fixteen, hath yet
turned his hãd to ẏ doing of ẏ Lattin mafters into our Englyche tong, with grete difcretion&much
applaus.   Alfo came with thefe ẏ famous Shaxpur.   A righte straunge mixing truly of mighty
bloud with meã, ẏ more in efpecial fyns ẏ queenes
grace was prefent, as likewyfe thefe following, *to
wit:* Ye Ducheffe of Bilgewater, twenty-two yeeres
of age ; ẏ Counteffe of Granby, twenty-fix ; her
doter, ẏ Lady Helen, fifteen ; as alfo thefe two
maides of honor, *to wit :* ẏ Lady Margery Boothy,
fixty-fiue, & ẏ Lady Alice Dilberry, turned feuen-
ty, fhee beeing two yeeres ẏ queenes graces elder.
    I beeing her mai^{ty's} cup-bearer,, hadde no
choyce but to remayne & behold ranke forgotte, &
ẏ high holde conuerfe w^h ẏ low as uppon equal
termes, a grete scandal did ẏ world heare therof.
    In ẏ heat of ẏ talke it befel ẏ one did breake

Figure 8. A specimen page from *1601*, secretly printed
at West Point by Lieutenant Charles Wood (USMA 1874).

Wood placed himself in a precarious position. As late as 31 December 1939, he wrote to Lieutenant Colonel E.E. Farman, then the West Point librarian, saying that, had he been discovered using the government's printing press for Mark Twain's *1601*, "I would have expected to be court-martialed."

Shortly after the February visit, on 3 April 1882, Mark Twain sent a copy of the 1880 edition of *1601* along with a letter asking Wood to "do me the kindness to make any and all corrections that suggest themselves to you." Taking Mark Twain at his word, Wood entered enthusiastically into the project, not only correcting occasional errors but also initiating cosmetic changes in the appearance of the text. Wood recorded his actions:

> When I read it, I felt that the character of it would be carried a little better by a printing which pretended to the eye that it was contemporaneous with the pretended "conversation."
>
> I wrote Mark that for literary effect I thought there should be a species of forgery, though of course there was no effort to actually deceive a scholar. Mark answered that I might do as I liked — that his only object was to secure a number of copies, as the demand for it was becoming burdensome, but he would be very grateful for any interest I brought to the doing.
>
> Well, [Sergeant] Tucker [foreman of the printing shop] and I soaked some handmade linen paper in weak coffee, put it as a wet bundle into a warm room to mildew, dried it to a dampness approved by Tucker and he printed the "copy" on a hand press. I had special punches cut for such Elizabethan abbreviations as the a, e, o, and u, when followed by m or n — and for the (commonly and stupidly pronounced ye).
>
> The only editing I did was as to the spelling and a few old English words introduced. The spelling, if I remember correctly is mine, but the text is exactly as written by Mark.

I wrote asking his view of making the spelling of the period and he was enthusiastic — telling me to do whatever I thought best and he was greatly pleased with the result. (*1601* 17)

Kevin MacDonnell, of Austin, Texas, a dealer in rare books, currently has in his possession two copies of the West Point edition of 1882. In one of them, once owned by Wood, an inserted two-by-four-inch fragment of paper from the 1880 edition contains a note to Wood in Mark Twain's handwriting: "I am sorry it is not cleaner, Colonel, (I mean the paper not the conversation) but it is all I have, except the original manuscript. Yrs truly, S.L.C." This note contradicts the generally accepted knowledge that Mark Twain sent Wood his manuscript and that Wood acted independently in fashioning the West Point edition. The handwritten note shows that the 1880 edition and Wood's West Point edition were both set in Caslon, a common typeface at that time (see fig. 8). Wood did not, as he said, create special type; rather, he "kerned" certain combinations of letters by filing off portions so that they would fit together to affect an Elizabethan appearance (MacDonnell).

As a gesture of appreciation for Wood's assistance with *1601*, Mark Twain sent him a copy of *The Stolen White Elephant, Etc.* (1882), a collection of stories. He had sent Wood a copy of *The Prince and the Pauper* following the February 1881 reading at West Point. Wood replied to him on 14 July 1882 that the collection "is far from being a White Elephant on my hands and I have already very much enjoyed looking over it."

An original West Point edition of *1601* is a much sought-after treasure among rare-book collectors today. Wood might have wished that he had been a bit more prescient and retained additional copies. On 21 March 1900 Mark Twain himself wrote to Wood requesting more: "I greatly need a couple of copies of '1601' to fulfill promises with. Can you help me? I've been out of the humble classic for many years." Unfortunately Wood had no more and could not send any to Mark Twain. Others also sent requests to Wood for copies. On 26 April 1907 Brainard Rorison of New York City wrote to Wood concerning *1601* (which Rorison erroneously calls "1604"), asking for copies that might be in Wood's possession. Wood sent back a brief reply: "Never have turned up. I have no idea where to find a copy. Very sorry. CESW."

Wood told Lieutenant Colonel Farman that when he printed *1601* he ran off sixty copies, sending fifty to Mark Twain and distributing the rest to friends, except for the one copy he kept for himself. Years later he gave his personal copy to his brother James M. Wood, who then "sent it to an unknown editor of a press."

Although his name is not as widely known as those of some of the famous generals who graduated from West Point, Wood takes his place in the history books for his activities as an officer in the Plains Indian campaigns, as a writer of poetry and fiction, and as a political activist in defense of radicals. We can see from a brief look at Wood's interesting life how Mark Twain would make friends with a person of such vitality.

Before becoming the adjutant at West Point, Wood served as General Howard's aide in October 1877, when Chief Joseph of the Nez Percé surrendered rather than face Howard's advancing cavalry. The credit for this victory over the Nez Percé belongs to Mark Twain's old friend Colonel Nelson A. Miles (later the commanding general of the army), who had been Howard's aide during the Civil War. Like other non-West Pointers, Miles had developed a deep mistrust of academy graduates (Johnson 44), and was convinced that Howard would claim the credit for Joseph's surrender when he arrived at Bear Paw Mountain in Montana Territory, where Miles had doggedly pursued the chief and held him in a state of siege. Howard sent two of his Nez Percé scouts to parley with Chief Joseph, and persuaded him to surrender in the face of certain defeat in combat with Miles's troopers (Johnson 205). To his credit Howard allowed Miles to accept Joseph's rifle, with Howard and Wood present.

When Wood published in *Harper's Weekly* what he claimed was a verbatim account of Chief Joseph's dramatic and touching surrender speech, he recast the event to portray Howard as the conqueror, not Miles. Some historians have questioned the authenticity of this published version of Joseph's famous speech (Bingham 17). Wood's literary imagination might have produced the poetically phrased proclamation to further his own and Howard's reputation. Most printed versions omit the first two sentences:

Tell General Howard I know his heart. What he told me before I have it in my heart. I am tired of fighting. Our chiefs are killed; Looking Glass is dead, Ta-Hool-hool-shute is dead. The old men are all dead. It is the young men who say, "Yes" or "No." He who led on the young men is dead. It is cold, and we have no blankets; the little children are freezing to death. My people, some of them, have run away to the hills, and have no blankets, no food. No one knows where they are — perhaps freezing to death. I want to have time to look for my children, and see how many of them I can find. Maybe I shall find them among the dead. Hear me, my chiefs! I am tired; my heart is sick and sad. From where the sun now stands I will fight no more forever. (Wood, "Surrender of Joseph" 906)

Wood, whose skill as an artist enhanced Mark Twain's *1601* text, illustrated his article in *Harper's Weekly* with a sketch of Joseph flanked by Miles and Howard. One of the most literate and cultured officers at West Point years later when Mark Twain visited there, he was a close friend of the talented Weir family, whose history is entwined with that of West Point. Robert Walter Weir (1803–89), a professor of drawing from 1834 to 1876 and a particular favorite of Ulysses S. Grant during his cadet days (McFeely, *Grant* 17), painted the allegorical *Peace and War* above the chancel in the old cadet chapel, now relocated to the post cemetery (Schaff 127). But he is best known outside West Point for his *Embarkation of the Pilgrims* in the rotunda of the Capitol in Washington. Wood became friends with Weir's two sons, the famous impressionist painter J. Alden Weir (1852–1919), and the artist and sculptor John Ferguson Weir (1841–1926), both of whom were born at West Point. Captain Truman Seymour (USMA 1846), one of the heroes of Fort Sumter on the Union side, was Weir's son-in-law.

Wood achieved some fame as a writer of both poetry and fiction. Clearly influenced by Walt Whitman, he published several volumes of poems promulgating themes of love, nature, the hypocrisy of politics, and social injustice. His long work "The Poet in the Desert" pays tribute to Chief Joseph, who "made bloody protest against Perfidy and Power" (Wood, *Collected Poems* 265); he praises the Nez Percé and other tribes as "A poor people who asked nothing but freedom, / Butchered in the dark" (268).

On 31 October 1904, Mark Twain wrote to Wood complimenting him on his poem "A Masque of Love," saying he had read it "with strong pleasure," deeming it "a beautiful poem & wise & deep. What Alp shall you subdue next? You were an able instructor of West Point lads in the science of war; then you took up the law & distinguished yourself in that profession; & now you have proven that you are a poet." He signed this letter "Mark," rather than his usual "S. L. Clemens," an indication of his close friendship with Wood and his recognition of him as a fellow writer.

When Wood resigned from the army in 1884, he became a successful lawyer in Portland, Oregon. He frequently traveled east to argue before the Supreme Court, using the time spent on trains to compose verses. Active in social causes, he spoke out in support of famous figures such as anarchists Nicola Sacco and Bartolomeo Vanzetti, both executed in 1927 following a celebrated trial, and socialist Tom Mooney, convicted of murder for his participation in a San Francisco bombing in 1916. Wood helped to overturn Mooney's death sentence. At the same time that Wood championed these socialist causes, he also served as land agent for Lazard Freres, a New York City banking and investment firm, the embodiment of American-style capitalism. When he concluded negotiations for a wagon-road grant and received a one-million-dollar commission for his efforts, he promptly retired from his law practice, left his wife and six children, and moved to California with his mistress, Sara Bard Field, who had divorced her husband, a minister (Bingham 8–9). One of Wood's daughters, Nan Wood Honeyman, became a congressional representative from Portland and promoted New Deal social issues (Frost 475).

In addition to poetry, Wood wrote fictional pieces, among them *Heavenly Discourse* (1928), a series of satiric conversations taking place in heaven. Some of the conversations were previously published in the magazine *Masses* (Tenney 93). Among the "cast" of these conversations are God, Jesus, St. Peter, Socrates, Confucius, Buddha, Mary Wollstonecraft, Margaret Fuller, and Rabelais. Mark Twain participates in a number of the conversations on topics such as "Freedom," "Censorship," "God on Catholicism and the K.K.K.," "God Advises Peter as to the Church," and "Satan Recovers His Reason."

One of these satires, "God's in His Heaven — All's Wrong with the World," depicts Sacco and Vanzetti appearing at heaven's gate. There Mark Twain, Abraham Lincoln, Daniel Webster, and others express indignation at their seeking admission. God hears their case and finally declares Sacco and Vanzetti not guilty. Wood's writing has been described as "marked by candor, the masculine humor and language of the growing West, and a penetrating knowledge of human nature" (Joughin and Morgan 428).

Mark Twain and Wood's friendship lasted many years. In 1895 in Oregon Wood gave a supper in his honor at the Portland Club, where Mark Twain entertained two dozen leading men of the city with his stories for about two hours (Gribben and Karonovich 12). When Wood died in California in 1944, one month short of his ninety-second birthday, he was the oldest living graduate of West Point (Wood, *Collected Poems* xxii).

V

"Greeted with Tumultuous Applause"

3 April 1886

Following the 1882 visit, Mark Twain did not return to the military academy for four years. We know from a letter to Wood that he wanted to make another visit to West Point two years after the *1601* episode. He wrote to Wood on 24 July 1884, saying, "I tried to get to West Point in June but made a failure of it; so I can't tell you any news from there." But in 1886 he returned on two occasions.

Shortly after the *1601* episode in 1882, though not related to it, Major General Wesley Merritt replaced Oliver O. Howard as superintendent. Merritt wrote to Mark Twain on 17 March 1886 to inquire about his appearing at the academy: "There is a great desire on the part of the Corps of Cadets and the Army people stationed at the Post to have you lecture at West Point. Can you gratify the wish?" Merritt offered Mark Twain several available dates, including 20 or 27 March or 3 April. He closed the letter by saying that "There are many pleasant recollections of a visit you made here some few years since" (appendix 3 contains full-text copies of the Mark Twain–Merritt correspondence).

Mark Twain wrote to Howells on 19 March: "I have nearly about decided to go to West Point & read to the cadets Saturday Apl 3d." He wanted to see his friend Howells, and told him about his upcoming engagements so that he and his family could arrange a visit to Hartford. When Mark Twain responded favorably Merritt replied on 22 March 1886 that he was "delighted that the prospects of your coming are good. You will find many friends and admirers here." Merritt told him on 30 March 1886: "Your note is just received. I am glad you are coming. Mrs. Merritt and I will be delighted to have you and the Rev. Mr. Twitchell [sic] as our guests." Merritt urged him not to worry about arriving late at the superintendent's home: "Our quarters are always open. There are stages at the station for all trains, and you can drive at once to my quarters." Twichell confirmed that he accompanied Mark Twain on this visit; writing in his journal for 2–5 April 1886, Twichell said that Mark Twain "read in the evening in the Mess Hall to the Cadets and general garrison for an hour-and-a-half with as great success as on the occasion of our previous visit" (qtd. in Smith and Gibson 2: 553n). Twichell refers to the last "official" visit, 28 February 1881, not the clandestine visit of 1882.

Post Circular No. 8 (see fig. 9), dated 2 April 1886, reads:

Mr. Samuel L. Clemens (Mark Twain) will deliver a lecture in the Cadet Mess Hall tomorrow (Saturday) evening at 8 o'clock.

The officers, ladies and residents of the post are invited to attend.

By order of Colonel Merritt:

W.C. Brown

1st Lieutenant 1st Cavalry, Adjutant.

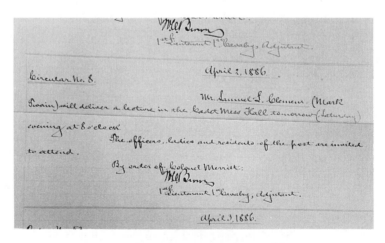

Figure 9. Announcement of Mark Twain's lecture in the Cadet Mess Hall, 3 April 1886.
SOURCE: USMA Archives

Several accounts of this 1886 visit exist. One of West Point's correspondents to the *Army and Navy Journal* (10 April 1886) sent a dispatch dated 7 April 1886:

Everyone on the post who could possibly do so went to the mess hall last Saturday evening to hear Mark Twain. The platform for the speaker was on the side of the hall, and the seats for the listeners were arranged in a semi-circle. The cadets were evidently in good humor, for when the head waiter of the mess went on the platform to arrange the table, he was greeted with tumultuous applause, which caused a number of officers who were in the mess parlor to hurry into the room, thinking that the lecture had begun.

When Mr. Clemens entered the hall at 8 o'clock he was warmly greeted. He was escorted to the platform by Prof. Postlethwaite and Lieut. O.J. Brown. After music the lecturer was introduced and gave a selection from Huckleberry Finn, illustrating Huck's interview with the escaped slave regarding the wisdom of Solomon [chapter 14]. The chapter on German Genders ["The Awful German Language"] was very funny. Meeting an American girl in a foreign restaurant ["An American Party"] and Cure for Stammering were next given. The evening's entertainment was ended with the Jumping Frog. The good hits were all generously and vigorously applauded, and it is safe to say that no lecturer ever had a more appreciative audience. ("West Point")

Cadet Mark Leslie Hersey (USMA 1887) was present and wrote another account of this visit:

He read from *Huckleberry Finn* in the mess hall, and I think not only the entire corps but all the officers and their families were present. Prof. Postlethwaite, our Chaplain, presided, and we never before had seen this dignified Chaplain lose complete control of himself, just as the whole audience did

in its outbursts of laughter that accompanied Mark's readings. He reached the climax when, by request, he told the
story of the "Jumping Frog of Calaveras County." That
inimitable drawl of his has never been duplicated. Of all the
many fine entertainments given during my four cadet years,
both amateur and professional, this reading of Mark Twain's
stands out preeminently the most wonderful of them all.
Literally, my sides were so lame from laughter that I did not
get over the pain of it for several days, and I fancy my
experience was that of most of the others. (6)

Apparently Cadet Hersey was so overcome with prolonged
mirth that he neglected his cadet duties. The 7 April 1886 *Army*

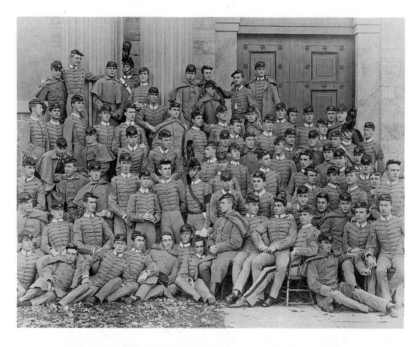

Figure 10. The West Point Class of 1886 heard Mark
Twain speak three times. He entertained the seniors in
Cadet First Captain John J. Pershing's barracks room.
SOURCE: USMA Archives

and *Navy Journal* account of Mark Twain's visit notes that "Cadet Nathaniel F. McClure, of the Second Class, has been appointed a sergeant in the Battalion of Cadets vice Hersey, reduced to the ranks" ("West Point").

This visit of 3 April 1886 is noteworthy for another reason. Charles Swift Riché (USMA 1886) recalled in "A Brief History of the Class" (see fig. 10) that Mark Twain, as usual, visited informally in the barracks after his address in the mess hall. Once again he sat with the cadets and, in Riché's words, "left a most delightful impression" (23). He entertained cadets in the room of a fellow Missourian, Cadet First Captain John J. Pershing (Reeder 32). Pershing (1860–1948) became one of West Point's most famous graduates, a superintendent of the academy, and hero of the war against Pancho Villa. President Theodore Roosevelt was so impressed with Pershing that he promoted him to brigadier general over 862 more senior officers (Reeder 33). He commanded the American Expeditionary Force during World War I, receiving a promotion to the army's highest rank of general of the armies in 1919.

VI

"Just to See a Little More"

5–7 May 1886

Wesley Merritt (see fig. 11) wrote to Mark Twain on 22 April 1886 to thank him for entertaining the cadets and for one of the "pleasantest recollections of our lives." He mentioned in that letter that he expected Mark Twain to return soon: "I hope that your promise to visit West Point in May will not constitute a patch of pavement of a nameless place. I am delighted to say our 'weather' promises to be all that ever you could desire for outdoor work." Mark Twain made good on his promise, once

Figure 11. Major General Wesley Merritt was a
personal friend of Mark Twain's as well as superintendent during three of his visits to West Point.
SOURCE: USMA Archives

again accompanied by Joseph Twichell, visiting West Point 5–7 May 1886. Twichell's journal says, "To West Point with M.T. — just to see a little more of the Academy than we were able to last month" (qtd. in Smith and Gibson 2: 557n). No evidence has been found in archival sources to indicate which stories he might have told, if any. There is evidence from Merritt that he encouraged Mark Twain to visit informally with the cadets, assuring him in a letter of 30 March 1886 that he would "let you do as you please as to hours of 'coming in' and returning. Our quarters are always open." Apparently the cadets wanted to demonstrate their skills in various infantry, artillery, and cavalry drills in Mark Twain's honor. Following the visit, Merritt wrote to Mark Twain on 22 April 1886 thanking him for "the honor we had of entertaining you."

Mark Twain took advantage of this visit to gather background material for his work in progress, *A Connecticut Yankee in King Arthur's Court*.

VII

Mark Twain's "Court-Martial" Offense

29–30 April 1887

Mark Twain next visited West Point less than one year later, on 30 April 1887, fulfilling a promise he had made to General Merritt the year before. Merritt assured him in a letter dated 17 April 1887 that he would be able to see "the artillery drill which was another important specification in your visit." He readily accepted Merritt's invitation to return to West Point to speak in the newly refurbished mess hall (see fig. 12), soon to be officially named Grant Hall in honor of his old friend General Ulysses S. Grant (U.S.M.A. 11: 337), who had died two years earlier.

Figure 12. The new Cadet Mess Hall, named Grant Hall in honor
of Ulysses S. Grant, whose portrait appears on the far wall.
SOURCE: USMA Archives

In the two weeks preceding this visit, Mark Twain was reflecting
on the Civil War, on both his own brief participation in it and the
role played by his friend Grant. In Baltimore on 8 April 1887,
before the twenty-second reunion banquet of the Union Veterans
Association of Maryland, Mark Twain delivered one of his
humorous speeches recounting his military experiences during
the Civil War. Long before, he had begun to exaggerate almost
every aspect of his two-week period of service. Whether he ever
held the rank of second lieutenant in the irregular unit the Marion
Rangers is suspect, and his tale of killing a man in a skirmish is
almost certainly a complete fabrication.

On 27 April, just three days before his return to West Point,
Mark Twain spoke in Hartford at the ninth annual reunion
banquet of the Army and Navy Club of Connecticut. This speech,
"General Grant's English," vigorously took to task the British
author Matthew Arnold, who had criticized some passages of
Grant's *Personal Memoirs*, which Mark Twain had published.

When he arrived at West Point, having recently met with Civil War veterans' groups, he was returning to a place he associated with patriotism, a sense of national history, and the prospect of future American greatness symbolized by the reunion of Northern and Southern cadets in the corps.

On this visit Mrs. Clemens accompanied her husband. The day before his speech in the mess hall, he observed an artillery drill with General Sherman, his younger brother Senator John Sherman, and Dr. Richard Jordan Gatling, the inventor of the machine gun that bears his name.

Mark Twain and Gatling both lived in Hartford, Gatling having moved there in 1870. The Colt Patent Fire Arms Manufacturing Company at Hartford, makers of Gatling's rapid-fire gun, plays a part in *A Connecticut Yankee in King Arthur's Court*; Hank Morgan is the "head superintendent" at the "great Colt arms factory" in Hartford (50).

The *Army and Navy Journal* of 23 May 1887 published an account of the reading in a dispatch from the academy dated 5 May: "On Saturday evening the cadet mess hall was thrown open for the first time since it has received its new and handsome decorations. Exclamations of surprise and pleasure greeted these changes, which are certainly fine. An unusually large and brilliant audience welcomed with a storm of applause the arrival of Mark Twain" ("West Point"). Having learned that the cadets regarded Professor Postlethwaite (see fig. 13) with great affection and that he had a sense of humor, Mark Twain once again used the chaplain as an obliging stage prop:

> He entered the room with Professor Postlethwaite and was escorted to the platform. The reading this time was on the article that appeared in the April "Century" "English as She is Taught" — which aroused simply roars of laughter, but the cream of the fun was in the remark, "There were donkeys in the Theological Seminary" [sic], and his immediately turning round to explain to the chaplain that nothing

Figure 13. Chaplain William M. Postlethwaite, who often appeared with Mark Twain and became an obliging foil for his jokes. Postlethwaite taught law and history at West Point.
SOURCE: USMA Archives

personal was intended, was so indescribably funny that the audience continued to laugh and applaud for fully five minutes.

On Saturday afternoon the corps of cadets was reviewed by Gen. Merritt. Mr. Clemens was invited to accompany the reviewing party. He committed a court-martial offence by forgetting to throw away his cigar before taking his place in line with the staff. ("West Point")

Mark Twain purposely tweaked the authorities by smoking in public, for he knew perfectly well that regulations forbade cadets from smoking. The use of tobacco in any form by cadets had been prohibited since 11 June 1881 (U.S.M.A. 10: 68), the very day after he had been at West Point for graduation exercises for the class of 1881. Permission to smoke tobacco was not returned to cadets until 4 September 1904. He enjoyed this intentional violation of the rules at West Point so much that he repeated the performance at the United States Naval Academy at Annapolis on 9 March 1907 by deliberately smoking in an area where marine guards twice told him to extinguish his cigar (Nolan and Tomlinson 5).

Cadet Charles Dudley Rhodes (USMA 1889), writing to his parents on 8 May 1887, mentioned that, in addition to his cigars, Mark Twain smoked an old corncob pipe. Rhodes wrote that "Mrs. Merritt says he is fascinated with West Point" (n. pag.). Rhodes had written his parents the week before, on 1 May 1887, and discussed this visit in detail:

Mark Twain has been visiting Gen. Merritt the past few days. Mrs. M. is from Hartford, Mark's home. He generally comes up two or three times a year & gives us a free lecture. Last night he lectured in the mess hall on "English As She Is Taught." It was very funny but I didn't enjoy it as much as I would had I not read it in the last *Century*. But then a fellow here is glad to hear anything and hardly any of the fellows had read it. He got off a pretty good "grind" on Prof.

Postlethwaite. The latter introduced Mr. Clemens & occupied a seat on the platform. In the course of his remarks,
Mr. C. gave as an instance in which children were deceived
by the sound of words: "There are many donkeys in the
theological gardens." The cadets clapped & yelled & Prof.
P. got red in proportion & finally got up and bowed. (n. pag.)

VIII

"A Lecture on Aristocracy"

11 January 1890

On 1 November 1889 Mark Twain received an invitation to
appear at West Point during the Christmas-holiday festivities from Colonel John M. Wilson, appointed superintendent
in July 1889. Wilson was "anxious to do something this winter for
the entertainment of the Cadets," he said. The colonel also
reminded Mark Twain that they had met in Washington on
several occasions (see appendix 3). As chief of protocol for
the White House, Wilson knew him from his many visits to
the capital, both at the White House and as a frequent witness
before Congress on copyright law.

Mark Twain accepted immediately. The original plans called
for him to speak on 7 December 1889. Colonel Wilson wrote to
him on 11 November, again extending the hospitality of his
residence and requesting that he telegraph his arrival time so that
Wilson could meet him at South Dock on the Hudson River.
Mark Twain wrote to Wilson and postponed the visit to 14
December. Wilson replied on 22 November: "Your kind note is
fast at hand and it will give us great pleasure to have you with us
at the time you indicate and unless something occurs to prevent
you from coming, we will look for and welcome you on Dec. 14th."
Wilson again pledged to meet him at the dock.

Alas, the scheduled appearance on 14 December was again postponed because Mark Twain became ill. When Mrs. Clemens sent regrets, Superintendent Wilson replied on 12 December: "Mrs. C's letter is just received and I regret that you are ill. I trust that you will soon be yourself once more, and that the pleasure of hearing you address the Cadets will be only temporarily postponed." On 18 December Mark Twain expressed his disappointment to his daughter Susy: "I have been laid up with a cold myself ever since I saw you, and only got out on the street yesterday. Of course I missed my West Point engagement, and it stands postponed for three weeks" (*Susy and Mark* 272).

On 9 January 1890 the *Post Orders*, Circular No. 2 (U.S.M.A. 12: 218), announced:

> Mr. Samuel L. Clemens (Mark Twain) will address the Cadets in Grant Hall on Saturday, the 11th instant, at 7:45 P.M. Officers and their families are cordially invited to attend.
>
> By Order of Colonel Wilson:
> (signed) William C. Brown
> 1st Lieutenant 1st Cavalry, Adjutant

We have Mark Twain's own words to tell us that on this occasion he read passages from *A Connecticut Yankee in King Arthur's Court*, published just two weeks before this visit. On 23 December 1889 he wrote to his friend and mentor William Dean Howells, editor of *Atlantic Monthly*:

> I am going to read to the Cadets at West Point Jan. 11. I go from here to New York the 9th, and up to the Point the 11th. Can't you go with me? It's great fun. I'm going to read the passages in the "Yankee" in which the Yankee's West Point cadets figure — and shall covertly work in a lecture on aristocracy to those boys. I am to be the guest of the Superintendent, but if you will go I will shake him and we

77

will go to the hotel. He is a splendid fellow, and I know him well enough to take that liberty. (Smith and Gibson 2: 625)

We know that he was at work on the book as early as 1884, five years before its publication; this date, significantly, denotes the chronological center of his visits to West Point. In chapter 3 we shall see the extent to which West Point influenced the writing of *A Connecticut Yankee*.

Howells did not share Mark Twain's enthusiasm for West Point. In fact, in his response from Boston on 29 December 1889, Howells denigrates the military academy: "I wish I could go to West Point with you, but I can't, or rather I won't; for I hate to shiver round in the shadow of your big fame, and I guess I hate the sight of a military-factory too, though I'm not sure; I suppose we must have 'em a while yet" (Smith and Gibson 2: 627). At this time Howells was increasingly outspoken about political matters. In the same letter he tells his friend that "there is no longer an American Republic, but an aristocracy-loving oligarchy in place of it." Howells probably viewed West Point as part of the apparatus that sustained the "oligarchy."

Howells's recalcitrance notwithstanding, Mark Twain's letter effectively serves as a summary of his consistently warm relationship with West Point. First, he clearly relished the prospect of this trip to the academy despite his full schedule and recent illness; his visits always elicited the excitement and anticipation he wanted to share with Howells. Second, he knew that this visit would be "great fun" because of his earlier experiences there; the cadets and staff tried, through their parades, hops, and military demonstrations, to entertain Mark Twain as much as he entertained them. Third, the fact that he would be the superintendent's personal house guest indicated that he enjoyed the hospitality usually extended to high-ranking military and government officials; he would doubtless have enjoyed letting Howells "shiver round in the shadow" of his popularity at the academy. Fourth, the letter indicates that he knew his way around the post, and felt comfortable in suggesting that he and Howells could stay at the old West Point Hotel, play billiards, and, perhaps, enjoy some libation. And fifth, he reveals that he had taken the trouble to create an original speech especially for the cadets, whom he had featured favorably in his recently published *A Connecticut Yankee*.

The record of his many visits to the academy at the close of the nineteenth century indicates that, as a literary observer of the social and political scene, he viewed West Point's historic contributions and its promise of future vitality as a positive influence on the evolving idea of American democracy. Mark Twain dissociated his well-known anti-imperialism — his revolt against political interests that often thrust the military into the spotlight as a visible extension of American policy — from his steadfast affection for West Point's unique articulation of a set of values sometimes at variance with the shifting ideologies of the time.

CHAPTER III

"One of My Deepest Secrets Was My West Point": West Point in *A Connecticut Yankee in King Arthur's Court*

I

When Mark Twain visited West Point 5–7 May 1886, he gathered additional material for his novel in progress, *A Connecticut Yankee in King Arthur's Court*. A few months later, on 11 November 1886, Mark Twain read from his manuscript before a meeting of the Military Service Institute at Governor's Island. This gathering served as a test audience for his forthcoming book, in which the military academy symbolizes courtly behavior. He knew that many important graduates of West Point, several of whom he knew well, would be present: General William T. Sherman (USMA 1840), General John M. Schofield (USMA 1853), General James B. Fry (USMA 1847), General William W. Burns (USMA 1847), General William D. Whipple (USMA 1851), General Daniel McClure (USMA 1849), General Oliver L. Shepherd (USMA 1840), Colonel John Hamilton (USMA 1847), and Captain Charles

Morris (USMA 1865). Dozens of other officers, civilians, and ladies attended the reading.

Mark Twain told this distinguished gathering of military professionals that the evening's entertainment would be "a story — a satire if you please — which I began to write some time ago and which is not finished; so what I propose to do under the circumstances is to read the first chapter just as it is and then in brief synopsis or outline tell the rest of it" (*Connecticut Yankee* 507).

When Mark Twain visited West Point on 11 January 1890, he had just published his novel the month before, and read passages from it to the cadets. While West Point and the cadets are by no means the central metaphor for the novel, he clearly intended for West Point to play an important role in representing an egalitarian institution in which merit counts above heredity.

This novel was not well received in England. The British publisher, Chatto and Windus, nervously invested in a book satirizing the Arthurian legends embodying a revered part of English history and literature. Some British readers resented Mark Twain's presuming to impose a nineteenth-century American notion of democratic government upon a nation steeped in a tradition of aristocracy and monarchy.

Hank Morgan, the central character who comes to be known as "The Boss," is a head superintendent at "the great Colt arms factory" in Hartford, Connecticut, Mark Twain's home. There he makes "guns, revolvers, cannon, boilers, engines, all sorts of labor-saving machinery" (50). He fights with a laborer named Hercules, who knocks him unconscious with a crowbar. When he awakens he finds himself magically transported back to sixth-century England, where a court page whom he names Clarence tells him the date is 19 June 528. But Hank refuses to believe that he has arrived somehow in King Arthur's court at Camelot. When he conveniently remembers — this is a burlesque, after all — that an eclipse of the sun occurred on 21 June 528 at three minutes past noon, he decides to humor what appear to him to be the inmates of an insane asylum for forty-eight hours, when the eclipse will or will not occur, thus confirming his whereabouts.

Merlin the magician persuades King Arthur that Hank is a dangerous lunatic who should be imprisoned and burned at the stake. Hank sends word to the king that he will extinguish the sun and that all life in Camelot and everywhere will perish. At the execution ceremony, when the solar eclipse occurs on schedule, everyone hails Hank as a magician superior to Merlin, and King Arthur promotes him to "perpetual minister and executive" with great power in the kingdom (95).

Mark Twain's use of a solar eclipse reflects his fascination with astronomy; he owned a dozen books on the subject. His interest perhaps derived from the fact that, just two weeks prior to his birth in 1835, Halley's comet was at the point nearest the sun in its orbit. With fitting situational irony, the comet was in the same position on 20 April 1910, the day before he died.

Hank brings nineteenth-century technology to King Arthur's England, transforming society with electricity, telephones, telegraphs, trains, steam engines, schools, and Protestantism. A controversial subtheme of the novel concerns the idea that the Roman Catholic Church perpetuated the domination by the aristocracy over the masses. Hank says that any established church eventually grows corrupt and tyrannical. He also creates a West Point to produce professionally trained officers for the army, but in so doing runs afoul of the tradition of hereditary knighthood that permitted only the nobility — no matter how unqualified — to be the officers.

Hank decides that much of his energy should be directed toward dismantling knighthood and chivalry. "Chivalry," in this context, does not mean gentlemanly behavior or courtesy, a tenet of the West Point experience in Mark Twain's day as well as today, when the athletic mascot is the Black Knight, emblematic of the chivalric code; rather, Mark Twain uses chivalry here to mean the archaic notion that one should receive special treatment because of one's hereditary title of king, earl, baron, or knight. American democratic principles in the nineteenth century were being shaped by management-labor disputes; the rise of trade unions on factory assembly lines; agitation by workers in iron, steel, and coal, upon whom industrial advancement depended; and an increasingly volatile national political arena.

In the first mention of West Point, Hank tells us of his clandestine activities as he discovers the nature of living in a monarchy:

> I had been going cautiously all the while. I had had confidential agents trickling through the country some time, whose office was to undermine knighthood by imperceptible degrees, and to gnaw a little at this and that and the other superstition, and so prepare the way gradually for a better order of things. I was turning on my light one candlepower at a time, and meant to continue to do so.
>
> I had scattered some branch schools secretly about the kingdom, and they were doing very well. I meant to work this racket more and more, as time wore on, if nothing occurred to frighten me. One of my deepest secrets was my West Point — my military Academy. I kept that most jealously out of sight; and I did the same with my naval Academy which I had established at a remote seaport. Both were prospering to my satisfaction. (129)

Later, when the king takes Hank's suggestion that a standing army should be formed, Hank is dismayed to find that the old hereditary rules have prevailed, precluding his "better order of things." Hank asks his faithful assistant Clarence:

> "Anything else in the way of news?"
>
> "The King hath begun the raising of the standing army ye suggested to him; one regiment is complete and officered."
>
> "The mischief! I wanted a main hand in that myself. There is only one body of men in the kingdom that are fitted to officer a regular army."

"Yes — and now ye will marvel to know there's not so much as one West Pointer in that regiment."

"What are you talking about? Are you in earnest?"

"It is truly as I have said."

"Why, this makes me uneasy. Who were chosen, and what was the method? Competitive examination?"

"Indeed, I know naught of the method. I but know this — these officers be all of noble family, and are born — what is it you call it? — chuckle-heads."

"There's something wrong, Clarence."

"Comfort yourself, then; for two candidates for a lieutenancy do travel hence with the king — young nobles both — and if you but wait where you are you will hear them questioned."

"That is news to the purpose. I will get one West Pointer in, anyway." (276–77)

The competitive examination becomes an important method for Mark Twain of revealing the hypocrisy of hereditary nobility. When he wrote *A Connecticut Yankee*, some, but not all, candidates were subjected to a competitive examination.

For about the first twenty-five years of West Point's existence, young men applied directly through the president or the secretary of war. Some of the men receiving appointments in those early years were barely literate. Beginning in 1826 the standards became more stringent, both for admission and for continuation. All applicants had to pass a basic reading, writing, and arithmetic test, which allowed them probationary admission. This test measured minimal competencies of those already attending West Point, and could not be considered "competitive" for admission. Then, each January, general examinations were administered to the cadets, just as they were to college students anywhere; those who passed were granted full admittance to the corps, but those who failed were immediately dismissed (Agnew xviii).

Even by 1863, in the middle of the Civil War, the standards had not increased. The only requirements were that a candidate "be able to read and write well, and perform with facility and accuracy the various operations of the four ground rules of Arithmetic, of Reduction, of simple and compound Proportion, and of vulgar and decimal Fractions." He should also be able to "write in a fair and legible hand" (Boynton 266–67).

A congressional nomination was not intended to be an appointment, but members of Congress came to view it as such. On 18 May 1864, twenty-five years before Mark Twain's novel appeared, a spirited debate occurred in the Senate concerning competitive examinations. Some senators wanted to protect their privilege, and insisted that they be allowed to continue to make nominations, tantamount to appointments, of young men from their constituencies without those men having to write a competitive examination (*Centennial Report* 2: 118). This practice of allowing new cadets to come to the academy and remain virtually untested until the first examinations in January was a wasteful tribute to the power of congressmen who could use their nominations for political purposes. In his superintendent's report of 1886, Mark Twain's friend Wesley Merritt emphasized that those who entered the academy through competitive examinations achieved better academic records (Coffman, *Old Army* 271).

Mark Twain's reading from his novel with members of the faculty, staff, and board of visitors present possibly, even probably, brought about a change in the law concerning admission to the academy. A lengthy article in the *New York Times*, discussing the festivities of June Week in 1890 (when the seniors to whom Mark Twain read his recently published novel graduated), described the selection system for admission:

It is provided by law that the corps of cadets shall consist of one from each Congressional district, one from each territory, one from the District of Columbia, and ten from the United States at large. They are appointed by the President, and with the exception of the ten appointed at large they must be actual residents of the districts from which it is claimed they are appointed. The appointments are made one year in advance of the time of admission.

Congressmen have long been permitted to nominate candidates, and this privilege has come to be abused in that many of them appear to think they have the right to make the appointments also. The law is with the President, however, and if he sees fit he may ignore the recommendations of any member. In some Congressional districts, the system of competitive examinations has been inaugurated, and it has proved very successful. By adopting it Congressmen are relieved from embarrassing promises, and the Academy secures a much brighter lot of young men than by the old system. The boy who can distance all competitors in an initial examination is naturally better qualified to win in the subsequent entrance examination imposed by the Academic Board. The present Board of Visitors favors the competitive system. The educational standards for admission requires a knowledge of the elements of English grammar, of descriptive geography, particularly that of the United States, and of the history of the United States. It is likely that the standard which was adopted many years ago will soon be raised to meet the advances science and general learning are constantly making. ("Needs of West Point")

Mark Twain's fictional observations regarding competitive examinations could well have influenced the policy change, for on 1 March 1892 entrance examinations for candidates were held, by order of the secretary of war, at various posts throughout the United States for all young men who desired to enter West Point (*Centennial Report* 2: 145). This idea of holding competitive examinations throughout the country proved so successful that on 2 March 1901 Congress enacted a law stating that "appointees shall be examined, under regulations to be framed by the Secretary of War, before they shall be admitted to the Academy, and shall be required to be well versed in such subjects as he may from time to time prescribe" (*Centennial Report* 1: 228). Although congressmen could still nominate, the academy, through local boards of officers, could insist on academic proficiency. The next year, in 1902, twelve years after the publication of *A Connecticut Yankee*, H. Irving Hancock published *Life at West Point*, in which he discusses the benefits of the competitive examinations then required for entrance:

> It may be that the candidate has not yet passed his examinations for entrance to the Academy. If he has not, he has an ordeal before him that will test his general education to a severe limit. It has been the rule, of late years, for Congressmen to appoint their candidates a year or so before the time of entrance. Candidates so appointed have, as a rule, been ordered before a board of army officers holding its sessions at one of the larger army stations. Upon passing this board, the candidate receives a certificate that admits him to the Academy without further examination. (31)

Mark Twain presciently depicts the board of officers in a critical scene in *A Connecticut Yankee*. When Clarence tells Hank that two noblemen are candidates for a lieutenancy in the new standing army, Hank declares that "I will get one West Pointer in, anyway" (277). He calls the superintendent at the academy on the recently installed telephone line (West Point obtained telephone service in 1887), and he tells him to send a good West Pointer to compete for the lieutenancy.

Chapter 25, entitled "A Competitive Examination," shows the West Pointer competing against the other two candidates, whose sole claim for becoming officers is that they are of noble birth. When Mark Twain told Howells that he would "covertly work in a lecture on aristocracy to those boys" at West Point on 11 January 1890, he probably had in mind Hank's remarks in "A Competitive Examination":

The master minds of all nations, in all ages, have sprung in affluent multitude from the mass of the nation, and from the mass of the nation only — not from its privileged classes; and so, no matter what the nation's intellectual grade was, whether high or low, the bulk of its ability was in the long ranks of its nameless and its poor, and so it never saw the day that it had not the material in abundance whereby to govern itself. Which is to assert an always self-proven fact: that even the best-governed and most free and enlightened monarch is still behind the best condition attainable by its people; and that the same is true of kindred governments of lower grades, all the way down to the lowest. (288)

Mark Twain had met enough cadets over the years to know that many of them came from humble backgrounds, that for every "aristocratic" Robert E. Lee from old Virginia stock the academy admitted a Ulysses S. Grant of the mercantile class of Ohio. In 1902 more than sixty percent of the cadets were sons of laborers, in keeping with the stated aim of many superintendents since Sylvanus Thayer "to create and foster a democratic spirit among the cadets" (Hancock 15).

Hank says King Arthur had disrupted his plans for an army chosen on a meritorious basis:

King Arthur had hurried up the army business altogether beyond my calculations. I had not supposed he would move in the matter while I was away; and so I had not mapped out a scheme for determining the merits of officers; I had only remarked that it would be wise to submit every candidate to a sharp and searching examination; and privately I meant to put together a list of military qualifications that nobody could answer to but my West Pointers. That ought to have been attended to before I left; for the king was so taken with the idea of a standing army that he couldn't wait but must get about it at once, and get up as good a scheme of examination as he could invent out of his own head.

I was impatient to see what this was; and to show, too, how much more admirable was the one which I should display to the Examining Board. I intimated this, gently, to the king, and it fired his curiosity. When the Board was assembled, I followed him in, and behind us came the candidates. One of these candidates was a bright young West Pointer of mine, and with him were a couple of my West Point professors. (288–89)

When the examining board discovers that the West Pointer is the son of a weaver, the chairman ends the interview with "It is sufficient. Get you hence" (289). But Hank appeals to the king to let the professors examine the candidate, because the board, "who were all well-born folk, implored the king to spare them the indignity of examining the weaver's son" (289). Hank says:

I had had a blackboard prepared, and it was put up now, and the circus began. It was beautiful to hear the lad lay out the science of war, and wallow in details of battle and siege, of supply, transportation, mining and countermining, grand tactics, big strategy and little strategy, signal service, infantry, cavalry, artillery, and all about siege-guns, field-guns, Gatling guns, rifled guns, smooth bores, musket practice, revolver practice — and not a solitary word of it all could these catfish make head or tail of, you understand. (289–90)

How close to an actual West Point examination was Mark Twain's fiction? The report of the commandant of cadets, 18 September 1898, just a few years after the publication of *A Connecticut Yankee*, contains this description of cadet military instruction: "The course of practical military instruction embraced . . . tactical and minor tactical exercises of . . . infantry, cavalry, and light artillery; target practice with rifle and revolver, and with field, siege, and seacoast guns" (*Centennial Report* I: 393);

"Launcelot swept in"

Figure 14. Daniel Carter Beard's illustration of Sir Launcelot
arriving to rescue Hank Morgan and King Arthur
in *A Connecticut Yankee in King Arthur's Court.*

"[i]nstruction in machine guns (10–barrel Gatling)" (401); "laying out camps" (402); and "the construction of shelter trenches" (402).

Hank says his West Point cadet acquitted himself so well that "I judged the cake was ours, and by a large majority" (290). But then the examining board interviews two noblemen who can neither read nor write. This burlesque scene reveals that the noblemen clearly have no qualifications to become officers. One nobleman, Sir Pertipole, Baron of Barley Mash, can prove "four generations of noble descent" (292), the founder of his line lifting "himself to the sacred dignity of the British nobility" by building a brewery (294). The other nobleman, when asked about his heritage, says his great-grandmother was "a king's leman [mistress] and did climb to that splendid eminence by her own unholpen merit from the sewer where she was born" (294). The chairman of the examining board, in statements fraught with Twainian satire, heartily responds, "Ah, this, indeed, is true nobility, this is the right and perfect intermixture. The lieutenancy is yours, fair lord. Hold it not in contempt; it is the humble step which will lead to grandeurs more worthy of the splendor of an origin like to thine" (294).

II

For all his opposition to the idea of an aristocracy suppressing a meritocracy, Hank allies himself with King Arthur, whom he regards as benevolent and good hearted. In chapter 38, "Sir Launcelot and Knights to the Rescue," Hank and King Arthur, about to be hanged outside the walls of London, are rescued by Launcelot, Galahad, and "five hundred mailed and belted knights on bicycles!" (425; see fig. 14). Often viewed as merely a humorous entrance in a comic scene, the rescue of Hank and King Arthur by knights astride bicycles instead of steeds might simply fit the pattern of anachronisms that Mark Twain establishes with the other nineteenth-century technological marvels introduced into

Arthurian England. In addition to the contemporary military use of bicycles in Britain, Mark Twain doubtless knew that the United States army seriously experimented with bicycles for infantrymen just at the time he was writing his novel. A manual describing the success of these experiments was published in 1892, and in 1895 his friend Major General Nelson A. Miles, citing the established military use of bicycles by European nations, appointed Second Lieutenant James A. Moss (see fig. 15), who graduated near the bottom of his West Point class in 1894, to organize the first unit: the Twenty-Fifth U.S. Infantry Bicycle Corps (see fig. 16). The Bicycle Corps recorded some impressive achievements, among them a 1,900–mile march from Fort Missoula to St. Louis in forty days (Coffman, *Old Army* 357). In 1898 Lieutenant Moss and the Bicycle Corps served on riot-control duty during the occupation of Cuba, rapidly encircling mobs and, in a show of force, dismounting with military precision. Moss retired as a colonel, having successfully parlayed his experiment with the bicycle as

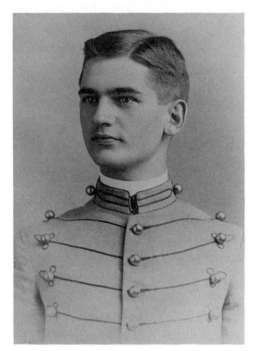

Figure 15.
Cadet James A. Moss
(USMA 1894)
commanded the
Twenty-Fifth U.S.
Infantry Bicycle Corps
in the West.
SOURCE: USMA Archives

Figure 16. Lieutenant James A. Moss leads his bicycle
corps on maneuvers near Fort Missoula, Montana.
SOURCE: Archives/Special Collections,
Mansfield Library, University of Montana

an instrument of war into a favorable reputation as a decisive and
resourceful officer.

Miles could have been one of Mark Twain's models for Hank
Morgan. Always resentful of the advantages West Pointers
enjoyed over nongraduates such as he, Miles was perhaps the
army's most innovative senior officer. Historians today regard him
as one of the most formidable Indian fighters of the western
campaigns. During the Civil War, at age twenty-seven, he had
gained the wartime rank of major general and had received the
Medal of Honor. When the war ended he became a colonel in
the regular army and gained unparalleled fame in the Plains
Indian campaigns. He drove Sitting Bull into Canada, subdued
Crazy Horse at Wolf Mountain, captured Chief Joseph of the
Nez Percé, captured Geronimo in New Mexico, and led the army

against the Sioux in the campaign that concluded with the battle at Wounded Knee.

In addition to his introduction of the bicycle, Miles initiated in 1886 the heliograph system for rapid communication between his troopers during his campaign on the Mexican border against Geronimo. In the same spirit of innovation in which Hank introduces technology to Arthurian England, Miles placed teams of five to eight soldiers on fortified mountain peaks, forming a network stretching for hundreds of miles, each team equipped with a heliostat, an instrument that flashed messages using mirrors (Kruz 88). The movements of the Indians were relayed along the heliograph system almost as fast as the telegraph, frustrating the Indians' attempts to evade the soldiers and to assemble into a body of any appreciable strength. After capturing Geronimo, Miles demonstrated the speed of these "spirit lights" so effectively that Geronimo realized Miles could not be defeated, and he subsequently convinced his ally Natchez, son of the legendary Cochise and hereditary chief of the Chiricahuas, to surrender (Johnson 249).

Mark Twain knew Miles for over thirty years, and liked him so well that he wrote a humorous story ("General Miles and the Dog") about how he swindled Miles out of a dog and three dollars. Miles also endeared himself to Mark Twain when he filed a report in 1902 of military abuses in the Philippines during the war there, a subject of intense interest to the writer as an outspoken anti-imperialist (Twain, *Mark Twain Speaking* 600–02).

Near the end of *A Connecticut Yankee*, when Hank returns from a trip to the Continent, he discovers that all his scientific and social innovations have been overturned by forces opposing King Arthur. Hank and Clarence assemble fifty-two boys from their "various works" (465), including West Point, and construct an elaborate defense against thirty thousand knights under the command of the church in what Hank calls the "last stand of chivalry of England," an inverted allusion to the "last stand" of ill-fated West Pointer George Armstrong Custer and his famously unsuccessful defense against overwhelming odds. This final combat scene shows a slaughter of twenty-five thousand noblemen, electrocuted on wire fences, drowned in moats, and cut down with Gatling guns (486). Some critics have faulted Mark Twain for depicting such a viciously gory battle as an inappropriate conclusion for his satirical novel.

The novel ends when Merlin, in disguise, puts a curse on Hank that induces a coma that will last for thirteen centuries (489). Awakening in his own time, Hank deliriously recalls that "Clarence and I, and a handful of my cadets fought and exterminated the whole chivalry of England!" (492). He dies, summoning his ghostly cadets to one more manning of the battlements (493).

III

The original edition of *A Connecticut Yankee in King Arthur's Court* was profusely illustrated by Daniel Carter Beard (1850–1941), whom Mark Twain selected to illustrate the novel because he was impressed with Beard's work in *Cosmopolitan*. Mark Twain's publishing business needed a best-seller to extricate it from financial difficulty, and Mark Twain wanted the book in the best possible format, including illustrations (Long and LeMaster 112.)

Two of the more intriguing illustrations in the first edition of *A Connecticut Yankee* are Beard's rendition of a dandyish West Point cadet and a title page for chapter 25 depicting the West Point cadet who undergoes the competitive examination. In the first instance, the cadet's androgynous appearance — far removed from the manly image of real West Pointers — has caused some consternation (see fig. 17). The second rendition of a West Pointer, selected as one of sixteen illustrations forming the publisher's publicity announcement, shows a more traditional double-buttoned tunic with high collar (with a "W" and "P" visible). The cadet's left hand is turned palm forward, the correct position of attention for a cadet at that time. An 1891 account in the *New York Times* tells of a new cadet "reporting in" and being accosted by two upperclassmen: "Two of them caught a hand apiece, jerked it down the sides of my legs, pulled the thumbs back, and jammed the little finger of each hand along the seams of my trousers, flattening out the palms full to the front. . . . I was informed that that was the first position of a soldier" ("Plebe at West Point"; see fig. 18).

Mark Twain himself enthusiastically endorsed Beard's conception (Inge 64). In a speech to the Society of Illustrators, 22 December 1905, he discussed how Beard's drawings complemented his ideas in the novel:

> Now, Beard got everything that I put into that book and a little more besides. Those pictures of Beard's in that book — oh, from the first page to the last is one vast sardonic laugh at the trivialities, the servilities of our poor human race, and also at the professions and the insolence of priestcraft and kingcraft — those creatures that make slaves of themselves and have not the manliness to shake it off. Beard put it all in that book. I meant it to be there. I put a lot of it there and Beard put the rest. (*Mark Twain Speaking* 473)

Beard, a socialist, appreciated Mark Twain's theme of exploding the myth of hereditary nobility and "kingcraft." One of the founders of the Boy Scouts of America in 1910, he wrote about twenty books for boys and served as associate editor of *Boys' Life* magazine for many years. As one who devoted himself to an organization of hardy, uniformed, disciplined young men, Beard would not likely have wanted to disparage the values of West Point through his art, nor would Mark Twain, with his well-documented affection for West Point, have allowed him to do so. America's greatest humorist understood that satire usually relies upon reversals and unexpected oppositions; he also understood that Beard's drawings might satirically depict West Pointers not

A WEST POINTER.

Figure 17. Daniel Carter Beard's illustration of a West Pointer for *A Connecticut Yankee in King Arthur's Court.*

Figure 18. Daniel Carter Beard's illustration of a West Point cadet appearing before a competitive examination board for a lieutenancy. Notice the "W" and "P" on the cadet's stand-up collar.

as the robust young men whom Mark Twain met at the academy but as effeminate, dainty adolescents who, through education and resourcefulness, could defeat over twenty-five thousand knights in mortal combat.

While West Point has assumed a place in our culture as an "elite" or "special" place for future military professionals, Mark Twain knew that it drew cadets from every level of society — even more true today than in his time. As a place where energetic and bright young people can thrive in a competitive setting, West Point serves as an essential motif in his complex and ambitious attack upon antidemocratic institutions.

"Four Happy Years of Young Manhood": West Point in "Which Was the Dream?"

I

In chapter 2 we learned of Mark Twain's friendship with Cadet Oberlin M. Carter, who led his class of 1880 academically. As the guest of honor at the January 1940 meeting of the Mark Twain Society of Chicago, Carter reminisced about seeing Mark Twain at West Point and of visiting the humorist at his home in Hartford. A controversial episode in Carter's background adds a further dimension to the relationship of Mark Twain and West Point.

Carter, a tall, handsome officer, appeared destined to ascend to the highest levels of leadership in the army following his graduation from West Point. Posted to Savannah, Georgia, in 1884, he became the chief district engineer there four years later. The upper social circles of the historic port city welcomed Carter and his strikingly beautiful wife, the daughter of a wealthy businessman from New York City.

Following his assignment in Savannah, Carter assumed a highly visible and important position as a military attaché to the Court of St. James's in London, where the attractive couple became the darlings of Mayfair society. But their glamorous life in cosmopolitan London would soon end in disgrace.

Captain Cassius E. Gillette (USMA 1884), who replaced Carter as district engineer in Savannah, brought charges of corruption against his predecessor. Summoned back from London, Carter was convicted at a sensational court-martial for "misappropriation of funds, of bad work, of corrupt practices in letting contracts as well as in gross irregularities of conduct in other matters" ("Case of Capt. Carter").

He had accepted a substantial personal loan from another West Pointer, Benjamin D. Greene (USMA 1866; see fig. 19), a contractor who had influential friends in Savannah's political circles. Carter also became friends with John F. Gaynor, president of the Atlantic Contracting Company. Both of these men were involved with

Figure 19.
Cadet Benjamin D. Greene (USMA 1866) was convicted along with Captain Oberlin M. Carter for defrauding the government in connection with engineering projects in Savannah, Georgia.
SOURCE: USMA Archives

engineering projects (totaling over $3,500,000) for which Carter had responsibility. In 1899 a federal grand jury indicted Greene and Gaynor in Savannah for conspiracy to defraud the government. Fleeing to Canada, they were captured, extradited, and, after lengthy litigation, found guilty in 1906 (Gordon Smith).

Carter's sentence required him "to be dismissed from the service of the United States, to suffer a fine of $5,000, [and] to be confined at hard labor for five years" at the federal prison at Leavenworth (Ooms 27). Mark Twain would have known of Carter's ongoing case and its outcome because of the dozens of articles, often on the front page, in the *New York Times*.

After serving his sentence Carter became a consulting engineer in Chicago, and spent the rest of his life trying unsuccessfully to clear his name with petitions to the military and to the Congress ("Death Ends Fight"). In 1914 West Point dropped his name from the roster of the class of 1880 because of his conviction.

Late in life Mark Twain composed a short story with some parallels to Captain Carter's legal difficulties and to those of French army Captain Alfred Dreyfus (1859–1935), whose controversial conviction by court-martial for treason prompted a vigorous outcry of public indignation. The cases of both officers occurred at the same time and involved protracted efforts to clear their names. Carter's sobriquet was "the American Dreyfus" (Ooms 23).

In "From the 'London Times,' 1904," a science fiction short story published in *Century* magazine in November 1898, Mark Twain, as narrator, sends three dispatches from Chicago (Carter's hometown) to the London *Times*, telling of the unfortunate case of Captain John Clayton, a military attaché with whom he had socialized in Europe. The narrator says, "I had met him at West Point years before, when he was a cadet. It was when General Merritt was superintendent. He had the reputation of being an able officer, and also of being quick-tempered and plain-spoken" (*Science Fiction* 127). There was, coincidentally, a Cadet Clayton in the class of 1886, when Merritt was superintendent, but Bertram T. Clayton later served as a Congressman from Alabama and died in combat in World War I in France, and thus should not be construed as the model for the fictional character ("Col. B.T. Clayton Killed").

Lacking the equanimity of West Pointers in Mark Twain's other fiction and essays, the fictional, hot-headed academy graduate loses his temper and engages in a fistfight with Jan Szczepanik, an actual friend of Mark Twain's who, as a character in this story, invents the telelectroscope, a device similar to a closed-circuit television, which allows a viewer instantaneously to see and hear events from around the world through the telephone wires. Clayton swears it will never prove feasible or practical.

Three years later, in 1901, when the inventor arrives in Chicago, the two men resume their mutual antipathy and quarrel publicly. When Szczepanik disappears and the authorities find a decomposed body beneath Clayton's house, the officer is tried for murder, convicted, and sentenced to death by hanging. But, says Mark Twain, "Clayton swore that he did not commit the murder, and that he had nothing to do with it. . . . He had numerous and powerful friends, and they worked hard to save him, for none of them doubted the truth of his assertion" (129). A former mayor of Savannah said Oberlin Carter's friends there "continued to accept his claims of innocence" (Gamble 34), many of whom were among that city's most prominent citizens (Barber and Gann 68). He received a strong defense from prominent attorney Frank Preston Blair, son of the emissary from Lincoln who offered command of the Union army to Robert E. Lee at the start of the Civil War (Gamble 34).

Like Alfred Dreyfus, Oberlin Carter and the fictional John Clayton were tried twice for the same crime. Dreyfus was found guilty in 1894, but, because of public sentiment espoused by novelist Émile Zola, who exposed gross irregularities in the case through his famous open letter "J'accuse" (Kleeblatt ix), and others who supported his cause, he was retried in 1899 (Friedman 42). Astonishingly, and to the subsequent embarrassment of the

French government, the court reconvicted Dreyfus. His appeals, known as *L'affaire*, dragged on for eight years until he was finally freed in 1906. Dreyfus died in obscurity in 1935.

In the case of Carter, a board of inquiry, tantamount to a trial, first cleared him of all charges, and he left for his glamorous assignment in London in 1897. Having been promoted to captain, and thinking his career was once more assured, he was summoned back in September of that year, with great publicity, to stand trial by a court-martial convened in January 1898. This second trial resulted in his conviction four months later. Relentlessly petitioning officials in Congress and the War Department to review the case and restore his good name, he died in 1944 without having accomplished his goal.

In Mark Twain's short story, Clayton is spared just moments before the hangman is to execute him when Mark Twain, gazing forlornly into the telelectroscope, spots Szczepanik alive and well in Peking, in hiding because of his desire to shun publicity for his invention. When the governor of Illinois halts the execution, Clayton's vindication, like Carter's, seems assured. But then, at a second trial, the United States Supreme Court invokes "French justice," declaring that, while Clayton clearly did not murder Szczepanik, *someone* had been murdered, and, because Clayton had been found guilty in the first trial, he should conveniently be executed according to the original sentence. When an associate justice protests, "But Szczepanik is still alive," the chief justice, named Lemaitre, perhaps after the well-known critic and anti-Dreyfusard Jules Lemaître (Chapman 250), confoundingly responds, "So is Dreyfus" (135).

The story concludes: "Poor Clayton was hanged yesterday. The city is draped in black, and indeed, the like may be said of the State. All America is vocal with scorn of 'French justice,' and of the malignant little soldiers who invented it and inflicted it upon the other Christian lands" (135).

Striking similarities suggest that Mark Twain drew upon both Carter and Dreyfus as models for his fictional Captain Clayton:

the concurrent chronologies of events, the accusations against military attachés, the fact that Mark Twain places in his story a former West Point cadet whom he had known years before, and the attendant publicity of both the Dreyfus and Carter cases.

"From the 'London Times,' 1904" appears to have derived from a mixture of cases known to Mark Twain of actual military figures whose otherwise promising and exemplary lives become stained with dishonor, a theme that he explored earlier in "Which Was the Dream?" (1897), a poignant story to which we now turn.

II

Mark Twain's stories from this period typically portray a successful man who suddenly finds himself in a nightmarish existence. Resembling the classic tragic hero, the narrator, having considered himself lucky or fortunate throughout his life, falls from his high position, his ruin taking the form of financial disgrace or social scandal. His reversal does not come about through his own malfeasance but through betrayal by others whom he trusts. Most of these narrators also resemble Mark Twain himself, who, in the later years of his life, suffered from depression because of a succession of unfortunate events: his personal bankruptcy from his unwise investment in the Paige typesetting machine from 1880 to 1894, with the concomitant failure of his publishing firm, Charles L. Webster and Company; the unexpected death of his favorite child, Susy, in 1896; and the death of his wife in 1904. The central character in these stories wonders whether he has awakened from a dream of happiness into the true world of misery, or whether he finds himself in a nightmare from which he may eventually awaken and return to his former happy state.

"Which Was the Dream?" contains a West Point motif that becomes an important element in the author's portrait of the central character, West Point graduate General Tom X., an amalgam of General Ulysses S. Grant, General John C. Frémont, and Mark Twain himself. Interestingly in this later writing, he resurrects the name Tom, fraught with associations with his innocent and insouciant character Tom Sawyer. Mark Twain originally described General X. as being from Ohio, Grant's home state, but changed the state to Kentucky. General X.'s wife is Alice Sedgewick, "short for Alison" (35), says Tom. Her name recalls Alisande from the dreamlike *A Connecticut Yankee*. (Later, Mark Twain would blend both names in the character General Tom Alison from "A Horse's Tale" [1906].) General X. tells us that he and Alice met as children in a Tom Sawyer–Becky Thatcher–like courtship (31) and pledged their love to each other in a state of innocence. Alice becomes the source of much of General X.'s happiness.

References to happiness and dreams abound in the story. Tom says his boyhood was "followed by four happy years of young manhood, spent at the Military Academy of West Point, whence I was graduated in the summer of 1841, aged 21 years" (38). He says his life began in 1845 with his marriage, a "happiness which made all previous happinesses of little moment.... Our days were a dream, we lived in a world of enchantment" (38). Tom and Alice have two daughters, Bessie and Jessie, with distinctly different personalities.

Soon Tom and Alice come into great fortune through an inheritance from her father's estate, and their poverty disappears "in a night" (39). He goes to war in Mexico as a colonel in command of a regiment, and draws the attention of Generals Winfield Scott and Zachary Taylor, propelling him to the rank of general — "by many years the youngest of that rank in our armies"; thereafter he becomes a senator, "the youngest that was ever elected" (39). Amid all this happiness and good fortune, Tom foreshadows his coming ruin:

> Those were memorable days, marvelous days for us. More than ever we seemed to be living in a world of enchantment.

It all seemed so strange, indeed so splendidly impossible, that these bounties, usually reserved for age, should be actually ours, and we so young; for she was but 22 and I but 28. Every morning one or the other of us laughed and said, "Another day gone, and it isn't a dream *yet!*" For we had the same thought, and it was a natural one: that the night might rob us, some time or other, and we should wake bereaved. (40)

Tom describes Bessie as a poet, "a dreamer," while Jessie has "adventurous ways and manly audacities" (42). Critics generally agree that Bessie represents Mark Twain's favorite daughter, Susy, who died in 1896, one year before Mark Twain wrote the incomplete draft of "Which Was the Dream?" (31). The tone for this story of unexpected loss derives from his grief over Susy's sudden death. Bessie has recurring dreams that she is "being eaten up by bears. It is the main horror of her life" (46). Tom says, "while you are *in* a dream it *isn't* a dream — it is reality, and the bear-bite hurts; hurts in a perfectly real way" (47).

An unnumbered chapter shows Tom, now a senator, about to be plunged into ruin when his palatial home in Washington, DC, catches fire. A burned house was Mark Twain's private metaphor for Susy's death (John Davis 788). The house is crowded with fifty children and thirty mothers who have come to see a play and celebrate Bessie's eighth birthday. Panic ensues among the women and children: "But fortunately, and by a mere chance, there was a man there; and by still happier chance he was a soldier; a soldier of the best sort, the sort that is coolest in circumstances which make other people lose their heads. This was a young man named Grant, who was a third class man at West Point when I was a first" (50–51).

Not to be confused with General X., who was, in part, modeled after Ulysses S. Grant, Lieutenant Grant, nicknamed "Useless," takes command of the situation in a "calm and confident voice," and "in orderly procession the column fell in and filed out like a battalion leaving the field on dress parade" (51). Mark Twain then offers an encomium to West Point:

> But for West Point's presence there, I should be setting down a pathetic tragedy now. Lieutenant Grant had served under me for a while in the beginning of the Mexican war, and lately he had come to Washington on a business visit from his home in the West, and we had renewed our acquaintanceship. I think he had in him the stuff for a General, or certainly a Colonel; I do not know why he achieved no distinction in the war — but then, such things go a good deal by luck and opportunity. (51)

That there exists in the story this character, also a West Pointer, named "Useless" Grant adds to the confusion and creates critical interest in Mark Twain's effort to present characters to whom good or bad fortune falls without warning. While young Lieutenant Grant feels that, "if ever there was a useless man in the world, and one for whom there was plainly no place and no necessity, he was the one" (51), he fortuitously is on hand to take command and become a hero by leading the women and children to safety when the house catches fire. Far from being useless in this scene of panic, "by a mere chance" Lieutenant Grant is the most useful person there, a reversal of his own view of himself. As we have seen, Mark Twain was fascinated with situations involving duality of characters, confusion of genders, changelings, twins, princes exchanging places with paupers, or characters displaced in time through circumstances beyond their control.

While good people sometimes have good or bad fortune, evil characters often set events in motion that affect others. Such a character in this story is Tom's business manager and confidential secretary, Jeff Sedgewick, Alice's cousin, of whom she is not fond. Charles L. Webster, who married Mark Twain's niece, Annie Moffett (Sammy Moffett's sister), influenced Mark Twain's depiction of Sedgewick. Together Mark Twain and Webster formed Charles L. Webster and Company, which published the highly profitable two-volume *Personal Memoirs* (1885–86) of Ulysses S. Grant. But Mark Twain ultimately regarded Webster as stupid and incompetent, blaming him for the subsequent failure and bankruptcy of the firm (Cook). Webster's son, Samuel Charles Webster, refuted Mark Twain's disdain in *Mark Twain, Business Man* (1946), a collection of letters purporting to show Twain's own lack of business acumen.

Jeff, who doubtless set the fire, leaves the house about five minutes before the fire alarm sounds. We learn that he has relieved Tom of the wearisome task of signing official documents by perfecting Tom's signature, so that no one could "tell the genuine signature from the imitation" (53). Tom tells us that he gave Jeff "full power of attorney, quite naturally, and thenceforth I was saved from even the bother of consulting and confirming" (53). Tom trusts Jeff even though Alice warns him that Jeff "will do you an ill turn some day — the worst turn he can invent" because he envies Tom's fame and prosperity (53). Tom allows Jeff to invest his wife's fortune in a California gold mine named, appropriately enough, the "Golden Fleece," for it soon becomes apparent that Jeff has "fleeced" his trusting employer in this mythic venture.

When Jeff does not appear several hours after the fire, Tom has "a vague, indefinable, oppressive sense of impending trouble in the air" (56). His happiness begins to decline almost immediately after the fire when he writes a check for three thousand dollars in gratitude to the engine company for fighting his housefire. The president of the bank calls upon the senator and with great deference tells him his account is overdrawn. The gloom deepens when Tom learns that this bank president has met with other bank presidents and discovered that Tom is "heavily overdrawn all around" (59). General X. tells the bank president that the insurance from the destruction of his house "will far more than pay you gentlemen, and henceforth I shall keep clear of this kind of thing. Even if I owed a million or two I should still be solvent, by grace of my Californian mining venture" (59).

The next chapter takes Tom further into ruination. A delegation of three bank presidents and a Mr. Collins from New York call upon him in his fire-damaged house and inform him that the Golden Fleece mine does not exist and that his house was uninsured. These financial catastrophes stun the incredulous Tom, but another stinging insult to his character follows when Collins, an agent of the insurance company, accuses him of purposely making fraudulent entries in an insurance payment ledger. Collins further informs him that Jeff has sailed "for the other side of the world" (66), thus leaving Tom to answer to these overwhelming charges. In a dramatic moment, when one of the bank presidents accuses him of forgery, the assault upon his honor is more than he can bear, and he falls into a coma lasting eighteen months. Tom's coma, induced by an emotional and psychological blow, functions much like the dreamlike state that Hank Morgan enters as a result of a powerful physical blow to the head delivered by the mythically named worker Hercules in *A Connecticut Yankee*.

The unfinished manuscript closes with a fragment of an unnumbered chapter in which Alison tells Tom that "all our friends stood by her, none of them discarded her; new ones came; and new and old together would have helped her out of their pockets if she would have consented" (72). When Mark Twain experienced financial difficulty, friends such as Henry Huttleston Rogers of the Standard Oil Company advised him and assisted him in reestablishing his credit. Mark Twain similarly stood by his friend Grant and helped to restore his family to economic health through the sale of his *Personal Memoirs*.

When Grant left office at the end of his second term, his final message to Congress admitted that his administration had been plagued with scandal, but he asserted that "Failures have been errors of judgment, not of intent" (qtd. in Hesseltine 417). In a similar voice Mark Twain concludes "Which Was the Dream?" with a tribute both to General X. and to West Point and all that the institution represents: "The officers of the army believed my story, and believed it entirely. They said that a man trained at West

Point might be a fool in business matters, but never a rascal and never a liar; that he was a gentleman, and would remain one" (73).

III

Mark Twain drew upon his long friendship with Ulysses S. Grant and his association with West Point in constructing the fragmentary and disjointed "Which Was the Dream?" We must remember that Mark Twain did not finish the narrative, and that we do not have a seamless story that invites close critical interpretation. Nevertheless, "Which Was the Dream?" belongs in that body of symbolic writings revealing much about the author's state of mind as he reflected upon his professional successes and failures and his personal triumphs and tragedies. In this troubled time he returns to his memories of West Point as a source of constancy and reliability.

Mark Twain's friendship with Grant began in 1870 when the humorist called upon the eighteenth president (1869–77) at the White House. When Mark Twain savagely attacked the government in *The Gilded Age* (1872), he satirized Congress but not the president. On 12 November 1879 the two were together in Chicago for a reunion of the Army of the Tennessee. At Haverly's Theater Mark Twain gave a brief speech at the grand banquet in Grant's honor on 13 November (Gold 157). He was the fifteenth and final speaker of the evening; his speech, a response to the toast "To the Babies," put Grant's significant accomplishments in the context of his childhood, the state of innocence that begins the succession of experiences that can make us great, as with Grant, or merely ordinary. Mark Twain considered this speech one of his finest.

Another historic person informing the character of General X. is General John C. Frémont, the famous explorer and Civil War general who opened up routes to the American West, where six cities are named for him. The Civil War brought Twain, Grant, and Frémont together for a brief moment. At the outbreak of the war, Grant, then a civilian, sought a commission in the Union army; he was rebuffed by Frémont, who refused to see him in his headquarters in St. Louis (Hesseltine 20). Grant, as commanding general of Union forces, would later outrank Frémont. When Grant obtained a colonelcy as commander of the Twenty-First Illinois Volunteer Regiment (McFeely, *Grant* 80), Frémont ordered him to take his force into Missouri to disrupt the wide-spread Confederate guerrilla operations there. One of those guer-rillas was Mark Twain. In 1885, the year of Grant's death, Mark Twain wrote "The Private History of a Campaign that Failed," a fanciful account of his short stint with the Confederate army at the opening of the Civil War. He says the impetus for his leaving Missouri and heading out West, where he began the writing career that would make him famous, was the impending approach of Union forces under the command of Colonel Grant (281). Denying any hint of cowardice on his part, Mark Twain later claimed that his flight from harm's way allowed him to survive and later rescue the impoverished Grant by publishing his *Personal Memoirs*.

The parallels between Mark Twain, Grant, Frémont, and Gen-eral X. are striking. General X. tells us he was born in 1820, but we do not see his death in the unfinished story. Mark Twain (1835–1910) and the two models, Grant (1822–85) and Frémont (1813–90), were approximate contemporaries, sharing a period of history — the expansion of the American West, the Civil War, the gilded age of corrupt politicians and robber barons — when an ambitious person could both rise to great economic or political heights and plunge into bankruptcy and disgrace. General X. distinguishes himself in the war with Mexico, declared by the United States in May 1846 and ended with a treaty in February 1848. As mentioned above, Mark Twain had no glorious military past, having served a brief two weeks in a Missouri volunteer unit. General X. most nearly resembles Grant in military service. Like General X., Grant captured the attention of Generals Taylor and Scott in Mexico, advancing with Scott to occupy Mexico City.

Frémont did not serve in Mexico, but, as a captain during this war, he organized the California Battalion to cement American rights to California, conducting several successful campaigns and gaining valuable military experience. Both Grant and Frémont served as generals on the Union side in the Civil War, with Grant becoming the foremost commander of the conflict.

These figures had similarities in the political realm also. Mark Twain found in politics a rich source of humor for his jokes and speeches, but did not venture into politics personally. General X. becomes the youngest man up to that time elected to the Senate, and would, he says, "be President and First Citizen of the United States now, if I were of lawful age" (40–41). When Grant entered the White House in March 1869, he was the youngest man elected president at that time. Frémont was, like General X., a senator from California, and he was a presidential nominee. Courted by the Democratic Party, Frémont, then just forty-three years old, accepted instead the nomination of a new antislavery Republican Party in 1856 (Nevins 437). The victim of a massive campaign assaulting his character as well as his antislavery views, Frémont lost the presidency to James Buchanan. In 1878 President Rutherford B. Hayes appointed Frémont territorial governor of Arizona (Nevins 603).

One of the more intriguing parallels concerns Mark Twain's use of families and family names for his sketch of General X. The general's mother tells him "we were as good blood as the best in the town — good old Virginian stock, like the Sedgewicks and the Dents" (35). Mark Twain's paternal grandparents were Virginians, and his father made it a point to impress young Sam Clemens with their Virginian roots. His mother's family came to Missouri from Kentucky. Mark Twain selects the family name Dent for one of the leading families of his fictional Pawpaw Corners, Kentucky. Ulysses S. Grant married Julia Boggs Dent, daughter of a well-to-do Missouri planter. General Frémont's wife knew the Dents and saw Grant when he was a lieutenant courting Julia at the Dent plantation near St. Louis (Nevins 186).

General X. marries well also; Alison Sedgewick's father "was the principal lawyer and had run for Congress once" (35). Mark Twain married Olivia Langdon, daughter of a coal-mining magnate in upstate New York. Jervis Langdon lent Mark Twain $25,000, enabling him to buy the Buffalo *Express* newspaper; he bought Mark and Olivia an expensive house in Buffalo as a wedding present. Like Alison Sedgewick, Mark Twain's wife inherited a fortune upon the death of her father. John C. Frémont came from humble origins, but he married the daughter of powerful Senator Thomas Hart Benton from Mark Twain's home state of Missouri. Each of these men had the good fortune to marry into wealthy families, but their wealth was transitory; both Grant and Frémont were virtually penniless when they died.

Names of the characters in "Which Was the Dream?" find parallels in the people upon whom Mark Twain drew for his story. In his earliest drafts of the story, he used the initials "S" and "C" for the two daughters, doubtless representing his own daughters Susy and Clara, later changing them to Jessie and Bessie respectively. Frémont's wife's name was Jessie; she was an intelligent, iron-willed force behind many of his successes. In a remarkable coincidence, Grant named one of his sons Jesse, after Grant's father.

The fictional General X. graduates from West Point in 1841; General Grant graduated in 1843, a lackluster twenty-first out of thirty-nine. Like Mark Twain, General Frémont was not a West Point graduate, and, throughout his career as an explorer in the West and his Civil War service, he possessed a paranoid suspicion that West Pointers were jealous of his accomplishments (Nevins 133), although one of his sons, John C. Frémont Jr., attended West Point, and the other, Frank P. Frémont, attended Annapolis.

The catastrophe or reversal of fortune befalling the fictional General X. mirrors the lives of Mark Twain, Grant, and Frémont. General X. trusts his private secretary, Jeff Sedgewick, allowing him to duplicate his signature and giving him complete power of attorney. There never was a "Golden Fleece" mine (a complete invention by Sedgewick), and the house is uninsured against the devastating fire. General Frémont's San Francisco mansion was similarly destroyed by fire in 1851 (Nevins 399). (Wealthy Silas Lapham, in William Dean Howells's novel of 1885, *The Rise of Silas Lapham*, ruined when his mansion burns, is glad that his insurance has lapsed because the catastrophe ironically proves his honesty.) Frémont also entered the unfamiliar world of business through his speculative investments in gold mines in the Mariposas in California. His reputation was tainted in 1870 by charges, later proved false, that he had fraudulently resold bonds of the Memphis and El Paso Railroad. Left penniless and despairing, Frémont survived largely through the sale of his wife's stories and articles to popular magazines. Once possessing a fortune in the tens of millions and a viable contender for the presidency of the United States, he had nothing to leave to his wife when he died in 1890 (Nevins 610). Despite the fiscally sound beginning of their marriage through Olivia's inheritance, Mark Twain later declared bankruptcy through his unwise investment in the Paige typesetting machine. He recovered from his bankruptcy by launching a successful speaking tour, paying each creditor one hundred cents on the dollar. This money-making speaking tour resulted in his least successful travel book, *Following the Equator: A Journey around the World* (1897).

During Grant's presidency his administration frequently suffered from scandals, none of his own doing. His private secretary, Orville E. Babcock, was involved in the Whiskey Ring that defrauded the government of tax revenues (McFeely, *Grant* 416), and his secretary of war, William W. Belknap, with whom Mark Twain had corresponded in 1874, resigned amid charges of accepting bribes from an Indian agent (Hesseltine 396). Other scandals created suspicion about Grant's ability to manage his administration. But his personal financial problems most closely resembling those of General X. stemmed from his involvement with his son's investment firm of Grant and Ward in New York City. Grant put $100,000, all of his liquid capital, under the direction of the firm, and encouraged other family members to do so (Hesseltine 446). In 1884 the firm collapsed; Frederick Ward, another model for Jeff Sedgewick, fled after swindling the entire Grant family and other investors, further sullying Grant's reputation. Mark Twain's purposeful guiding of Grant toward completion of his *Personal Memoirs* enabled the family to recoup its losses. Bankrupt and suffering from throat cancer, Grant summoned all his personal courage and labored to finish his manuscript, completing it just before his death. Royalties from the sale of the two-volume set netted his family over $400,000. In a bitter irony Mark Twain's publishing firm went bankrupt in part because he sank capital from the sales of Grant's book into his Paige typesetter.

Mark Twain steadfastly liked Grant from their first meeting in 1870 to Grant's death in 1885. When Grant's *Personal Memoirs* appeared, the English writer and critic Matthew Arnold committed what was to Mark Twain a blasphemous act by attacking Grant's grammar. Arnold had a longstanding supercilious view of Americans and their writing, and his two-part article in the English *Murray's Magazine*, reprinted in Boston in 1887, infuriated his American readership (Arnold 7). James B. Fry (USMA 1847), who served as provost marshal general during the Civil War, counterattacked Arnold in the *North American Review* in 1887. Mark Twain soon joined the fray. Although he and Arnold liked each other personally (he had entertained Arnold cordially at his home in Hartford), Arnold disdained the American's "philistine" writings and humor. In a speech at the annual reunion of the Army and Navy Club of Connecticut, on 27 April 1887, Mark Twain defended his old friend Grant:

> When we think of General Grant our pulses quicken and his grammar vanishes: we only remember that this is the simple soldier who, all untaught of the silken phrasemakers, linked words together with an art surpassing the art of the schools, and put into them a something which will still bring to American ears, as long as America shall last, the roll of

his vanished drums and the thread of his marching hosts. What do we care for grammar when we think of the man that put together that thunderous phrase, "Unconditional and immediate surrender!" And those others: "I propose to move immediately upon your works!" "I propose to fight it out on this line if it takes all summer!" Mr. Arnold would doubtless claim that that last sentence is not strictly grammatical; and yet nevertheless it did certainly wake up this nation as a hundred million tons of A1, forty proof, hard-boiled, hide-bound grammar from another mouth couldn't have done. And finally we have that gentler phrase: that one which shows you another true side of the man; shows that in his soldier heart there was room for other than gory war mottoes, and in his tongue the gift to fitly phrase them: "Let us have peace." (qtd. in Arnold 57–58)

CHAPTER V

"Bullies and Cowards": Mark Twain on Hazing

I

Hazing, in its various forms, has constituted a part of cadet life at West Point since the inception of the academy, and, from time to time, it has caused sensationally negative publicity. Two celebrated cases of hazing drew the attention of Mark Twain. The first case, still hotly debated over one hundred years after it occurred in 1880, involved racism; the second, occurring late in 1898, as West Point approached its centennial year of 1902, caused such a storm of indignation that the continued existence of the academy was threatened. Mark Twain expressed outrage at both of these incidents.

The term "hazing" goes back at least as far as the fifteenth century, and was used in the military, particularly the navy, to mean scolding, upbraiding, frightening, or punishing those in the enlisted ranks; the word possibly derives from "hazard." In nineteenth-century America the term came to be associated almost exclusively with the first year of collegiate life as a rite of passage (a coming-of-age experience), particularly at the service academies and among social fraternities at civilian colleges.

On 8 June 1890 the *New York Times* published an account of a new cadet undergoing the usual first-day humiliations, including some humorous ribbing:

> Hazing is prohibited at the Academy, and each new man is instructed to report all cases of improper treatment at the hands of cadets, but nevertheless the graybacks who get an opportunity to humiliate prospective "plebes" seldom fail to improve it, and the victims dare not make any complaint.
>
> It is a question whether there is any wisdom in turning these raw men over to the tender mercies of Second Class men. But it is the custom here, and West Point customs seldom change. ("Put through Their Paces")

As late as 1891 hazing was still viewed as a necessary ritual in getting a new cadet started in the right direction. That year an unnamed ex-cadet who entered West Point in 1873 wrote an article for the *New York Times*, "A Plebe at West Point." The subhead of the article, "He Furnishes Amusement to the Cadets," reveals that some plebes were hazed in the spirit of fun, and the light tone of the article reinforces this view (see fig. 20).

The writer mentioned physical contact, but did so in a comic vein; nothing he wrote suggested that he felt threatened or endangered when the upperclassmen began a form of mental hazing:

> "What's your name?"
> "Age?"
> "How's your mother?"
> "Got any dynamite in your grip?"
> "Where'd you get that hat?"

"Where were you born?"
"Sorry or glad that you were born?"
"Don't you think it was a waste of material?"
"Think you'll make a good soldier?"
"Married?"
"How many children?"
"How much is twice two?"
"Why?"

PLEBE DRILL.

Figure 20. "Plebe Drill" in 1886. Sometimes the
"drill" got out of hand and became hazing.
SOURCE: *Harper's New Monthly Magazine* (July 1887)

"How far is it from here to somewhere else and back if you run both ways?"

"Are you white or colored?"

"Read and write?"

"Pa alive?"

"What for?"

"Grandma got any teeth?"

"How many?"

"Why didn't you count 'em?"

"Is she a flirt?"

" 'Fraid of a nigger man in the dark?"

"Ever scalp a wooden Indian?"

"How many fingers on each hand?"

"How many thumbs?"

"Both alike, ain't they?"

"Any insane people in your family except yourself?"

These and a hundred other entertaining questions were put to me. Although I was all afire, I could not help but laugh at some of the conundrums.

The ex-cadet said that, when he and a dozen of his classmates withdrew from the academy at the end of summer camp in August, "the country was deprived of the valuable services of that number of possible Indian fighters." The writer expressed no bitterness and did not indicate a desire to retaliate for the hazing he received almost twenty years before. He clearly enjoyed the verbal repartee, the rapid firing of "conundrums" or unanswerable questions intended to confuse him.

Quite apart from the badinage and more humorous aspects of hazing, occasionally incidents of genuine brutality and cruelty occurred. West Point and the other service academies, since their inception and until the present day, have sought to control hazing, realizing that attempts to eradicate it would be futile. In 1864, upon the orders of Secretary of War Edwin Stanton, all cadets wanting to go on furlough were required to sign a certificate that they had not in any way "interfered with, or molested, harassed, or injured new cadets" (*Centennial Report* 2: 118).

Another dimension of hazing at West Point involved the admission of African Americans into the corps of cadets following the Civil War. For the most part black cadets were not targets for hazing through direct contact with upperclassmen; rather, they were generally ostracized by both Northern and Southern cadets, perhaps just as cruel a form of hazing in its own fashion because it excluded blacks from the humorous aspects of the practice. Whites refused to share a barracks room with blacks, and frequently protested their assignment with a black cadet to the same table in the mess hall. The lack of hazing at least allowed the few black cadets who entered the academy in the years following the Civil War to concentrate on the demanding academic requirements; slaves had been forbidden by law to read and write, a short legacy of literacy among the black cadets, most of whom came from the South.

In 1870 James Webster Smith from South Carolina became the first black to be admitted to West Point. After four years of social isolation at the academy, Smith had advanced only to second-class (junior) standing when he was dismissed for academic deficiencies. In March 1996 President Bill Clinton approved a posthumous commission for Smith at the request of several members of the South Carolina congressional delegation (Piacente 3-B). The first black to graduate was Henry O. Flipper, from Georgia, who was appointed in 1873. A white student from Atlanta offered Flipper five thousand dollars, a princely sum in those days, not to take the appointment, but Flipper refused (Guttman 22). Like Smith, Flipper was virtually ignored by his classmates, but managed to finish a respectable fiftieth out of seventy-six in the class of 1877.

A second black cadet, Johnson C. Whittaker from South Carolina, joined Flipper, with whom he shared a room, in 1876. In 1879, when Mark Twain began visiting West Point, Whittaker was the lone black cadet. That year Whittaker was found deficient by the academic board. Rather than follow the recommendation for dismissal, Superintendent Schofield put Whittaker back a year and allowed him to continue his lackluster academic career, a decision that Schofield would later regret.

Hazing and racism became linked when a tactical officer found Whittaker tied to his bunk and bleeding from head wounds on the morning of 6 April 1880. He claimed that three masked cadets had entered his room and beat him the night before, but he was unable to identify any of them. The case caused a stir in the newspapers, and the public generally sided with Whittaker. Schofield hired private detectives to get to the bottom of the matter, and the evidence presented in an official inquiry convinced the West Point authorities that Whittaker had concocted the story to gain sympathy and divert attention from his academic deficiencies, which he feared the upcoming examinations would reveal.

Schofield had a reputation for being prejudiced against blacks. He opposed universal suffrage for black men during Reconstruction because most of them were former illiterate slaves. Schofield felt that illiterates of any race were unfit to vote on important issues or to be candidates for office (McDonough 161). In his memoirs he deplored the public's sympathy for Whittaker, saying that the results of the investigation showing that the black cadet himself was to blame "did not suffice to allay the public clamor for protection to the recently emancipated negroes in the enjoyment of privileges in the national institutions for which they had not become either mentally or morally fitted" (445–46). He placed the blame for the controversy outside the walls of the academy: "A presidential election was pending, and the colored vote and that in sympathy with it demanded assurance of the hearty and effective support of the national administration" (446). And he saw himself as a scapegoat: "Nothing less than a radical change at West Point would satisfy that demand, and who could be a more appropriate victim to offer as a sacrifice to that Moloch than one who had already gone beyond the limits of duty, of justice, and of wisdom in his kind treatment of the colored cadet?" (446).

Because of his known fondness for social issues, particularly his espousal of causes advancing the newly emancipated blacks, Oliver O. Howard was specifically selected to replace Schofield, for whom, to avoid embarrassing him, a new army department had been created for the purpose of transferring him to a command commensurate with his rank of major general.

On 31 December 1880 a court-martial was established in New York City at the request of Whittaker and his supporters in order to clear his name. The president of the court was Mark Twain's old friend Brigadier General Nelson A. Miles, a non-West Pointer. The court-martial began on 20 January 1881 and lasted until 10 June 1881 (Marszalek 238).

In "June Week" of 1881, when Mark Twain was at West Point for graduation, the attorney for the prosecution, Major Asa Bird Gardiner, made his final address to the court on 6 June, arguing that Whittaker "had an abundant motive for his deceit in the prospect of exciting public sympathy and procuring relief from his threatened discharge on account of inability to pass the examinations, as well as in revenge against the white cadets to whom he was hostile" (qtd. in "Whittaker Court Martial"). Although the defense attorneys called dozens of witnesses on Whittaker's behalf, the court convicted him, largely on the basis of a handwriting analysis of a note they believed Whittaker had forged.

On 21 March 1882 (about the time Mark Twain was at West Point arranging for the printing of *1601*), the adjutant general of the army issued an order finding Whittaker guilty of "conduct unbecoming an officer and a gentleman" and "false swearing to the prejudice of good order and military discipline." He was sentenced to "be dishonorably dismissed from the military service of the United States and to pay a fine of $1, and to be thereafter confined at hard labor for one year in such penitentiary as the reviewing authority may direct" ("National Capital Topics"). But President Chester A. Arthur issued an order — timed precisely for concurrent release to the press — dissolving the court-martial and setting aside the sentence of a fine and imprisonment because the allegedly forged note and other handwriting samples had not been properly introduced as evidence (Marszalek 248–49). Cadet Whittaker was released from arrest and officially dismissed from West Point for academic deficiency ("National Capital Topics"). In July 1995 President Clinton granted Whittaker a posthumous commission as a second lieutenant, the commission that had been denied him at West Point over a century earlier. Clinton said, "Today, finally, we can pay tribute to a great American and we can acknowledge a great injustice" (qtd. in Purdum).

Mark Twain knew about this case and felt strongly that Whittaker had received unjust treatment. Howells characterized Mark Twain as the "most desouthernized Southerner I ever knew" (35) in the context of recalling their conversation about the Whittaker case:

> About that time a colored cadet was expelled from West Point for some point of conduct "unbecoming an officer and gentleman," and there was the usual shabby philosophy in a portion of the press to the effect that a negro could never feel the claim of honor. The man was fifteen parts white, but, "Oh yes," Clemens said, with bitter irony, "it was that one part black that undid him." It made him a "nigger" and incapable of being a gentleman. It was to blame for the whole thing. The fifteen parts white were guiltless. (34–35)

II

Although racism became the specific issue dominating the Whittaker case, hazing in general was brought into the spotlight as never before, and signaled a change in the public's view of the activity from a harmless collegiate tradition to a pernicious and dangerous practice.

Authorities at West Point unswervingly insisted that hazing had been abolished. In an article in *Harper's* magazine in 1887, Charles King, who had served with Custer in the West, said of hazing:

> It took hard work to uproot it, for the ingenuity and activity of the corps are something phenomenal; but the thing has been done, and to-day the ancient and objectionable custom is but the shadow of a formerly vigorous substance. The plebes are drilled as sharply and disciplined as thoroughly as ever before, the line of demarcation between theirs and the senior classes is still maintained, but the tricks and pranks, the fagging that rendered life a burden, and the "yanking" that made night hideous, and with them all that had a tendency to the harmful, have been practically abolished. (219)

Despite King's optimistic view that hazing had ended, the most notorious case of hazing at West Point, involving a cadet with the unfortunate last name of Booz, occurred over a decade later and, as in the Whittaker case, attracted the attention of Mark Twain. From Bristol, Pennsylvania, Oscar L. Booz entered West Point on 20 June 1898 and immediately became a target for hazing by upperclassmen who thought he had a superior attitude. They also thought Booz put too fine an interpretation on regulations, refusing to carry out orders that crossed the line from normal military discipline to hazing.

In their justification of hazing, cadets often cited the same factors. The arguments have changed little over the years: hazing developed both mental acumen and physical stamina, qualities essential to an officer in combat; hazing helped to bond the corps through their shared experience; hazing taught a plebe that he must accept orders from upperclassmen without question as preparation for the "real world" of military discipline; hazing helped a plebe to shed the notion that he is a superior person, even though he might have won a congressional appointment from his hometown for his outstanding qualities. Plebes whose fathers were famous generals or otherwise noteworthy received more than the usual ration of hazing: Philip Sheridan Jr., Ulysses S. Grant III, and Douglas MacArthur were all subjected to severe hazing ("West Point Inquiry").

Oscar Booz, in one way or another, seemed to violate all expectations of the plebe system. Although he was not from a famous lineage, within the corps his name (which invited mockery) quickly became known. For an accumulation of misdemeanors, on 6 August 1898 Booz was "called out" to fight an upperclassman before the assembled corps of cadets away from tactical officers, who tacitly allowed hazing. In the first round of the fight, Booz held his own against a more experienced boxer named Frank Keller. But as the second round got under way, Booz fell almost immediately to the ground and claimed that he could not rise. That was the rule — fight until one man could rise no more. So the fight ended ("Booz's West Point Fight").

But word quickly spread through the corps that Booz had bragged about beating the system using its own rules. Rumor had it that he was not hurt at all, and, therefore, he must not have sufficiently learned his lesson.

Soon Booz was forced to drink large amounts of Tabasco sauce, a standard practice in the corps for dealing with "mouthy" plebes. But upperclassmen subjected him at every meal to far more than the customary amount. This form of hazing lasted until September, when classes began. He resigned on 31 October 1898 and returned to Pennsylvania, claiming complete exhaustion as a result of his ordeal.

But the story does not end there. The *New York Times* on 1 December 1900 printed an article declaring "Cadet Dying from Hazing," compellingly linking hazing with mortal danger. Tragically, on 3 December 1900, Booz died of tubercular laryngitis, a condition his parents traced directly to his repeated consumption of excessive amounts of Tabasco sauce. In other words, they argued, upperclassmen at West Point had killed a member of the corps through institutionally sanctioned brutality ("Former Cadet Booz Dead").

The ensuing investigation kept West Point and hazing in the public's eye for months. On 11 December 1900 the matter was debated in the House of Representatives. Congressman John Hull from Iowa, chairman of the Committee on Military Affairs, called upon Secretary of War Elihu Root to conduct an intensive investigation and to report back to Congress. Congressman Edmund Driggs of New York claimed that the practice of hazing plebes was "notorious," citing the Whittaker case of 1880 (qtd. in "House Looks into Hazing").

On 19 December 1900 sixty-eight members of the class of 1902 were summoned before a court of inquiry; fourteen of them, including the son of General Phil Sheridan, testified that they had not received brutal or degrading treatment and that Booz had not received any worse treatment than they had. The first witness, Cadet Raymond L. Linton of Michigan, described "bracing," an exaggerated position of attention, but he said unpopular cadets, such as Booz, were often ignored, while more popular plebes received more attention. Cadet Stephen Abbott of Illinois said he knew of several instances of upperclassmen receiving punishment for inflicting bracing on plebes. Superintendent Albert L. Mills questioned Cadet Albert B. Dockery of Mississippi about Tabasco sauce: "Do you know any other name for it?" Cadet Dockery replied with hesitation that "cadets sometimes call it hell sauce" (qtd. in "Cadets Describe Hazing").

Booz's fellow Pennsylvanian, Cadet Charles McH. Eby, swore that Booz was "not held in very high regard by the cadets, as he had not shown courage in his fight with Keller." Eby, struggling valiantly to avoid direct answers, went on under questioning to describe various forms of hazing that, he said, used to be prevalent but had not been practiced for two years: "bracing," an exaggerated form of a soldierly position; "wooden willie," continuous gun drill; "football," lying on the back and raising the legs to a perpendicular position and back again several times, probably for six or seven minutes; "eagling," standing on the toes; "hanging on stretcher," suspended by the hands from a bar, with the feet not on the floor. Eby answered a series of questions regarding hazing:

> "Did you ever see a man faint while undergoing any of these exercises?"
> "Well, I have known a man to feign."
> "Under what form of exercise?"
> "Eagling, I think, Sir."
> "How long did he exercise?"
> "I can't exactly say, about five or six minutes, I think."
> "Who was that man?"
> "Myself, Sir." (qtd. in "Cadets Describe Hazing")

Cadet John K. Herr of New Jersey had acted as Booz's second during the fight with Keller. Under oath Herr said that, when Booz fell down and swore he could not get up, he "told Booz that his actions were cowardly and were so regarded by the others, and that he could remove the stigma by fighting another upper class man his own size or smaller, but he paid no attention to me." Cadet Philip H. Sheridan of Illinois, a classmate of Booz's, said that he himself had not been subjected to humiliating acts, even though he had, on occasion, been forced to ride broom handles and to sit in wash bowls in the company street (qtd. in "Cadets Describe Hazing").

Perhaps conscious of the Whittaker case and its implicit racism, the court inquired of Cadet Samuel Frankenberger whether he or Booz's tent mate, Cadet Sigmond S. Albert, both of whom were Jewish, had ever been discriminated against because of their religious faith. Frankenberger replied that they had not been (qtd. in "Cadets Describe Hazing").

The next day an editorial supported West Point, saying that

> the boys are evidently telling the truth, the whole truth, and nothing but the truth.... There is nothing in their evidence

that hints at all strongly at the existence among them of anything approaching serious brutality in spirit or conduct. ... With all due sympathy for [Booz's] sorrowing parents, the general public can await the result of the investigation with equanimity, in perfect confidence that for any real wrongs that have been done adequate justice will be allotted, and equally sure that West Point is now what it always has been, one of the most admirable of our National institutions, a training school for patriots, for heroes, and for gentlemen. ("Careful Reading")

When the inquiry resumed on 21 December, Cadet Keller testified that he had been selected by others to fight Booz, who was taller and weighed two pounds more than Keller. Keller maintained that he was unable to deliver a knockout punch because Booz kept running away, Keller's blows landing ineffectively on Booz's back. Others also testified that Booz had not been hit hard enough to cause him to stay down. Still others said that Booz had been "slack" while performing guard duty and that he had been discovered reading a novel or some other secular book hidden between the covers of his Bible. Cadet James Prentice of New York said Booz hid the book in that manner "so as to take advantage of the fact that no one would interfere with him while reading the Bible" (qtd. in "Booz's West Point Fight").

The court of inquiry was an official military court, internal to the army and the institution. But as the case went on, politicians began to take notice, and some members of Congress wanted to hold hearings about abolishing West Point. An editorial in the *New York Times* on 23 December 1900 again gave direct support to West Point:

Cannot the hair-trigger critics in Congress overlook an occasional fist fight, or even the more reprehensible experiments with Tabasco sauce, for the sake of a prank so truly delightful as that of forcing a new cadet to learn by heart and frequently repeat, while his companions eyed him up and down, the perfervid narration of his virtues and beauties, published by his home paper at the time of his appointment? That was discipline the effects of which could not have been anything else than good. Is it nothing that these boys hate a lie, that they loathe even the appearance of cowardice, that they are not less fit than eager to follow — no, to carry, the Stars and Stripes wherever duty calls? Abolish the Military Academy, indeed! What for? In order that Congressmen may have more patronage in times of National peril? We can think of no other reason. ("Small Politicians")

On 4 January 1901 the congressional committee began hearing testimony in Philadelphia to inquire into the cause of Cadet Booz's death. Three sessions were held this first day, lasting from 9:00 a.m. until midnight. Most of the testimony involved hearing physicians who offered medical opinions on the likelihood that drinking Tabasco sauce might cause susceptibility to tuberculosis germs.

On the same day former cadet Sigmond S. Albert contradicted the testimony of his friend Samuel Frankenberger to the military court of inquiry when he told the congressmen that he was more severely hazed than other cadets of his class because of his religion. Albert said he had been called "a damned Jew" by upperclassmen. His testimony bore echoes of the charges of racial or ethnic motivations for hazing such as West Point had encountered years earlier with the Whittaker case (qtd. in "Congressional Booz Inquiry").

Secretary of War Elihu Root in Washington said on 9 January 1901 that Booz's death was not due to hazing and that there would be no censure of anyone at West Point; he praised Superintendent Albert L. Mills for his efforts to eliminate or control hazing (qtd. in "No Censure in Booz Report"). Mills graduated from West Point in 1879, and likely heard Mark Twain when he appeared at the academy that spring. The same day the congressional committee moved to West Point and heard testimony from Mills. Over the course of the next several weeks, public interest in the case increased because of the political aspects of having congressmen conduct the inquiry ("Congressional Investigation").

The congressmen continued to question Mills when the inquiry resumed on 12 January. Congressman Driggs of New York asked Mills, "Is it not cowardly on the part of upper-class men to call out fourth-class men to fight against men who have better physical advantages?"

"Yes I think it is wrong, and to a certain extent cowardly," was the reply.

In speaking of the ideas of outsiders on hazing, Col. Mills said that many thought it commendable, and former graduates of the Academy looked upon it in the same light. This encouraged the young men as they advanced from the fourth class to do the same to their successors as had been done to themselves.

"Many parents," said the witness, "are sympathetic when their sons are fourth class men, but their feelings undergo a change when their sons advance to the upper classes."

"Then you think they enjoy their sons getting even?" said Mr. [Irving] Wanger [congressman from Pennsylvania, Booz's home state].

"Yes, Sir, they do, particularly the women," was the Colonel's answer, which caused a good deal of laughter among the women who were listening. ("Methods at West Point")

The *New York Times* scolded the academy for not bringing to light the facts of the Booz case, which the congressional inquiry was able to unearth, but an editorial expressed the belief that "harmless" hazing such as quizzing and teasing of plebes was acceptable as "boyish follies," but that "the system of conducting fights between upper and lower class men was outrageous in every sense and cowardly in some" ("Appreciably Serious").

Mark Twain focused on fighting as part of hazing when he spoke out on the case. His remarks appeared on the front page of the *New York Times* on 20 January 1901 in an article entitled "Mark Twain on Hazing":

WASHINGTON, JAN. 19. — Mark Twain, in an interview to-day, spoke about hazing at West Point, and denounced the practice as a brutal one and the men who indulge in it as bullies and cowards. "Why," he said, "the fourth class man who is compelled to fight a man from the first class hasn't a show in the world, and it is not intended that he should. I have read the rules provided to prevent such practices, and they are wholly deficient, because one provision is omitted. I would make it the duty of a cadet to report to the authorities any case of hazing which came to his notice; make such reports a part of the vaunted West Point 'code of honor' and the beating of young boys by upper class men will be stopped.

"I am not opposed to fights among boys as a general thing. If they are conducted in a spirit of fairness, I think it makes boys manly, but I do oppose compelling a little fellow to fight some man big enough to whip two of him. When I was a boy, going to school down in the Mississippi Valley, we used to have our fights, and I remember one occasion on which I got soundly trounced, but we always matched boys as nearly of a size as possible, and there was none of the cowardly methods that seem to prevail at West Point."

Mark Twain's comments appear carefully worded, and might have been part of an organized campaign by a West Point protective group. Although the story is datelined Washington, evidence shows that Mark Twain was not in Washington that day but in New York City. Significantly his statement does not condemn the institution as a whole, as did some congressmen, nor hazing as a general practice; it focuses on the unfairness of "calling out" a smaller fourth classman by more developed upper classmen, the same point made by representatives of the four classes at West Point.

This "interview" appeared next to a story headlined "Cadets Abolish Hazing," saying in part: "When the congressmen were hurrying their inquiries to a termination, the cadets of all four classes held a meeting in Grant Hall and unanimously decided to abolish exercising and hazing of every form, as well as the practice of 'calling out' fourth-class men."

Shortly after this meeting Superintendent Mills handed the chairman of the inquiry, General George Dick, a letter signed by representatives of each of the four classes pledging to abolish hazing. General Dick called the four representatives to the inquiry and commended them for their pledge, saying that their taking this action would "be read by the country with feelings of merited approbation." He added that he would return to Congress "with the kindest feelings and best wishes for the Academy and all connected with it." Thus, Mark Twain's public statements were in accord both with the cadets who promised to cease the cruelty of "calling out" and with the congressional inquiry that recommended West Point should continue.

To say that the Booz case, the culmination of a series of unfortunate hazing incidents over the years, threatened to close West Point is not an overstatement. When egregious cases of hazing or an organized-cheating scandal become public knowledge, the service academies undergo scrutiny and evaluation — and rightly so. The public has a right to expect the highest standards of behavior from future officers. Certainly the unfavorable attention from cases such as those of Whittaker and Booz caused West Point to examine the entire institution of hazing and to eliminate, insofar as possible, the most brutal aspects. Although Mark Twain's comments appeared late in the argument, his precisely timed statement was consistent with his steadfast affection for the academy.

Seven years later, when Mark Twain read in the *New York Times* the obituary of his beloved nephew Samuel E. Moffett, who drowned on 1 August 1908 (see "Editor Moffett Dies"), he must surely have noticed with dismay the headline, four columns away on the same page, "President Upsets His Own Hazing Law." The article reported that President Theodore Roosevelt, to considerable controversy, had reinstated eight upperclassmen at West Point who ten days before "were found guilty of hazing in some of its worst forms."

Mark Twain's
West Point Readings

While we cannot know all the stories and jokes Mark Twain told the cadets during his informal visits with them in the barracks, we do have a reliable record of his presentations to the larger audiences of cadets, faculty, staff, and guests in the mess hall. We can only imagine the mirth of the cadets as they heard America's favorite storyteller's inimitable delivery of these stories. "The Wisdom of Solomon," chapter 14 of *Adventures of Huckleberry Finn*, is widely available and not reproduced here.

DATE OF VISIT	READINGS
1876–80	No readings; at least three informal visits with cadets.
28 February 1881	"Clarence and Eugene" "How I Escaped Being Killed in a Duel" "Cure for Stammering"
9–11 June 1881	No readings at West Point, but "The Benefit of Judicious Training," about West Point, told in Hartford on 8 June.

February 1882	Arranged for printing of *1601*.
3 April 1886	"The Wisdom of Solomon" (chapter 14 of *Adventures of Huckleberry Finn*) "The Awful German Language" "An American Party" "Cure for Stammering" "The Celebrated Jumping Frog of Calaveras County"
5–7 May 1886	No readings; informal visits with cadets.
30 April 1887	"English as She Is Taught"
11 January 1890	Selections from *A Connecticut Yankee in King Arthur's Court*

"Clarence and Eugene"
(Delivered at West Point 28 February 1881)

Twins fascinated Mark Twain. Siamese twins and sets of twins recur throughout his stories and novels. He wrote a sketch called "The Siamese Twins" as early as 1868, in which he discusses Chang and Eng Bunker (1811–74), the original Siamese twins. (His use of the names Clarence and Eugene in the West Point version retains the initials of Chang and Eng.) His sketch on the famous conjoined twins carries the "brother against brother" notion to extremes when he has them fighting on opposite sides in the Civil War. The story that Mark Twain told at West Point was one of several variations on this favorite story.

Years later, at a benefit to raise funds for a monument to Robert Fulton in New York City, on 19 April 1906, he related a similar tale in a mock interview with a reporter. The humorist said he told the reporter he was born a twin, but his brother, Samuel (Mark Twain's real first name), was perhaps dead. The reporter wanted to know if Samuel had been buried alive. Mark Twain replied:

> "That was a mystery," said I. "We were twins, and one day when we were two weeks old — that is, he was one week old and I was one week old — we got mixed up in the bathtub, and one of us drowned. We never could tell which. One of us had a strawberry birthmark on the back of his hand. There it is on my hand. This is the one that was drowned. There's no doubt about it."
>
> "Where's the mystery?" he said.
>
> "Why, don't you see how stupid it was to bury the wrong twin?" I answered. I didn't explain it any more because he said the explanation confused him. To me it is perfectly plain. (*Mark Twain Speaking* 516)

Mark Twain's "An Encounter with an Interviewer" departs from the West Point version also. A newspaper reporter questions a "man who has become notorious" (Mark Twain, *Complete Humorous Sketches* 257) about his dead twin brother, here named Bill, not Samuel:

> *A.* "You see, we were twins — defunct and I — and we got mixed in the bathtub when we were only two weeks old, and one of us was drowned. But we didn't know which. Some think it was Bill. Some think it was me."
>
> *Q.* "Well, that *is* remarkable. What do *you* think?"
>
> *A.* "Goodness knows! I would give whole worlds to know. This solemn, this awful mystery has cast a gloom over my whole life. But I will tell you a secret now, which I never have revealed to any creature before. One of us had a peculiar mark — a large mole on the back of his left hand; that was *me. That child was the one that was drowned!*" (259–60)

Mark Twain later used variants of this drowning device in both *Huckleberry Finn* and "Those Extraordinary Twins." In chapter

17 of *Huckleberry Finn,* Emmeline Grangerford writes a poem about young Stephen Dowling Bots, who "fell down a well and was drownded" (143). In 1890 Mark Twain wrote "Those Extraordinary Twins," an unsuccessful story that evolved into the short novel *The Tragedy of Pudd'nhead Wilson.* Mark Twain said in an introduction to "Those Extraordinary Twins" that he used the drowning device as a way of getting rid of unnecessary characters: Rowena, an irritating sentimentalist, goes "out into the back yard after supper to see the fireworks," but "she fell down the well and got drowned"; two boys "went out back one night to stone a cat and fell down the well and got drowned"; and two old ladies, Aunt Patsy Cooper and Aunt Betsy Hale, "went out back one night to visit the sick and fell down the well and got drowned" (*Pudd'nhead Wilson* 121).

The twins in this story, Angelo and Luigi Capello, are Italian Siamese twins! They share two legs and a torso, but have two heads and four arms. One is dark haired, the other blond. To depict these twins, Mark Twain drew upon his 1868 sketch about the original Siamese twins, in which "Eng is a Baptist, but Chang is a Roman Catholic; still, to please his brother, Chang consented to be baptized at the same time that Eng was, on condition that it should not 'count' " (*Sketches* 249). The idea that Siamese twins would embrace different religions allowed Mark Twain to combine contrary religions and his "drowning" motif. In a curtain speech at a performance of the play *Pudd'nhead Wilson* in New York in 1895, Mark Twain talked about the "extraordinary" Italian Siamese twins: "Angelo was a trouble to Luigi, the infidel, because he was always changing his religion, trying to find the best one, and he always preferred sects that believed in baptism by immersion, and this was a constant peril and discomfort to Luigi, who couldn't stand water outside or in; and so every time Angelo got baptized Luigi got drowned and had to be pumped out and resuscitated" (*Mark Twain Speaking* 277).

Pudd'nhead Wilson involves not only a set of separate (i.e., non-Siamese) twins, also named Angelo and Luigi, but also a pair of changelings, look-alike children who are switched, a device similar to the situation in *The Prince and the Pauper*. In *Pudd'nhead Wilson*, a slave switches her light-skinned infant with the son of her master. Mark Twain's long-standing fascination with twins possibly reflects his own complex duality as Samuel Clemens–Mark Twain. Some scholars enjoy analyzing his writings in an effort to form a psychological portrait; I have discussed this approach more fully in chapter 4. Suffice it to say that the cadets at West Point were not concerned with the manifold psychological difficulties encountered in his works. They simply enjoyed seeing the master storyteller performing at his finest.

"How I Escaped Being Killed in a Duel"
(Delivered at West Point 28 February 1881)

While the cadets thought this story was hilarious, its real-life origin was a deadly serious matter; Mark Twain once found himself in a dispute of his own making, a quarrel that could have cost him his life in a duel.

In April and May 1864, years before this visit to West Point, when Mark Twain was a reporter for the Virginia City *Territorial Enterprise* in Nevada Territory, he became embroiled with a rival newspaper editor over a charitable organization called the Sanitary Fund (sometimes called Sanitary Commissions or Sanitary Societies) established to provide medical care for wounded Union soldiers. Mark Twain's beloved older sister, Pamela Clemens Moffett, worked for the United States Sanitary Commission in St. Louis during the war. As a money-raising enterprise, a sack of flour would be auctioned off but never claimed by the winning bidder; thus, the same sack of flour made its way around the territory, eliciting hundreds of thousands of dollars for the charity.

Mark Twain, whose sympathies lay with the South, had too much to drink one night and wrote a wildly untrue story about misappropriation of the money by the deceiving women of the Sanitary Fund, who had organized a fund-raising ball in nearby Carson City for, of all things, a "Miscegenation Society" somewhere in the East! He intended to entertain friends privately with the story, but a typesetter at the *Territorial Enterprise*, searching for copy, found it and, thinking it legitimate, ran the piece with Mark Twain's byline. The reaction from the good-hearted women and their husbands was understandably hostile. The Virginia City *Union*, a rival newspaper, was only too happy to heat up the controversy, turning Mark Twain on a spit like a roasting pig.

Mark Twain exchanged angry letters with James L. Laird and challenged him to a duel. This challenge passed to *Union* reporter J.W. Wilmington, whom he did not know. He was dismayed when he subsequently discovered that Wilmington had been a captain in an Ohio infantry unit, a veteran of Shiloh, and doubtless more adept with firearms than he.

Mark Twain's good friend Steve Gillis, a hot-tempered, feisty little man, became his "second" for the duel, which seemed destined to take place. As the appointed day approached, Gillis and Mark Twain practiced their marksmanship. Their efforts to obtain some minimal competency became the genesis of the story of a man practicing for a duel. The danger of the duel actually occurring abated when Gillis shot the head off a sparrow at thirty-five yards and managed to convince Wilmington's nearby seconds that Mark Twain had done it. Tempers cooled while Wilmington thought the situation over.

The matter ended when Mark Twain and Gillis suddenly departed Virginia City for San Francisco in the middle of the night on 29 May 1864. Mark Twain claimed a victory because his challenge had not been taken up and the duel not fought, but he and everyone else involved knew that he had behaved boorishly by not forthrightly admitting his bibulous mistake and by not offering a convincingly abject apology.

Several versions of the duel story exist. A reliable chronicle of the actual events of 1864 may be found in volume one of *Mark Twain's Letters 1853–1866* (281–301), showing in their own words the escalating exchange of insults between Mark Twain, Laird (called "Lord" in the fictional account of the incident), and Wilmington. Volume one of *Mark Twain's Autobiography* (350–61) gives the famous writer's slanted version composed in 1906. But the story the West Point cadets enjoyed was probably a variation on "How I Escaped Being Killed in a Duel," appearing in the magazine *Every Saturday*, 21 December 1872, reprinted in Louis J. Budd's *Mark Twain: Collected Tales, Sketches, Speeches, and Essays* (1992).

How I Escaped Being Killed in a Duel

The only merit I claim for the following narrative is that it is a true story. It has a moral at the end of it, but I claim nothing on that, as it is merely thrown in to curry favor with the religious element.

After I had reported a couple of years on the Virginia City (Nevada) *Daily Enterprise*, they promoted me to be editor-in-chief — and I lasted just a week, by the watch. But I made an uncommonly lively newspaper while I *did* last, and when I retired I had a duel on my hands, and three horse-whippings promised me. The latter I made no attempt to collect; however, this history concerns only the former. It was the old "flush times" of the silver excitement, when the population was wonderfully wild and mixed: everybody went armed to the teeth, and all slights and insults had to be atoned for with the best article of blood your system could furnish. In the course of my editing I made trouble with a Mr. Lord, editor of the rival paper. He flew up about some little trifle or other that I said about him — I do not remember now what it was. I suppose I called him a thief, or a body-snatcher, or an idiot, or something like that. I was obliged to make the paper readable, and I could not fail in my duty to a whole community of subscribers merely to save the exaggerated sensitiveness of an individual. Mr. Lord was offended, and replied vigorously in his paper. Vigorously means a great deal when it refers to a personal editorial in a frontier newspaper. Duelling was all the fashion among the upper classes in that country, and very few gentlemen would throw away an opportunity of fighting one. To kill a person in a duel caused a man to be even more looked up to than to kill two men in the ordinary way. Well, out there, if you abused a man, and that man did not like it, you had to call him out and kill him; otherwise you would be disgraced. So I challenged Mr. Lord, and I did hope he would not accept; but I knew perfectly well that he did not want to fight, and so I challenged him in the most violent and implacable manner. And then I sat down and suffered and suffered till the answer came. All our boys — the editors — were in our office, "helping" me in the dismal business, and telling about duels, and discussing the code with a lot of aged ruffians who had experience in such things, and altogether there was a loving interest taken in the matter, which made me unspeakably uncomfortable. The answer came — Mr. Lord declined. Our boys were furious, and so was I — on the surface.

I sent him another challenge, and another and another; and the more he did not want to fight, the bloodthirstier I became. But at last the man's tone changed. He appeared to be waking up. It was becoming apparent that he was going to fight me, after all. I ought to have known how it would be — he was a man who never could be depended upon. Our boys were exultant. I was not, though I tried to be.

It was now time to go out and practise. It was the custom there to fight duels with navy six-shooters at fifteen paces — load and empty till the game for the funeral was secured. We went to a little ravine just outside of town, and borrowed a barn-door for a target — borrowed it of a gentleman who was absent — and we stood this barn-door up, and stood a rail on end against the middle of it, to represent Lord, and put a squash on top of the rail to represent his head. He was a very tall, lean creature, the poorest sort of material for a duel — nothing but a line shot could "fetch" him, and even then he might split your bullet. Exaggeration aside, the rail was, of course, a little too thin to represent his body accurately, but the squash was all right. If there was any intellectual difference between the squash and his head, it was in favor of the squash.

Well, I practised and practised at the barn-door, and could not hit it; and I practised at the rail, and could not hit that; and I tried hard for the squash, and could not hit the squash. I would have been entirely disheartened, but that occasionally I crippled one of the boys, and that encouraged me to hope.

At last we began to hear pistol-shots near by, in the next ravine. We knew what that meant! The other party were out practising, too. Then I was in the last degree distressed; for of course those people would hear our shots, and they would send spies over the ridge, and the spies would find my barn-door without a wound or a scratch, and that would simply be the end of me — for of course that other man would immediately become as bloodthirsty as *I* was. Just at this moment a little bird, no larger than a sparrow, flew by, and lit on a sage-brush about thirty paces away; and my little second, Steve Gillis, who was a matchless marksman with a pistol — much better than I was — snatched out his revolver, and shot the bird's head off! We all ran to pick up the game, and sure enough, just at this moment, some of the other duellists came reconnoitring over the little ridge. They ran to our group to see what the matter was; and when they saw the bird, Lord's second said:

"That was a splendid shot. How far off was it?"
Steve said, with some indifference:
"Oh, no great distance. About thirty paces."
"Thirty paces! Heavens alive, who did it?"
"*My* man — Twain."
"The mischief he did! Can he do that often?"
"Well — yes. He can do it about — well — about four times out of five."

I knew the little rascal was lying, but I never said anything. I never told him so. He was not of a disposition to invite confidences of that kind, so I let the matter rest. But it was a comfort to see those people look sick, and see their underjaws drop, when Steve made these statements. They went off and got Lord, and took him home; and when we got home, half an hour later, there was a note saying that Mr. Lord peremptorily declined to fight!

It was a narrow escape. We found out afterwards that Lord hit *his* mark thirteen times in eighteen shots. If he had put those thirteen bullets through me, it would have narrowed my sphere of usefulness a good deal — would have well nigh closed it, in fact. True they could have put pegs in the holes, and used me for a hat-rack; but what is a hat-rack to a man who feels he has intellectual powers? I would scorn such a position.

I have written this true incident of my personal history for one purpose, and one purpose only — to warn the youth of the day against the pernicious practice of duelling, and to plead with them to war against it. If the remarks and suggestions I am making can be of any service to Sunday-school teachers, and newspapers interested in the moral progress of society, they are at liberty to use them, and I shall even be grateful to have them widely disseminated, so that they may do as much good as possible. I was young and foolish when I challenged that gentleman, and I thought it was very fine and very grand to be a duellist, and stand upon the "field of honor." But I am older and more experienced now, and am inflexibly opposed to the dreadful custom. I am glad, indeed, to be enabled to lift up my voice against it. I think it is a bad, immoral thing. I think it is every man's duty to do everything he can to *discourage* duelling. I always do now; I discourage it upon every occasion.

If a man were to challenge me *now* — now that I can fully appreciate the iniquity of that practice — I would go to that man, and take him by the hand, and lead him to a quiet, retired room — and kill him. (543–46)

"Cure for Stammering"

(Delivered at West Point
28 February 1881 and 3 April 1886)

*"Cure for Stammering" was one of Mark Twain's favorite stories
and one of the greatest challenges to perform.*

As nearly as I can cipher it out, the newspaper reporter has
got us lecturers at a disadvantage. He can either make a
synopsis or do most anything he wants to. He ought to be
generous, and praise us or abuse us, but not print our speeches.
Artemus Ward was bothered by a shorthand reporter, and he
begged him not to do him the injustice to garble his speech. He
says, "You can't take it all down as I utter it." The reporter said,
"If you utter anything I can't take down I will agree not to print
the speech." Along in the lecture he tipped the reporter a wink
and he told the following anecdote. Whistle wherever the stars
occur. If you can't, get somebody that can.

He said that several gentlemen were conversing in a hotel parlor
and one man sat there who didn't have anything to say. By and by
the gentlemen all went out except one of the number and the
silent man. Presently the man reached out and touched the
gentleman and says "* * I think, sir, I have seen you somewhere
before. I am not * * sure where it was or * * when it was * * but I
know I have * * seen you." The gentleman says, "Very likely; but
what do you whistle for?" "* * I'll tell you all about it. * * I used to
stammer * * fearfully and I courted a * * girl and she wouldn't have
me because I was afflicted with such an * * infirmity. I went to a
doctor and * * he * * told me that every time I * * went to stammer
* * that I must whistle, which I * * did, and it * * completely cured
me. But don't you know that * * girl * * wouldn't have me at last,
for she * * said that * * she wouldn't talk to a man that whistled as
I did * *. She'd as soon hold a conversation with a wheelbarrow
that wanted * * greasing." (qtd. in Lorch 320–21)

"The Benefit of Judicious Training"

Delivered by Mark Twain at the twelfth annual reunion of the Army of the Potomac, Hartford, Connecticut, 8 June 1881, the day before he and other dignitaries departed for West Point and "June Week" activities. The text of this speech appeared in Army and Navy Journal *11 June 1881: 944–45. Some reprinted versions of this speech are entitled "The Art of War" or "Instructing the Soldier."*

Let but the thoughtful civilian instruct the soldier in his duties, and the victory is sure.
    — *Martin Farquhar Tupper on the Art of War*

M r. Chairman, — I gladly join with my fellow-townsmen in extending a hearty welcome to these illustrious generals and war-scarred soldiers of the Republic. This is a proud day for us, and, if the sincere desire of our hearts has been fulfilled, it has not been an unpleasant day for them. I am in full accord, sir, with the sentiment of the toast — for I have always maintained, with enthusiasm, that the only wise and true way is for the soldier to fight the battle and the unprejudiced civilian to tell him how to do it; yet when I was invited to respond to this toast and furnish this advice and instruction, I was almost as embarrassed as I was gratified; for I could bring to this great service but the one virtue of absence of prejudice and set opinion.

Still, but one other qualification was needed, and it was of only minor importance — I mean, knowledge of the subject — therefore I was not disheartened, for I could acquire that, there being two weeks to spare. A general of high rank in this Army of the Potomac said two weeks was really more than I would need for the purpose — he had known people of my style who had learned enough in forty-eight hours to enable them to advise an army. Aside from the compliment, this was gratifying, because it confirmed the impression I had had before. He told me to go to the United States Military Academy at West Point — said in his flowery professional way that the cadets would "load me up." I went there and stayed two days, and his prediction proved correct. I make no boast on my own account — none; all I know about military matters I got from the gentlemen at West Point, and to them belongs the credit. They treated me with courtesy from the first; but when my mission was revealed, this mere courtesy blossomed into the warmest zeal. Everybody, officers and all, put down their work and turned their whole attention to giving me military information. Every question I asked was promptly and exhaustively answered. Therefore I feel proud to state that in the advice which I am about to give you, as soldiers, I am backed up by the highest military authority in the land, yes, in the world, if an American does say it — West Point!

To begin, gentlemen. When an engagement is meditated, it is best to feel the enemy first. That is, if it is night; for, as one of the cadets explained to me, you do not need to feel him in the daytime, because you can see him then. I never should have thought of that, but it is true — perfectly true. In the daytime the methods of procedure are various; but the best, it seems to me, is one which was introduced by General Grant. General Grant always sent an active young redoubt to reconnoitre and get the enemy's bearings. I got this from a high officer at the Point, who told me he used to be a redoubt on General Grant's staff and had done it often.

When the hour for the battle is come, move to the field with celerity — fool away no time. Under this head I was told of a favorite maxim of General Sheridan's. General Sheridan always said, "If the siege train isn't ready, don't wait; go by any train that is handy; to get there is the main thing." Now that is the correct idea. As you approach the field it is best to get out and walk. This gives you a better chance to dispose your forces judiciously for the assault. Get your artillery in position, and throw out stragglers to right and left to hold your lines of communication against surprise. See that every hodcarrier connected with the mortar battery is at his post. They told me at the Point that Napoleon despised mortar batteries and never would use them; he said that for real efficiency he wouldn't give a hatful of brickbats for a ton of mortar. However, that is all *he* knew about it.

Everything being ready for the assault, you want to enter the field with your baggage to the front. This idea was invented by our renowned guest, General Sherman. They told me General Sherman said the trunks and steamer chairs make a good protection for the soldiers, but that chiefly they attract the attention and rivet the interest of the enemy and this gives you an opportunity to whirl the other end of the column around and attack him in the rear. I have given a good deal of study to this tactic since I learned about it, and it appears to me it is a rattling-good idea. Never fetch on your reserves at the start. This was Napoleon's first mistake at Waterloo; next he assaulted with his bomb proofs and embrasures and ambulances, when he ought to have used a heavier artillery; thirdly, he retired his right by ricochet — which uncovered his pickets — when his only possibility of success lay in doubling up his center flank by flank and throwing out his chevaux-de-frise by the left oblique to relieve the skirmish line and confuse the enemy — and at West Point they said it would. It was about this time that the emperor had two horses shot under him. How often you see the remark that General So-and-So in such and such a battle had two or three horses shot under him. General Burnside and many great European military men — as I was informed by a high artillery officer at West Point, has justly characterized this as a wanton waste of projectiles, and he impressed upon me a conversation held in the tent of the Prussian chiefs at Gravelotte, in the course of which our honored guest just referred to — General Burnside — observed that if you can't aim a horse so as to hit the general with it, shoot it over him and you may bag somebody on the other side, whereas a horse shot under a general does no sort of damage. I agree cordially with General Burnside, and Heaven knows I shall rejoice to see the artillerists of this land and all lands cease from this wicked and idiotic custom.

At West Point they told me of another mistake at Waterloo, *viz.*, that the French were under fire from the beginning of the fight until the end of it, which was plainly a most effeminate and ill-timed attention to comfort, and a fatal and foolish division of military strength; for it probably took as many men to keep up the fires as it did to do the fighting. It would have been much better to have a small fire in the rear and let the men go there by detachments and get warm, and not try to warm up the whole army at once. All the cadets said that. An assault along the whole line was the one thing which could have restored Napoleon's advantages at this juncture; and he was actually rising in his stirrups to order it when a sutler burst at his side and covered him with dirt and debris; and before he could recover his lost opportunity Wellington opened a tremendous and devastating fire upon him from a monster battery of vivandières, and the star of the great captain's glory set, to rise no more. The cadet wept while he told me these mournful particulars.

When you leave a battlefield, always leave it in good order. Remove the wreck and rubbish and tidy up the place. However, in the case of a drawn battle, it is neither party's business to tidy up anything — you can leave the field looking as if the city government of New York had bossed the fight.

When you are traversing in the enemy's country in order to destroy his supplies and cripple his resources, you want to take along plenty of camp followers — the more the better. They are a tremendously effective arm of the service, and they inspire in the foe the liveliest dread. A West Point professor told me that the wisdom of this was recognized as far back as Scripture times. He quoted the verse. He said it was from the new revision and was a little different from the way it reads in the old one. I do not recollect the exact wording of it now, but I remember that it wound up with something about such-and-such a devastating agent being as "terrible as any army with bummers."

I believe I have nothing further to add but this: The West Pointer said a private should preserve a respectful attitude toward his superiors, and should seldom or never proceed so far as to offer suggestions to his general in the field. If the battle is not being conducted to suit him it is better for him to resign. By the etiquette of war, it is permitted to none below the rank of newspaper correspondent to dictate to the general in the field.

1601

(Printed at the West Point printing press in 1882)

Although not delivered at West Point, 1601 appears here because of its connection with West Point. When Lieutenant Charles Erskine Scott Wood printed 1601 on the West Point printing press in 1882 as a favor to his friend Mark Twain, he risked a court-martial. This salty Elizabethan burlesque is not for the squeamish.

[Date, 1601.]
OR
CONVERSATION, AS IT WAS BY THE SOCIAL FIRESIDE, IN THE TIME OF THE TUDORS

Yesternight toke her maiste ye queene a fantasie such as she sometimes hath, and hadde to her closet certain that doe write playes, bokes, and such like, these being my lord Bacon, his worship Sr. Walter Ralegh, Mr. Ben Jonson, and ye childe Francis Beaumonte, which being but sixteen, hath yet turned his hande to ye doing of ye Latin masters into our Englishe tong, wh grete discretion and much applaus. Also came wh these ye famous Shaxpur. A righte straunge mixing truly of mightie blode wh mean, ye more in especial since ye queenes grace was present, as likewise these following, to wit: Ye Duchess of Bilgewater, twenty-two yeres of age; ye Countesse of Granby, twenty-six; her doter, ye Lady Helen, fifteen; as also these two maides of honour, to wit: ye Lady Margery Boothy, sixty-five, and ye Lady Alice Dilberry, turned seventy, she being two yeres ye queenes graces elder.

I being her maistes cup-bearer, hadde no choice but to remaine and beholde rank forgot, and ye high holde converse wh ye low as uppon equal termes, a grete scandal did ye world heare therof.

In ye heat of ye talk it befel yt one did breake wynde, yielding all exceding mightie and distresful stink, wherat all did laffe full sore, and then —

Ye Queene. — Verily in mine eight and sixty yeres have I not heard the fellow to this fart. Meseemeth, by ye grete sounde and clamour of it, it was male; yet ye belly it did lurk behinde shoulde now fall leane and flat against ye spine of him yt hath bene delivered of so stately and so vaste a bulk, wheras ye guts of them yt doe quiff-splitters beare, stande comely still and rounde. Prithee let ye author confes ye offspring. Will my Lady Alice testify?

Lady Alice. — Good your grace, an' I hadde room for such a thunderbust within mine ancient bowels, 'tis not in reason I coulde discharge ye same and live to thank God for yt He did choose handmaide so humble wherby to shew his power. Nay, 'tis not I yt have broughte forth this rich o'ermastering fog, this fragrant gloom, so pray ye seeke ye further.

Ye Queene. — Mayhap ye Lady Margery hath done ye companie this favour?

Lady Margery. — So please ye madam, my limbs are feeble wh ye weighte and drouth of five and sixty winters, and it behoveth yt I be tender unto them. In ye good providence of God, an' *I* hadde contained this wonder, forsoothe wolde I have gi'en ye whole evening of my sinking life to ye dribbling of it forth, wh trembling and uneasy soul, not launched it sudden in its matchless might, taking mine own life wh violence, rending my weak frame like rotten rags. It was not I, your maiste.

Ye Queene. — O' God's name who hath favoured us? Hath it come to pass yt a fart shall fart *itself?* Not such a one as this, I trow. Young Master Beaumonte — but no; 'twolde have wafted him to heav'n like downe of goose's boddy. 'Twas not ye little Lady Helen — nay, ne'er blush, my childe; thoul't tickle thy tender maidenhedde with many a mousie-squeak before thou learnest to blow a harricane like this. Was't you, my learned and ingenious Jonson?

Jonson. — So fell a blast hath ne'er mine ears saluted, nor yet a stench so all-pervading and immortal. 'Twas not a novice did it, good your maiste, but one of veteran experience — else hadde he failed of confidence. In soothe it was not I.

Ye Queene. — My lord Bacon?

Lord Bacon. — Not from mine leane entrailes hath this prodigie burst forth, so pleas your grace. Naught doth so befit ye grete as grete performance; and haply shall ye finde yt 'tis not from mediocrity this miracle hath issued.

[Tho' ye subject be but a fart, yet will this tedious sink of learning pondrously phillosophize. Meantime did the foul and deadly stink pervade all places to that degree, yt never smelt I ye like, yet dare I not to leave ye presence, albeit I was like to suffocate.]

Ye Queene. — What saith ye worshipful Master Shaxpur?

Shaxpur. — In the grete hand of God I stande and so proclaim mine innocence. Though ye sinless hosts of heav'n hadde fore-tolde ye coming of this most desolating breath, proclaiming it a work of uninspired man, its quaking thunders, its firmament-clogging rottenness, its own achievement in due course of nature, yet hadde not I believed it; but hadde said the pit itself hath furnished forth the stink, and heav'ns artillery hath shook the globe in admiration of it.

[Then there was a silence, and each did turn him toward the worshipful Sr Walter Ralegh that browned, embattled, bloody swashbuckler, who rising up did smile, and simpering say]

Sr W. — Most gracious maiste, 'twas I that did it, but indeed it was so poor and frail a note, compared wh such as I am wont to furnish, yt in sooth I was ashamed to call the weakling mine in so august a presence. It was nothing — less than nothing, madam — I did it but to clear my nether throat; but hadde I come prepared, then hadde I delivered something worthie. Bear wh me, pleas your grace, till I can make amends.

[Then delivered he himself of such a godless and rock-shivering blast that all were fain to stoppe their ears, and following it did come so dense and foul a stink that yt which went before did seem a poor and trifling thing beside it. Then saith he, feigning that he blushed and was confused, *I perceive that I am weak to-day, and cannot justice do unto my powers:* and sat him down as who shoulde say, *There it is not much; yet he yt hath an arse to spare, let him fellow yt, an think he can.* By God, an I were ye Queene, I wolde e'en tip this swaggering braggart out o' the court, and let him air his grandeurs and break his intolerable wynde before ye deaf and such as suffocation pleaseth.] ·

Then felle they to talk about ye manners and customs of many peoples, and Master Shaxpur spake of ye boke of ye sieur Michael de Montaine, wherein was mention of ye customs of widows of Perigord to wear uppon ye headdress, in signe of widowhood, a jewel in ye similitude of a man's member wilted and limber, wherat ye queene did laffe and say, *Widows in England doe wear prickles too, but betwixt the thighs, and not wilted neither, till coition hath done that office for them.* Master Shaxpur did likewise observe how yt ye sieur de Montaine hath also spoken of a certain emperor of such mightie prowess yt he did take ten maidenheddes in ye compass of a single night, ye while his empress did entertain two and twenty lusty knights between her sheetes, yet was not satisfied; wherat ye merrie Countesse Granby saith a ram is yet ye emperor's superior, sith he will tup a hundred yewes 'twixt sun and sun; and after, if he can have none more to shag, will masturbate until he hath enrich'd whole acres wh his seed.

Then spake ye damned windmill, Sr Walter, of a people in ye uttermost parts of America, yt copulate not until they be five and thirty yeres of age, ye women being eight and twenty, and do it then but once in seven yeres.

Ye Queene. — How doth yt like mine little Lady Helen? Shall we send thee thither and preserve thy belly?

Lady Helen. — Please your highness grace, mine old nurse hath told me there are more ways of serving God than by locking the thighs together; yet am I willing to serve him yt way too, sith your highnesses grace hath set ye ensample.

Ye Queene. — God's wowndes, a good answer, childe.

Lady Alice. — Mayhap 'twill weaken when ye hair sprouts below ye navel.

Lady Helen. — Nay, it sprouted two yeres syne. I can scarce more than cover it with my hand now.

Ye Queene. — Hear ye that, my little Beaumonte? Have ye not a little birde about ye yt stirs at hearing tell of so sweete a neste?

Beaumonte. — 'Tis not insensible, illustrious madam; but mousing owls and bats of low degree may not aspire to bliss so whelming and ecstatic as is founde in ye downie nestes of birdes of Paradise.

Ye Queene. — By ye gullet of God, 'tis a neat-turned compliment. With such a tong as thine, lad, thou'lt spread the ivory thighs of many a willing maide in thy good time, an thy cod-piece be as handie as thy speeche.

Then spake ye queene of how she met olde Rabelais when she was turned of fifteen, and he did tell her of a man his father knew yt hadde a double pair of bollocks, wheron a controversy followed as concerning the most just way to spell the word, ye contention running high betwixt ye learned Bacon and ye ingenious Jonson, until at last ye olde Lady Margery, wearying of it all, saith, *Gentles, what mattereth it how ye shall spell the word? I warrant ye when ye use your bollocks ye shall not think of it; and my Lady Cranby be ye content; let the spelling be, ye shall enjoy the beating of them on your buttocks just the same, I trow. Before I hadde gained my fourteenth yere I hadde learned yt them yt wolde explore a cunte stop't not to consider the spelling o't.*

Sr W. — In soothe, when a shift's turned uppe, delay is mete for naught but dalliance. Boccaccio hath a story of a prieste yt did beguile a maide into his cell, then knelt him in a corner to praye for grace to be rightly thankful for this tender maidenhedde ye Lord hath sent him; but ye abbot, spying through ye key-hole, did see a tuft of brownish hair with fair white flesh about it, wherfore when ye priestes prayer was done, his chance was gone, forasmuch as ye little maide hadde but ye one cunte, and yt was already occupied to be content.

Then conversed they of religion, and ye mightie work ye olde dead Luther did doe by ye grace of God. Then next about poetry, and Master Shaxpur did rede a part of his King Henry IV, ye which, it seemeth unto me, is not of the value of an arseful of ashes, yet they praised it bravely, one and all.

Ye same did rede a portion of his "Venus and Adonis" to their prodigious admiration, wheras I, being sleepy and fatigued withal, did deme it but paltrie stuff, and was the more discomfited in yt ye blodie bucanier hadde got his secconde wynde, and did turn his mind to farting wh such villain zeal that presently I was like to choke once more. God damn this wyndie ruffian and all his breed. I wolde yt hell mighte get him.

They talked about ye wonderful defense which olde Sr Nicholas Throgmorton did make for himself before ye judges in ye time of Mary; which was an unlucky matter to broach, sith it fetched out ye queene wh a *Pity yt he having so much wit, hadde yet not enough to save his doter's maidenhedde sounde for her marriage-bedde.* And ye queene did give ye damn'd Sr Walter a look yt made hym wince — for she hath not forgot he was her own lover in yt olde day. There was silent uncomfortableness now; 'twas not a good turn for talk to take, sith if ye queene must find offense in a little harmless debauching, when prickes were stiff and cuntes not loath to take ye stiffness out of them, who of this companie was sinless? Beholde, was not ye wife of Master Shaxpur four months gone wh childe when she stood uppe before ye altar? Was not her Grace of Bilgewater roger'd by four lords before she hadde a husband?

Was not ye little Lady Helen borne on her mother's wedding-day? And, beholde, were not ye Lady Alice and ye Lady Margery there, mouthing religion, whores from ye cradle?

In time came they to discourse of Cervantes, and of the new painter, Rubens, that is beginning to be heard of. Fine words and dainty-wrought phrases from the ladies now, one or two of them being, in other days, pupils of yt poor arse, Lille himself; and I marked how that Jonson and Shaxpur did fidget to discharge some venom of sarcasm, yet dared they not in the presence, ye queenes grace being ye very flower of ye Euphuists herself. But beholde, these be they yt, having a specialtie, and admiring in it themselves, be jealous when a neighbour doth essaye it, nor can abide it in them long. Wherfore 'twas observable yt ye queene waxed uncontent; and in time a labor'd grandiose speeche out of ye mouthe of Lady Alice, who manifestly did mightily pride herself theron, did quite exhauste ye queenes endurance, who listened till ye gaudie speeche was done, then lifted uppe her brows, and wh vaste ironie, mincing saith, *O shitte!* Wherat they alle did laffe, but not ye Lady Alice, yt olde foolish bitche.

Now was Sr Walter minded of a tale he once did heare ye ingenious Margarette of Navarre relate, about a maide, which being like to suffer rape by an olde archbishoppe, did smartly contrive a device to save her maidenhedde, and said to him, *First, my lord, I prithee, take out they holy tool and pisse before me;* which doing, lo! his member felle, and wolde not rise again.

"The Awful German Language"
(Delivered at West Point 3 April 1886)

Mark Twain probably did not read this entire speech to his West Point audience. In his usual fashion, he would have modified the basic material to fit his audience. Present for this reading was Cadet First Captain John J. Pershing, who would later command the American Expeditionary Forces against the German army in World War I. "The Awful German Language" appeared in appendix D of A Tramp Abroad *(1880). All footnotes are Mark Twain's.*

A little learning makes the whole world kin.
— *Proverbs* xxxii, 7.

I went often to look at the collection of curiosities in Heidelberg Castle, and one day I surprised the keeper of it with my German. I spoke entirely in that language. He was greatly interested; and after I had talked a while he said my German was very rare, possibly a "unique"; and wanted to add it to his museum.

If he had known what it had cost me to acquire my art, he would also have known that it would break any collector to buy it. Harris and I had been hard at work on our German during several weeks at that time, and although we had made good progress, it had been accomplished under great difficulty and annoyance, for three of our teachers had died in the mean time. A person who has not studied German can form no idea of what a perplexing language it is.

Surely there is not another language that is so slipshod and systemless, and so slippery and elusive to the grasp. One is washed about in it, hither and thither, in the most helpless way; and when at last he thinks he has captured a rule which offers firm ground to take a rest on amid the general rage and turmoil of the ten parts of speech, he turns over the page and reads, "Let the pupil make careful note of the following *exceptions*." He runs his eye down and finds that there are more exceptions to the rule than instances of it. So overboard he goes again, to hunt for another Ararat and find another quicksand. Such has been, and continues to be, my experience. Every time I think I have got one of these four confusing "cases" where I am master of it, a seemingly insignificant preposition intrudes itself into my sentence, clothed with an awful and unsuspected power, and crumbles the ground from under me. For instance, my book inquires after a certain bird — (it is always inquiring after things which are of no sort of consequence to anybody): "Where is the bird?" Now the answer to this question — according to the book — is that the bird is waiting in the blacksmith shop on account of the rain. Of course no bird would do that, but then you must stick to the book. Very well, I begin to cipher out the German for that answer. I begin at the wrong end, necessarily, for that is the German idea. I say to myself, "*Regen* (rain) is masculine — or maybe feminine — or possibly neuter — it is too much trouble to look now. Therefore, it is either *der* (the) Regen, or *die* (the) Regen, or *das* (the) Regen, according to which gender it may turn out to be when I look. In the interest of science, I will cipher it out on the hypothesis that it is masculine. Very well — then *the* rain is der Regen, if it is simply in the quiescent state of being *mentioned*, without enlargement or discussion — Nominative case; but if this rain is lying around, in a kind of a general way on the ground, it is then definitely located, it is *doing something* — that is, *resting* (which is one of the German grammar's ideas of doing something), and this throws the rain into the Dative case, and makes it *dem* Regen. However, this rain is not resting, but is doing something *actively* — it is falling — to interfere with the bird, likely — and this indicates *movement*, which has the effect of sliding it into the Accusative case and changing *dem* Regen into *den* Regen." Having completed the grammatical horoscope of this matter, I answer up confidently and state in German that the bird is staying in the blacksmith shop "wegen (on account of) *den* Regen." Then the teacher lets me softly down with the remark that whenever the word "wegen" drops into a sentence, it *always* throws that subject into the *Genitive* case, regardless of consequences — and that therefore this bird stayed in the blacksmith shop "wegen *des* Regens."

N.B. — I was informed, later, by a higher authority, that there was an "exception" which permits one to say "wegen *den* Regen" in certain peculiar and complex circumstances, but that this exception is not extended to anything *but* rain.

There are ten parts of speech, and they are all troublesome. An average sentence, in a German newspaper, is a sublime and impressive curiosity; it occupies a quarter of a column; it contains all the ten parts of speech — not in regular order, but mixed; it is built mainly of compound words constructed by the writer on the spot, and not to be found in any dictionary — six or seven words compacted into one, without joint or seam — that is, without hyphens; it treats of fourteen or fifteen different subjects, each inclosed in a parenthesis of its own, with here and there extra parentheses which reenclose three or four of the minor parentheses, making pens within pens: finally, all the parentheses and reparentheses are massed together between a couple of king-parentheses, one of which is placed in the first line of the majestic sentence and the other in the middle of the last line of it — *after which comes the* VERB, and you find out for the first time what the man has been talking about; and after the verb — merely by way of ornament, as far as I can make out — the writer shovels in *"haben sind gewesen gehabt haben geworden sein,"* or words to that effect, and the monument is finished. I suppose that this closing hurrah is in the nature of the flourish to a man's signature — not necessary, but pretty. German books are easy enough to read when you hold them before the looking-glass or stand on your head — so as to reverse the construction — but I think that to learn to read and understand a German newspaper is a thing which must always remain an impossibility to a foreigner.

Yet even the German books are not entirely free from attacks of the Parenthesis distemper — though they are usually so mild as to cover only a few lines, and therefore when you at last get down to the verb it carries some meaning to your mind because you are able to remember a good deal of what has gone before.

Now here is a sentence from a popular and excellent German novel — with a slight parenthesis in it. I will make a perfectly literal translation, and throw in the parenthesis-marks and some hyphens for the assistance of the reader — though in the original there are no parenthesis marks or hyphens, and the reader is left to flounder through to the remote verb the best way he can:

"But when he, upon the street, the (in-satin-and-silk-covered-now-very-unconstrainedly-after-the-newest-fashion-dressed) government counselor's wife *met*," etc., etc.*

That is from *The Old Mamselle's Secret*, by Mrs. Marlitt. And that sentence is constructed upon the most approved German model. You observe how far that verb is from the reader's base of operations; well, in a German newspaper they put their verb away over on the next page; and I have heard that sometimes after stringing along on exciting preliminaries and parentheses for a column or two, they get in a hurry and have to go to press without getting to the verb at all. Of course, then, the reader is left in a very exhausted and ignorant state.

We have the Parenthesis disease in our literature, too; and one may see cases of it every day in our books and newspapers: but with us it is the mark and sign of an unpracticed writer or a cloudy intellect, whereas with the Germans it is doubtless the mark and sign of a practiced pen and of the presence of that sort of luminous intellectual fog which stands for clearness among these people. For surely it is *not* clearness — it necessarily can't be clearness. Even a jury would have penetration enough to discover that. A writer's ideas must be a good deal confused, a good deal out of

---

* *Wenn er aber auf der Strasse der in Sammt und Seide gehüllten jetz sehr ungenirt nach der neusten mode gekdeideten Regierungsrathin begegnet.*

line and sequence, when he starts out to say that a man met a counselor's wife in the street, and then right in the midst of this so simple undertaking halts these approaching people and makes them stand still until he jots down an inventory of the woman's dress. That is manifestly absurd. It reminds a person of those dentists who secure your instant and breathless interest in a tooth by taking a grip on it with the forceps, and then stand there and drawl through a tedious anecdote before they give the dreaded jerk. Parentheses in literature and dentistry are in bad taste.

The Germans have another kind of parenthesis, which they make by splitting a verb in two and putting half of it at the beginning of an exciting chapter and the *other half* at the end of it. Can any one conceive of anything more confusing than that? These things are called "separable verbs." The German grammar is blistered all over with separable verbs; and the wider the two portions of one of them are spread apart, the better the author of the crime is pleased with his performance. A favorite one is *reiste ab* — which means *departed*. Here is an example which I culled from a novel and reduced to English:

> "The trunks being now ready, he DE-after kissing his mother and sisters, and once more pressing to his bosom his adored Gretchen, who, dressed in simple white muslin, with a single tuberose in the ample folds of her rich brown hair, had tottered feebly down the stairs, still pale from the terror and excitement of the past evening, but longing to lay her poor aching head yet once again upon the breast of him whom she loved more dearly than life itself, PARTED."

However, it is not well to dwell too much on the separable verbs. One is sure to lose his temper early; and if he sticks to the subject, and will not be warned, it will at last either soften his brain or petrify it. Personal pronouns and adjectives are a fruitful nuisance in this language, and should have been left out. For instance, the same sound, *sie*, means you, and it means *she*, and it means *her*, and it means *it*, and it means *they*, and it means *them*. Think of the ragged poverty of a language which has to make one word do the work of six — and a poor little weak thing of only three letters at that. But mainly, think of the exasperation of never knowing which of these meanings the speaker is trying to convey. This explains why, whenever a person says *sie* to me, I generally try to kill him, if a stranger.

Now observe the Adjective. Here was a case where simplicity would have been an advantage; therefore, for no other reason, the inventor of this language complicated it all he could. When we wish to speak of our "good friend or friends," in our enlightened tongue, we stick to the one form and have no trouble or hard feeling about it; but with the German tongue it is different. When a German gets his hands on an adjective, he declines it, and keeps on declining it until the common sense is all declined out of it. It is as bad as Latin. He says, for instance:

SINGULAR

Nominative — Mein gut*er* Freund, my good friend.
Genitive — Mein*es* guten Freund*es*, of my good friend.
Dative — Meinem *guten* Freund, to my good friend.
Accusative — Mein*en* guten Freund, my good friend.

PLURAL

N. — Mein*e* gut*en* Freund*e*, my good friends.
G. — Mein*er* gut*en* Freund*e*, of my good friends.
D. — Mein*en* gut*en* Freund*en*, to my good friends.
A. — Mein*e* gut*en* Freund*e*, my good friends.

Now let the candidate for the asylum try to memorize those variations, and see how soon he will be elected. One might better go without friends in Germany than take all this trouble about them. I have shown what a bother it is to decline a good (male) friend; well this is only a third of the work, for there is a variety of new distortions of the adjective to be learned when the object is feminine, and still another when the object is neuter. Now there are more adjectives in this language than there are black cats in Switzerland, and they must all be as elaborately declined as the examples above suggested. Difficult? — troublesome? — these words cannot describe it. I heard a Californian student in Heidelberg say, in one of his calmest moods, that he would rather decline two drinks than one German adjective.

The inventor of the language seems to have taken pleasure in complicating it in every way he could think of. For instance, if one is casually referring to a house, *Haus*, or a horse, *Pferd*, or a dog, *Hund*, he spells these words as I have indicated; but if he is referring to them in the Dative case, he sticks on a foolish and unnecessary *e* and spells them *Hause, Pferde, Hunde*. So, as an added *e* often signifies the plural, as the *s* does with us, the new student is likely to go on for a month making twins out of a Dative dog before he discovers his mistake; and on the other hand, many a new student who could ill afford loss, has bought and paid for two dogs and only got one of them, because he ignorantly bought that dog in the Dative singular when he really supposed he was talking plural — which left the law on the seller's side, of course, by the strict rules of grammar, and therefore a suit for recovery could not lie.

In German, all the Nouns begin with a capital letter. Now that is a good idea; and a good idea, in this language, is necessarily conspicuous from its lonesomeness. I consider this capitalizing of nouns a good idea, because by reason of it you are almost always able to tell a noun the minute you see it. You fall into error occasionally, because you mistake the name of a person for the name of a thing, and waste a good deal of time trying to dig a meaning out of it. German names almost always do mean something, and this helps to deceive the student. I translated a passage one day, which said that "the infuriated tigress broke loose and utterly ate up the unfortunate fir forest" *(Tannenwald)*. When I was girding up my loins to doubt this, I found out that Tannenwald in this instance was a man's name.

Every noun has a gender, and there is no sense or system in the distribution; so the gender of each must be learned separately and by heart. There is no other way. To do this one has to have a memory like a memorandum-book. In German, a young lady has no sex, while a turnip has. Think what overwrought reverence that shows for the turnip, and what callous disrespect for the girl. See how it looks in print — I translate this from a conversation in one of the best of the German Sunday-school books:

"*Gretchen.* — Wilhelm, where is the turnip?
"*Wilhelm.* — She has gone to the kitchen.
"*Gretchen.* — Where is the accomplished and beautiful English maiden?
"*Wilhelm.* — *It* has gone to the opera."

To continue with the German genders: a tree is male, its buds are female, its leaves are neuter; horses are sexless, dogs are male, cats are female — tomcats included, of course; a person's mouth, neck, bosom, elbows, fingers, nails, feet, and body are of the male sex, and his head is male or neuter according to the word selected to signify it, and *not* according to the sex of the individual who wears it — for in Germany all the women wear either male heads or sexless ones; a person's nose, lips, shoulders, breast, hands, and toes are of the female sex; and his hair, ears, eyes, chin, legs, knees, heart, and conscience haven't any sex at all. The inventor of the language probably got what he knew about a conscience from hearsay.

Now, by the above dissection, the reader will see that in Germany a man may *think* he is a man, but when he comes to look into the matter closely, he is bound to have his doubts; he finds that in sober truth he is a most ridiculous mixture; and if he ends by trying to comfort himself with the thought that he can at least depend on a third of this mess as being manly and masculine, the humiliating second thought will quickly remind him that in this respect he is no better off than any woman or cow in the land.

In the German it is true that by some oversight of the inventor of the language, a Woman is a female; but a Wife *(Weib) is* not — which is unfortunate. A Wife, here, has no sex; she is neuter; so, according to the grammar, a fish is *he*, his scales are *she*, but a fishwife is neither. To describe a wife as sexless may be called under-description; that is bad enough, but over-description is surely worse. A German speaks of an Englishman as the *Engländer;* to change the sex, he adds *inn*, and that stands for Englishwoman — *Engländerinn*. That seems descriptive enough, but still it is not exact enough for a German; so he precedes the word with that article which indicates that the creature to follow is feminine, and writes it down thus: *"die* Engländer*inn,"* — which means "the *she-Englishwoman."* I consider that that person is over-described.

Well, after the student has learned the sex of a great number of nouns, he is still in a difficulty, because he finds it impossible to persuade his tongue to refer to things as *"he"* and *"she,"* and *"him"* and *"her,"* which it has been always accustomed to refer to as *"it."* When he even frames a German sentence in his mind, with the hims and hers in the right places, and then works up his courage to the utterance point, it is no use — the moment he begins to speak his tongue flies the track and all those labored males and females come out as *"its."* And even when he is reading German to himself, he always calls those things "it," whereas he ought to read in this way:

TALE OF THE FISHWIFE AND ITS SAD FATE[*]

It is a bleak Day. Hear the Rain, how he pours, and the Hail, how he rattles; and see the Snow, how he drifts along, and oh the Mud, how deep he is! Ah the poor Fishwife, it is stuck fast in the Mire; it has dropped its Basket of Fishes;

---

[*] I capitalize the nouns, in the German (and ancient English) fashion.

and its Hands have been cut by the Scales as it seized some of the falling Creatures; and one Scale has even got into its Eye, and it cannot get her out. It opens its Mouth to cry for Help; but if any Sound comes out of him, alas he is drowned by the raging of the Storm. And now a Tomcat has got one of the Fishes and she will surely escape with him. No, she bites off a Fin, she holds her in her Mouth — will she swallow her? No, the Fishwife's brave Mother-dog deserts his Puppies and rescues the Fin — which he eats, himself, as his Reward. O, horror, the Lightning has struck the Fish-basket; he sets him on Fire; see the Flame, how she licks the doomed Utensil with her red and angry Tongue; now she attacks the helpless Fishwife's Foot — she burns him up, all but the big Toe, and even *she* is partly consumed; and still she spreads, still she waves her fiery Tongues; she attacks the Fishwife's Leg and destroys it; she attacks its Hand and destroys *her*; she attacks its poor worn Garment and destroys *her* also; she attacks its Body and consumes him; she wreathes herself about its Heart and it is consumed; next about its Breast, and in a Moment *she* is a Cinder; now she reaches its Neck — *he* goes; now its Chin — it goes; now its Nose — *she* goes. In another Moment, except Help come, the Fishwife will be no more. Time presses — is there none to succor and save? Yes! Joy, joy, with flying Feet the she-Englishwoman comes! But alas, the generous she-Female is too late: where now is the fated Fishwife? It has ceased from its Sufferings, it has gone to a better Land; all that is left of it for its loved Ones to lament over, is this poor smoldering Ash-heap. Ah, woeful, woeful Ash-heap! Let us take him up tenderly, reverently, upon the lowly Shovel, and bear him to his long Rest, with the Prayer that when he rises again it will be in a Realm where he will have one good square responsible Sex, and have it all to himself, instead of having a mangy lot of assorted Sexes scattered all over him in Spots.

There, now, the reader can see for himself that this pronoun business is a very awkward thing for the unaccustomed tongue.

I suppose that in all languages the similarities of look and sound between words which have no similarity in meaning are a fruitful source of perplexity to the foreigner. It is so in our tongue, and it is notably the case in the German. Now there is that troublesome word *vermählt*: to me it has so close a resemblance — either real or fancied — to three or four other words, that I never know whether it means despised, painted, suspected, or married; until I look in the dictionary, and then I find it means the latter. There are lots of such words and they are a great torment. To increase the difficulty there are words which *seem* to resemble each other, and yet do not; but they make just as much trouble as if they did. For instance, there is the word *vermiethen* (to let, to lease, to hire); and the word *verheirathen* (another way of saying to *marry*). I heard of an Englishman who knocked at a man's door in Heidelberg and proposed, in the best German he could command, to "*verheirathen*" that house. Then there are some words which mean one thing when you emphasize the first syllable, but mean something very different if you throw the emphasis on the last syllable. For instance, there is a word which means a runaway, or the act of glancing through a book, according to the placing of the emphasis; and another word which signifies to *associate* with a man, or to *avoid* him, according to where you put the emphasis — and you can generally depend on putting it in the wrong place and getting into trouble.

There are some exceedingly useful words in this language. *Schlag*, for example; and *Zug*. There are three-quarters of a column of *Schlags* in the dictionary, and a column and a half of *Zugs*. The word *Schlag* means Blow, Stroke, Dash, Hit, Shock, Clap, Slap, Time, Bar, Coin, Stamp, Kind, Sort, Manner, Way, Apoplexy, Wood-cutting, Inclosure, Field, Forest-clearing. This is its simple and *exact* meaning — that is to say, its restricted, its fettered meaning; but there are ways by which you can set it free, so that it can soar away, as on the wings of the morning, and never be at rest. You can hang any word you please to its tail, and make it mean anything you want to. You can begin with *Schlag-ader*, which means artery, and you can hang on the whole dictionary, word by word, clear through the alphabet to *Schlag-wasser*, which means bilge-water — and including *Schlag-mutter*, which means mother-in-law.

Just the same with *Zug*. Strictly speaking, *Zug* means Pull, Tug, Draught, Procession, March, Progress, Flight, Direction, Expedition, Train, Caravan, Passage, Stroke, Touch, Line, Flourish, Trait of Character, Feature, Lineament, Chess-move, Organ-stop, Team, Whiff, Bias, Drawer, Propensity, Inhalation, Disposition: but that thing which it does *not* mean — when all its legitimate pennants have been hung on, has not been discovered yet.

One cannot overestimate the usefulness of *Schlag* and *Zug*. Armed just with these two, and the word *Also*, what cannot the foreigner on German soil accomplish? The German word *Also is* the equivalent of the English phrase "You know," and does not mean anything at all — in *talk*, though it sometimes does in print. Every time a German opens his mouth an *Also* falls out; and every time he shuts it he bites one in two that was trying to *get* out.

Now, the foreigner, equipped with these three noble words, is master of the situation. Let him talk right along, fearlessly; let him pour his indifferent German forth, and when he lacks for a word, let him heave a *Schlag* into the vacuum; all the chances are that it fits it like a plug, but if it doesn't let him promptly heave a Zug after it; the two together can hardly fail to bung the hole; but if, by a miracle, they *should* fail, let him simply say *Also!* and this will give him a moment's chance to think of the needful word. In Germany, when you load your conversational gun it is always best to throw in a *Schlag* or two and a *Zug* or two, because it doesn't make any difference how much the rest of the charge may scatter, you are bound to bag something with *them*. Then you blandly say *Also*, and load up again. Nothing gives such an air of grace and elegance and unconstraint to a German or an English conversation as to scatter it full of "Also's" or "You-knows."

In my note-book I find this entry:

July 1. — In the hospital yesterday, a word of thirteen syllables was successfully removed from a patient — a North German from near Hamburg; but as most unfortunately the surgeons had opened him in the wrong place, under the impression that he contained a panorama, he died. The sad event has cast a gloom over the whole community.

That paragraph furnishes a text for a few remarks about one of the most curious and notable features of my subject — the length of German words. Some German words are so long that they have a perspective. Observe these examples:

Freundschaftsbezeigungen.
Dilettantenaufdringlichkeiten.
Stadtverordnetenversammlungen.

These things are not words, they are alphabetical processions. And they are not rare; one can open a German newspaper any time and see them marching majestically across the page — and if he has any imagination he can see the banners and hear the music, too. They impart a martial thrill to the meekest subject. I take a great interest in these curiosities. Whenever I come across a good one, I stuff it and put it in my museum. In this way I have made quite a valuable collection. When I get duplicates, I exchange with other collectors, and thus increase the variety of my stock. Here are some specimens which I lately bought at an auction sale of the effects of a bankrupt bric-a-brac hunter:

GENERALSTAATSVERORDNETENVERSAMMLUNGEN
ALTERTHUMSWISSENSCHAFTEN.
KINDERBEWAHRUNGSANSTALTEN.
UNABHAENGIGKEITSERKLAERUNGEN.
WIEDERERSTELLUNGSBESTREBUNGEN.
WAFFENSTILLSTANDSUNTERHANDLUNGEN.

Of course when one of these grand mountain ranges goes stretching across the printed page, it adorns and ennobles that literary landscape — but at the same time it is a great distress to the new student, for it blocks up his way; he cannot crawl under it, or climb over it, or tunnel through it. So he resorts to the dictionary for help, but there is no help there. The dictionary must draw the line somewhere — so it leaves this sort of words out. And it is right, because these long things are hardly legitimate words, but are rather combinations of words, and the inventor of them ought to have been killed. They are compound words with the hyphens left out. The various words used in building them are in the dictionary, but in a very scattered condition; so you can hunt the materials out, one by one, and get at the meaning at last, but it is a tedious and harassing business. I have tried this process upon some of the above examples. *"Freundschaftsbezeigungen"* seems to be "Friendship demonstrations," which is only a foolish and clumsy way of saying "demonstrations of friendship." *"Unabhaengigkeitserklaerungen"* seems to be "Independencedeclarations," which is no improvement upon "Declarations of Independence," so far as I can see. *"Generalstaatsverordnetenversammlungen"* seems to be "Generalstates-representativesmeetings," as nearly as I can get at it — a mere rhythmical, gushy euphuism for "meetings of the legislature," I judge. We used to have a good deal of this sort of crime in our literature, but it has gone out now. We used to speak of a thing as a "never-to-be-forgotten" circumstance, instead of cramping it into the simple and sufficient word "memorable" and then going calmly about our business as if nothing had happened. In those days we were not content to embalm the thing and bury it decently, we wanted to build a monument over it.

But in our newspapers the compounding-disease lingers a little to the present day, but with the hyphens left out, in the German fashion. This is the shape it takes: instead of saying "Mr. Simmons, clerk of the county and district courts, was in town yesterday," the new form puts it thus: "Clerk of the County and District Courts Simmons was in town yesterday." This saves neither time nor ink, and has an awkward sound besides. One often sees a remark like this in our papers: *"Mrs.* Assistant District Attorney

Johnson returned to her city residence yesterday for the season." That is a case of really unjustifiable compounding; because it not only saves no time or trouble, but confers a title on Mrs. Johnson which she has no right to. But these little instances are trifles indeed, contrasted with the ponderous and dismal German system of piling jumbled compounds together. I wish to submit the following local item, from a Mannheim journal, by way of illustration:

"In the daybeforeyesterdayshortlyaftereleveno'clock Night, the inthistownstandingtavern called 'The Wagoner' was downburnt. When the fire to the onthedownburninghouseresting Stork's Nest reached, flew the parent Storks away. But when the by-theraging, firesurrounded Nest *itself* caught Fire, straightway plunged the quickreturning Motherstork into the Flames and died, her Wings over her young ones outspread."

Even the cumbersome German construction is not able to take the pathos out of that picture — indeed, it somehow seems to strengthen it. This item is dated away back yonder months ago. I could have used it sooner, but I was waiting to hear from the Father-stork. I am still waiting.

"Also!" If I have not shown that the German is a difficult language, I have at least intended to do it. I have heard of an American student who was asked how he was getting along with his German, and who answered promptly: "I am not getting along at all. I have worked at it hard for three level months, and all I have got to show for it is one solitary German phrase — '*Zwei glas*'" (two glasses of beer). He paused a moment, reflectively; then added with feeling: "But I've got that *solid!*"

And if I have not also shown that German is a harassing and infuriating study, my execution has been at fault, and not my intent. I heard lately of a worn and sorely tried American student who used to fly to a certain German word for relief when he could bear up under his aggravations no longer — the only word in the whole language whose sound was sweet and precious to his ear and healing to his lacerated spirit. This was the word *Damit*. It was only the *sound* that helped him, not the meaning;* and so, at last, when he learned that the emphasis was not on the first syllable, his only stay and support was gone, and he faded away and died.

I think that a description of any loud, stirring, tumultuous episode must be tamer in German than in English. Our descriptive words of this character have such a deep, strong, resonant sound, while their German equivalents do seem so thin and mild and energyless. Boom, burst, crash, roar, storm, bellow, blow, thunder, explosion; howl, cry, shout, yell, groan; battle, hell. These are magnificent words; they have a force and magnitude of sound befitting the things which they describe. But their German equivalents would be ever so nice to sing the children to sleep with, or else my awe-inspiring ears were made for display and not for superior usefulness in analyzing sounds. Would any man want to die in a battle which was called by so tame a term as a *Schlacht?* Or would not a consumptive feel too much bundled up, who was about to go out, in a shirt-collar and a seal-ring, into a storm which the bird-song word *Gewitter* was employed to describe? And observe the strongest of the several German equivalents for explosion — *Ausbruch*. Our word Toothbrush is more powerful than that. It seems to me that the Germans could do worse than import it into their language to describe particularly tremendous explosions with. The German word for hell — Hölle — sounds more like *helly* than anything else; therefore, how necessarily chipper, frivolous, and unimpressive it is. If a man were told in German to go there, could he really rise to the dignity of feeling insulted?

Having pointed out, in detail, the several vices of this language, I now come to the brief and pleasant task of pointing out its virtues. The capitalizing of the nouns I have already mentioned. But far before this virtue stands another — that of spelling a word according to the sound of it. After one short lesson in the

---

* It merely means, in its general sense, "herewith."

alphabet, the student can tell how any German word is pronounced without having to ask; whereas in our language if a student should inquire of us, "What does B, O, W, spell?" we should be obliged to reply, "Nobody can tell what it spells when you set it off by itself; you can only tell by referring to the context and finding out what it signifies — whether it is a thing to shoot arrows with, or a nod of one's head, or the forward end of a boat."

There are some German words which are singularly and powerfully effective. For instance, those which describe lowly, peaceful, and affectionate home life; those which deal with love, in any and all forms, from mere kindly feeling and honest good will toward the passing stranger, clear up to courtship; those which deal with outdoor Nature, in its softest and loveliest aspects — with meadows and forests, and birds and flowers, the fragrance and sunshine of summer, and the moonlight of peaceful winter nights; in a word, those which deal with any and all forms of rest, repose, and peace; those also which deal with the creatures and marvels of fairyland; and lastly and chiefly, in those words which express pathos, is the language surpassingly rich and effective. There are German songs which can make a stranger to the language cry. That shows that the sound of the words is correct — it interprets the meanings with truth and with exactness; and so the ear is informed, and through the ear, the heart.

The Germans do not seem to be afraid to repeat a word when it is the right one. They repeat it several times, if they choose. That is wise. But in English, when we have used a word a couple of times in a paragraph, we imagine we are growing tautological, and so we are weak enough to exchange it for some other word which only approximates exactness, to escape what we wrongly fancy is a greater blemish. Repetition may be bad, but surely inexactness is worse.

There are people in the world who will take a great deal of trouble to point out the faults in a religion or a language, and then go blandly about their business without suggesting any remedy. I am not that kind of a person. I have shown that the German language needs reforming. Very well, I am ready to reform it. At least I am ready to make the proper suggestions. Such a course as this might be immodest in another; but I have devoted upward of nine full weeks, first and last, to a careful and critical study of this tongue, and thus have acquired a confidence in my ability to reform it which no mere superficial culture could have conferred upon me.

In the first place, I would leave out the Dative case. It confuses the plurals; and, besides, nobody ever knows when he is in the Dative case, except he discover it by accident — and then he does not know when or where it was that he got into it, or how long he has been in it, or how he is ever going to get out of it again. The Dative case is but an ornamental folly — it is better to discard it.

In the next place, I would move the Verb further up to the front. You may load up with ever so good a Verb, but I notice that you never really bring down a subject with it at the present German range — you only cripple it. So I insist that this important part of speech should be brought forward to a position where it may be easily seen with the naked eye.

Thirdly, I would import some strong words from the English tongue — to swear with, and also to use in describing all sorts of vigorous things in a vigorous way.*

---

* *"Verdammt,"* and its variations and enlargements, are words which have plenty of meaning, but the *sounds* are so mild and ineffectual that German ladies can use them without sin. German ladies who could not be induced to commit a sin by any persuasion or compulsion, promptly rip out one of these harmless little words when they tear their dresses or don't like the soup. It sounds about as wicked as our "My gracious." German ladies are constantly saying, *"Ach! Gott!" "Mein Gott!" "Gott in Himmel!" "Herr Gott!" "Der Herr Jesus!"* etc. They think our ladies have the same custom, perhaps; for I once heard a gentle and lovely old German lady say to a sweet young American girl: "The two languages are so alike — how pleasant that is; we say *'Ach! Gott!'* you say 'Goddam.'"

Fourthly, I would reorganize the sexes, and distribute them according to the will of the Creator. This as a tribute of respect, if nothing else.

Fifthly, I would do away with those great long compounded words; or require the speaker to deliver them in sections, with intermissions for refreshments. To wholly do away with them would be best, for ideas are more easily received and digested when they come one at a time than when they come in bulk. Intellectual food is like any other; it is pleasanter and more beneficial to take it with a spoon than with a shovel.

Sixthly, I would require a speaker to stop when he is done, and not hang a string of those useless *"haben sind gewesen gehabt haben geworden seins"* to the end of his oration. This sort of gewgaws undignify a speech, instead of adding a grace. They are, therefore, an offense, and should be discarded.

Seventhly, I would discard the Parenthesis. Also the reparenthesis, the re-reparenthesis, and the re-re-re-re-re-reparentheses, and likewise the final wide-reaching all-inclosing king-parenthesis. I would require every individual, be he high or low, to unfold a plain straightforward tale, or else coil it and sit on it and hold his peace. Infractions of this law should be punishable with death.

And eighthly, and last, I would retain *Zug* and *Schlag*, with their pendants, and discard the rest of the vocabulary. This would simplify the language.

I have now named what I regard as the most necessary and important changes. These are perhaps all I could be expected to name for nothing; but there are other suggestions which I can and will make in case my proposed application shall result in my being formally employed by the government in the work of reforming the language.

My philological studies have satisfied me that a gifted person ought to learn English (barring spelling and pronouncing) in thirty hours, French in thirty days, and German in thirty years. It seems manifest, then, that the latter tongue ought to be trimmed down and repaired. If it is to remain as it is, it ought to be gently and reverently set aside among the dead languages, for only the dead have time to learn it.

A FOURTH OF JULY ORATION IN THE GERMAN TONGUE, DELIVERED AT A BANQUET OF THE ANGLO-AMERICAN CLUB OF STUDENTS BY THE AUTHOR OF THIS BOOK*

GENTLEMEN: Since I arrived, a month ago, in this old wonderland, this vast garden of Germany, my English tongue has so often proved a useless piece of baggage to me, and so troublesome to carry around, in a country where they haven't the checking system for luggage, that I finally set to work, last week and learned the German language. Also! Es freut mich dass dies so ist, denn es muss, in ein hauptsächlich degree, höflich sein, dass man auf ein occasion like this, sein Rede in die Sprache des Landes worin he boards, aussprechen soll. Dafür habe ich, aus reinische Verlegenheit — no, Vergangenheit — no, I mean Höflichkeit — aus reinische Höflichkeit habe ich resolved to tackle this business in the German language, um Gottes willen! Also! Sie müssen so freundlich sein, und verzeih mich die interlarding von ein oder zwei Englischer Worte, hie und da, denn ich finde dass die deutsche is not a very copious language, and so when you've really got anything to say, you've got to draw on a language that can stand the strain.

Wenn aber man kann nicht meinem Rede verstehen, so werde ich ihm später dasselbe übersetz, wenn er solche Dienst verlangen wollen haben werden sollen sein hätte. (I don't know what wollen haben werden sollen sein hätte means, but I notice they always put it at the end of a German sentence — merely for general literary gorgeousness, I suppose.)

This is a great and justly honored day — a day which is worthy

---

* [*A Tramp Abroad*]

of the veneration in which it is held by the true patriots of all climes and nationalities — a day which offers a fruitful theme for thought and speech; und meinem Freunde — no, mein*en* Freund*en* — mein*es* Freund*es* — well, take your choice, they're all the same price; I don't know which one is right — also! ich habe gehabt haben worden gewesen sein, as Goethe says in his Paradise Lost — ich — ich — that is to say — ich — but let us change cars.

Also! Die Anblick so viele Grossbrittanischer und Amerikanischer hier zusammengetroffen in Bruderliche concord, ist zwar a welcome and inspiriting spectacle. And what has moved you to it? Can the terse German tongue rise to the expression of this impulse? Is it Freundschaftsbezeigungenstadtverordnetenversammlungenfamilieneigenthümlichkeiten? Nein, o nein! This is a crisp and noble word, but it fails to pierce the marrow of the impulse which has gathered this friendly meeting and produced diese Anblick — eine Anblick welche ist gut zu sehen — gut für die Augen in a foreign land and a far country — eine Anblick solche als in die gewohnliche Heidelberger phrase nennt man ein "schönes Aussicht!" Ja, freilich natürlich wahrscheinlich ebensowohl! Also! Die Aussicht auf dem Königsstuhl mehr grösserer ist, aber geistlische sprechend nicht so schön, lob' Gott! Because sie sind hier zusammengetroffen, in Bruderlichem concord, ein grossen Tag zu feiern, whose high benefits were not for one land and one locality only, but have conferred a measure of good upon all lands that know liberty to-day, and love it. Hundert Jahre vorüber, waren die Engländer und die Amerikaner Feinde; aber heute sind sie herzlichen Freunde, Gott sei Dank! May this good-fellowship endure; may these banners here blended in amity so remain; may they never any more wave over opposing hosts, or be stained with blood which was kindred, is kindred, and always will be kindred, until a line drawn upon a map shall be able to say: "*This* bars the ancestral blood from flowing in the veins of the descendant!"

"An American Party"
(Delivered at West Point 3 April 1886)

"An American Party" also comes from A Tramp Abroad *(1880).
Mark Twain and his wife and daughters traveled in Europe
from April 1878 until August 1879; this trip became the basis for
his imaginative stories. The narrator of the stories is not Mark
Twain himself but closely resembles him. He based the character
Harris on his good friend Joseph Twichell, who joined him in
August 1878 for a month-long tour of Switzerland, where this
story takes place at the Schweitzerhof Hotel in Lucerne.*

The seven-thirty table d'hôte at the great Schweitzerhof furnished a mighty array and variety of nationalities, but it
offered a better opportunity to observe costumes than people, for
the multitude sat at immensely long tables, and therefore the faces
were mainly seen in perspective; but the breakfasts were served at
small round tables, and then if one had the fortune to get a table
in the midst of the assemblage he could have as many faces to
study as he could desire. We used to try to guess out the nationalities, and generally succeeded tolerably well. Sometimes we
tried to guess people's names; but that was a failure; that is a thing
which probably requires a good deal of practice. We presently
dropped it and gave our efforts to less difficult particulars. One
morning I said:

"There is an American party."

Harris said:

"Yes — but name the state."

I named one state, Harris named another. We agreed upon one
thing, however — that the young girl with the party was very
beautiful, and very tastefully dressed. But we disagreed as to her
age. I said she was eighteen, Harris said she was twenty. The
dispute between us waxed warm, and I finally said, with a pretense
of being in earnest:

"Well, there is one way to settle the matter — I will go and ask her."

Harris said, sarcastically, "Certainly, that is the thing to do. All you need to do is to use the common formula over here: go and say, 'I'm an American!' Of course she will be glad to see you."

Then he hinted that perhaps there was no great danger of my venturing to speak to her.

I said, "I was only talking — I didn't intend to approach her, but I see that you do not know what an intrepid person I am. I am not afraid of any woman that walks. I will go and speak to this young girl."

The thing I had in my mind was not difficult. I meant to address her in the most respectful way and ask her to pardon me if her strong resemblance to a former acquaintance of mine was deceiving me; and when she should reply that the name I mentioned was not the name she bore, I meant to beg pardon again, most respectfully, and retire. There would be no harm done. I walked to her table, bowed to the gentleman, then turned to her and was about to begin my little speech when she exclaimed:

"I *knew* I wasn't mistaken — I told John it was you! John said probably wasn't, but I knew I was right. I said you would recognize me presently and come over; and I'm glad you did, for I shouldn't have felt much flattered if you had gone out of this room without recognizing me. Sit down, sit down — how odd it is — you are the last person I was ever expecting to see again."

This was a stupefying surprise. It took my wits clear away, for an instant. However, we shook hands cordially all around, and I sat down. But truly this was the tightest place I ever was in. I seemed to vaguely remember the girl's face, now, but I had no idea where I had seen it before, or what name belonged with it. I immediately tried to get up a diversion about Swiss scenery, to keep her from launching into topics that might betray that I did not know her, but it was of no use, she went right along upon matters which interested her more:

"Oh dear, what a night that was, when the sea washed the

forward boats away — do you remember it?"

"Oh, *don't* I!" said I — but I didn't. I wished the sea had washed the rudder and the smoke-stack and the captain away — then I could have located this questioner.

"And don't you remember how frightened poor Mary was, and how she cried?"

"Indeed I do!" said I. "Dear me, how it all comes back!"

I fervently wished it *would* come back — but my memory was a blank. The wise way would have been to frankly own up; but I could not bring myself to do that, after the young girl had praised me so for recognizing her; so I went on, deeper and deeper into the mire, hoping for a chance clue but never getting one. The Unrecognizable continued, with vivacity:

"Do you know, George married Mary, after all?"

"Why, no! Did he?"

"Indeed he did. He said he did not believe she was half as much to blame as her father was, and I thought he was right. Didn't you?"

"Of course he was. It was a perfectly plain case. I always said so."

"Why, no you didn't! — at least that summer."

"Oh, no, not that summer. No, you are perfectly right about that. It was the following winter that I said it."

"Well, as it turned out, Mary was not in the least to blame — it was all her father's fault — at least his and old Darley's."

It was necessary to say something — so I said:

"I always regarded Darley as a troublesome old thing."

"So he was, but then they always had a great affection for him, although he had so many eccentricities. You remember that when the weather was the least cold, he would try to come into the house."

I was rather afraid to proceed. Evidently Darley was not a man — he must be some other kind of animal — possibly a dog, maybe an elephant. However, tails are common to all animals, so I ventured to say:

"And what a tail he had!"

"*One!* He had a thousand!"

This was bewildering. I did not quite know what to say, so I only said:

"Yes, he was rather well fixed in the matter of tails."

"For a negro, and a crazy one at that, I should say he was," said she.

It was getting pretty sultry for me. I said to myself, "Is it possible she is going to stop there, and wait for me to speak? If she does, the conversation is blocked. A negro with a thousand tails is a topic which a person cannot talk upon fluently and instructively without more or less preparation. As to diving rashly into such a vast subject — "

But here, to my gratitude, she interrupted my thoughts by saying:

"Yes, when it came to tales of his crazy woes, there was simply no end to them if anybody would listen. His own quarters were comfortable enough, but when the weather was cold, the family were sure to have his company — nothing could keep him out of the house. But they always bore it kindly because he had saved Tom's life, years before. You remember Tom?"

"Oh, perfectly. Fine fellow he was, too."

"Yes he was. And what a pretty little thing his child was!"

"You may well say that. I never saw a prettier child."

"I used to delight to pet it and dandle it and play with it."

"So did I."

"You named it. What *was* that name? I can't call it to mind."

It appeared to me that the ice was getting pretty thin, here. I would have given something to know what the child's sex was. However, I had the good luck to think of a name that would fit either sex — so I brought it out:

"I named it Frances."

"From a relative, I suppose? But you named the one that died, too — one that I never saw. What did you call that one?"

I was out of neutral names, but as the child was dead and she had never seen it, I thought I might risk a name for it and trust to luck. Therefore I said:

"I called that one Thomas Henry."

She said, musingly:

"That is very singular . . . very singular."

I sat still and let the cold sweat run down. I was in a good deal of trouble, but I believed I could worry through if she wouldn't ask me to name any more children. I wondered where the lightning was going to strike next. She was still ruminating over that last child's title, but presently she said:

"I have always been sorry you were away at the time — I would have had you name my child."

"*Your* child! Are you married?"

"I have been married thirteen years."

"Christened, you mean."

"No, married. The youth by your side is my son."

"It seems incredible — even impossible. I do not mean any harm by it, but would you mind telling me if you are any over eighteen? — that is to say, will you tell me how old you are?"

"I was just nineteen the day of the storm we were talking about. That was my birthday."

That did not help matters, much, as I did not know the date of the storm. I tried to think of some non-committal thing to say, to keep up my end of the talk, and render my poverty in the matter of reminiscences as little noticeable as possible, but I seemed to be about out of non-committal things. I was about to say, "You haven't changed a bit since then" — but that was risky. I thought of saying, "You have improved ever so much since then" — but that wouldn't answer, of course. I was about to try a shy at the weather, for a saving change, when the girl slipped in ahead of me and said:

"How I have enjoyed this talk over those happy old times — haven't you?"

"I never have spent such a half-hour in all my life before!" said I, with emotion; and I could have added, with a near approach to truth, "and I would rather be scalped than spend another one like it." I was holily grateful to be through with the ordeal, and was about to make my good-bys and get out, when the girl said:

"But there is one thing that is ever so puzzling to me."

"Why, what is that?"

"That dead child's name. What did you say it was?"

Here was another balmy place to be in: I had forgotten the child's name; I hadn't imagined it would be needed again. However, I had to pretend to know, anyway, so I said:

"Joseph William."

The youth at my side corrected me, and said:

"No, Thomas Henry."

I thanked him — in words — and said, with trepidation:

"O yes — I was thinking of another child that I named — I have named a great many, and I get them confused — this one was named Henry Thompson —"

"Thomas Henry," calmly interposed the boy.

I thanked him again — strictly in words — and stammered out:

"Thomas Henry — yes, Thomas Henry was the poor child's name. I named him for Thomas — er — Thomas Carlyle, the great author, you know — and Henry — er — er — Henry the Eighth. The parents were very grateful to have a child named Thomas Henry."

"That makes it more singular than ever," murmured my beautiful friend.

"Does it? Why?"

"Because when the parents speak of that child now, they always call it Susan Amelia."

That spiked my gun. I could not say anything. I was entirely out of verbal obliquities; to go further would be to lie, and that I would not do; so I simply sat still and suffered — sat mutely and resignedly there, and sizzled — for I was being slowly fried to death in my own blushes. Presently the enemy laughed a happy laugh and said:

"I *have* enjoyed this talk over old times, but you have not. I saw very soon that you were only pretending to know me, and so as I had wasted a compliment on you in the beginning, I made up my mind to punish you. And I have succeeded pretty well. I was glad to see that you knew George and Tom and Darley, for I had never heard of them before and therefore could not be sure that you had; and I was glad to learn the names of those imaginary children, too. One can get quite a fund of information out of you if one goes at it cleverly. Mary and the storm, and the sweeping away of the forward boats, were facts — all the rest was fiction. Mary was my sister; her full name was Mary — *Now* do you remember me?"

"Yes," I said, "I do remember you now; and you are as hard-hearted as you were thirteen years ago in that ship, else you wouldn't have punished me so. You haven't changed your nature nor your person, in any way at all; you look just as young as you did then, you are just as beautiful as you were then, and you have transmitted a deal of your comeliness to this fine boy. There — if that speech moves you any, let's fly the flag of truce, with the understanding that I am conquered and confess it."

All of which was agreed to and accomplished, on the spot. When I went back to Harris, I said:

"Now you see what a person with talent and address can do."

"Excuse me, I see what a person of colossal ignorance and simplicity can do. The idea of your going and intruding on a party of strangers, that way, and talking for half an hour; why I never heard of a man in his right mind doing such a thing before. What did you say to them?"

"I never said any harm. I merely asked the girl what her name was."

"I don't doubt it. Upon my word I don't. I think you were capable of it. It was stupid in me to let you go over there and make such an exhibition of yourself. But you know I couldn't really believe you would do such an inexcusable thing. What will those people think of us? But how did you say it? — I mean the manner of it. I hope you were not abrupt."

"No, I was careful about that. I said 'My friend and I would like to know what your name is, if you don't mind.'"

"No, that was not abrupt. There is a polish about it that does you infinite credit. And I am glad you put me in; that was a delicate attention which I appreciate at its full value. What did she do?"

"She didn't do anything in particular. She told me her name."

"Simply told you her name. Do you mean to say she did not show any surprise?"

"Well, now I come to think, she did show something; maybe it was surprise; I hadn't thought of that — I took it for gratification."

"Oh, undoubtedly you were right; it must have been gratification; it could not be otherwise than gratifying to be assaulted by a stranger with such a question as that. Then what did you do?"

"I offered my hand and the party gave me a shake."

"I saw it! I did not believe my own eyes, at the time. Did the gentleman say anything about cutting your throat?"

"No, they all seemed glad to see me, as far as I could judge."

"And do you know, I believe they were. I think they said to themselves, 'Doubtless this curiosity has got away from his keeper — let us amuse ourselves with him.' There is no other way of accounting for their facile docility. You sat down. Did they *ask* you to sit down?"

"No, they did not ask me, but I suppose they did not think of it."

"You have an unerring instinct. What else did you do? What did you talk about?"

"Well, I asked the girl how old she was."

"*Un*doubtedly. Your delicacy is beyond praise. Go on, go on — don't mind my apparent misery — I always look so when I am steeped in a profound and reverent joy. Go on — she told you her age?"

"Yes, she told me her age, and all about her mother, and her grandmother, and her other relations, and all about herself."

"Did she volunteer these statistics?"

"No, not exactly that. I asked the questions and she answered them."

"This is divine. Go on — it is not possible that you forgot to inquire into her politics?"

"No, I thought of that. She is a democrat, her husband is a republican, and both of them are Baptists."

"Her husband? Is that child married?"

"She is not a child. She is married, and that is her husband who is there with her."

"Has she any children?"

"Yes — seven and a half."

"That is impossible."

"No, she has them. She told me herself."

"Well, but seven and a *half*? How do you make out the half? Where does the half come in?"

"There is a child which she had by another husband — not this one but another one — so it is a stepchild, and they do not count it full measure.

"Another husband? Has she had another husband?"

"Yes, four. This one is number four."

"I don't believe a word of it. It is impossible, upon its face. Is that boy there her brother?"

"No, that is her son. He is her youngest. He is not as old as he looks; he is only eleven and a half."

"These things are all manifestly impossible. This is a wretched business. It is a plain case: they simply took your measure, and concluded to fill you up. They seem to have succeeded. I am glad I am not in the mess; they may at least be charitable enough to think there ain't a pair of us. Are they going to stay here long?"

"No, they leave before noon."

"There is one man who is deeply grateful for that. How did you find out? You asked, I suppose?"

"No, along at first I inquired into their plans, in a general way, and they said they were going to be here a week, and make trips round about; but toward the end of the interview, when I said you and I would tour around with them with pleasure, and offered to bring you over and introduce you, they hesitated a little, and asked if you were from the same establishment that I was. I said you were, and then they said they had changed their mind and considered it necessary to start at once and visit a sick relative in Siberia."

"Ah, me, you struck the summit! You struck the loftiest altitude of stupidity that human effort has ever reached. You shall have a monument of jackasses' skulls as high as the Strasburg spire if you die before I do. They wanted to know if I was from the same 'establishment' that you hailed from, did they? What did they mean by 'establishment'?"

"I don't know; it never occurred to me to ask."

"Well I know. They meant an asylum — an *idiot* asylum, do you understand? So they *do* think there's a pair of us, after all. Now what do you think of yourself?"

"Well, I don't know. I didn't know I was doing any harm; I didn't *mean* to do any harm. They were very nice people, and they seemed to like me."

Harris made some rude remarks and left for his bedroom — to break some furniture, he said. He was a singularly irascible man; any little thing would disturb his temper.

I had been well scorched by the young woman, but no matter, I took it out on Harris. One should always "get even" in some way, else the sore place will go on hurting.

"The Celebrated Jumping Frog of Calaveras County"
(Delivered at West Point 3 April 1886)

Mark Twain's first literary masterpiece, "The Celebrated Jumping Frog of Calaveras County," initially appeared in 1865 as "Jim Smiley and His Jumping Frog."

I n compliance with the request of a friend of mine, who wrote me from the East, I called on good-natured, garrulous old Simon Wheeler, and inquired after my friend's friend, Leonidas

W. Smiley, as requested to do, and I hereunto append the result. I have a lurking suspicion that *Leonidas W.* Smiley is a myth; that my friend never knew such a personage; and that he only conjectured that if I asked old Wheeler about him, it would remind him of his infamous Jim Smiley, and he would go to work and bore me to death with some exasperating reminiscence of him as long and as tedious as it should be useless to me. If that was the design, it succeeded.

I found Simon Wheeler dozing comfortably by the bar-room stove of the dilapidated tavern in the decayed mining camp of Angel's, and I noticed that he was fat and bald-headed, and had an expression of winning gentleness and simplicity upon his tranquil countenance. He roused up, and gave me good day. I told him that a friend of mine had commissioned me to make some inquiries about a cherished companion of his boyhood named *Leonidas W.* Smiley — *Rev. Leonidas W.* Smiley, a young minister of the Gospel, who he had heard was at one time a resident of Angel's Camp. I added that if Mr. Wheeler could tell me anything about this Rev. Leonidas W. Smiley, I would feel under many obligations to him.

Simon Wheeler backed me into a corner and blockaded me there with his chair, and then sat down and reeled off the monotonous narrative which follows this paragraph. He never smiled, he never frowned, he never changed his voice from the gentle-flowing key to which he tuned his initial sentence, he never betrayed the slightest suspicion of enthusiasm; but all through the interminable narrative there ran a vein of impressive earnestness and sincerity, which showed me plainly that, so far from his imagining that there was anything ridiculous or funny about his story, he regarded it as a really important matter, and admired its two heroes as men of transcendent genius in *finesse.* I let him go on in his own way, and never interrupted him once.

"Rev. Leonidas W. H'm, Reverend Le — well, there was a feller here once by the name of Jim Smiley, in the winter of '49 — or maybe it was the spring of '50 — I don't recollect exactly, somehow, though what makes me think it was one or the other is because I remember the big flume warn't finished when he first come to the camp; but anyway, he was the curiousest man about always betting on anything that turned up you ever see, if he could get anybody to bet on the other side; and if he couldn't he'd change sides. Any way that suited the other man would suit *him* — any way just so's he got a bet, he was satisfied. But still he was lucky, uncommon lucky; he most always come out winner. He was always ready and laying for a chance; there couldn't be no solit'ry thing mentioned but that feller'd offer to bet on it, and take ary side you please, as I was just telling you. If there was a horse-race, you'd find him flush or you'd find him busted at the end of it; if there was a dog fight, he'd bet on it; if there was a cat-fight, he'd bet on it; if there was a chicken-fight, he'd bet on it; why, if there was two birds setting on a fence, he would bet you which one would fly first; or if there was a camp-meeting, he would be there reg'lar to bet on Parson Walker, which he judged to be the best exhorter about here, and so he was too, and a good man. If he even see a straddle-bug start to go anywheres, he would bet you how long it would take him to get to — to wherever he was going to, and if you took him up, he would foller that straddle-bug to Mexico but what he would find out where he was bound for and how long he was on the road. Lots of the boys here has seen that Smiley, and can tell you about him. Why, it never made no difference to *him* — he'd bet on *any* thing — the dangdest feller. Parson Walker's wife laid very sick once, for a good while, and it seemed as if they warn't going to save her; but one morning he come in, and Smiley up and asked him how she was, and he said she was considerable better — thank the Lord for his inf'nite mercy — and coming on so smart that with the blessing of Prov'dence she'd get well yet; and Smiley, before he thought, says 'Well, I'll resk two-and-a-half she don't anyway.'

"Thish-yer Smiley had a mare — the boys called her the fifteen-minute nag, but that was only in fun, you know, because of course she was faster than that — and he used to win money on that horse, for all she was so slow and always had the asthma, or the distemper, or the consumption, or something of that kind. They used to give her two or three hundred yards' start, and then pass her under way; but always at the fag end of the race she'd get excited and desperate like, and come cavorting and straddling up, and scattering her legs around limber, sometimes in the air, and sometimes out to one side among the fences, and kicking up m-o-r-e dust and raising m-o-r-e racket with her coughing and sneezing and blowing her nose — and *always* fetch up at the stand just about a neck ahead, as near as you could cipher it down.

"And he had a little small bull-pup, that to look at him you'd think he warn't worth a cent but to set around and look ornery and lay for a chance to steal something. But as soon as money was up on him he was a different dog; his under-jaw'd begin to stick out like the fo'castle of a steamboat, and his teeth would uncover and shine like the furnaces. And a dog might tackle him and bully-rag him, and bite him, and throw him over his shoulder two or three times, and Andrew Jackson — which was the name of the pup — Andrew Jackson would never let on but what *he* was satisfied, and hadn't expected nothing else — and the bets being doubled and doubled on the other side all the time, till the money was all up; and then all of a sudden he would grab that other dog jest by the j'int of his hind leg and freeze to it — not chaw, you understand, but only just grip and hang on till they throwed up the sponge, if it was a year. Smiley always come out winner on that pup, till he harnessed a dog once that didn't have no hind legs, because they'd been sawed off in a circular saw, and when the thing had gone along far enough, and the money was all up, and he come to make a snatch for his pet holt, he see in a minute how he'd been imposed on, and how the other dog had him in the door, so to speak, and he 'peared surprised, and then he looked sorter discouraged-like, and didn't try no more to win the fight, and so he got shucked out bad. He give Smiley a look, as much as to say his heart was broke, and it was his fault, for putting up a dog that hadn't no hind legs for him to take holt of, which was his main dependence in a fight, and then he limped off a piece and laid down and died. It was a good pup, was that Andrew Jackson, and would have made a name for hisself if he'd lived, for the stuff was in him and he had genius — I know it, because he hadn't no opportunities to speak of, and it don't stand to reason that a dog could make such a fight as he could under them circumstances if he hadn't no talent. It always makes me feel sorry when I think of that last fight of his'n, and the way it turned out.

"Well, thish-yer Smiley had rat-tarriers, and chicken cocks, and tomcats and all them kind of things, till you couldn't rest, and you couldn't fetch nothing for him to bet on but he'd match you. He ketched a frog one day, and took him home, and said he cal'lated to educate him; and so he never done nothing for three months but set in his back yard and learn that frog to jump. And you bet you he *did* learn him, too. He'd give him a little punch behind, and the next minute you'd see that frog whirling in the air like a doughnut — see him turn one summerset, or maybe a couple, if he got a good start, and come down flat-footed and, all right, like a cat. He got him up so in the matter of ketching flies, and kep' him in practice so constant, that he'd nail a fly every time as fur as he could see him. Smiley said all a frog wanted was education, and he could do 'most anything — and I believe him. Why, I've seen him set Dan'l Webster down here on this floor — Dan'l Webster was the name of the frog — and sing out, 'Flies, Dan'l, flies!' and quicker'n you could wink he'd spring straight up and snake a fly off'n the counter there, and flop down on the floor ag'in as solid as a gob of mud, and fall to scratching the side of his head with his hind foot as indifferent as if he hadn't no idea he'd been doin' any more'n any frog might do. You never see a frog so modest and straightfor'ard as he was, for all he was so gifted. And when it come to fair and square jumping on a dead level, he could get over more ground at one straddle than any animal of his breed you ever see. Jumping on a dead level was his strong suit, you understand; and when it come to that, Smiley would ante up money on him as long as he had a red. Smiley was monstrous proud of his frog, and well he might be, for fellers that had traveled and been everywheres all said he laid over any frog that ever *they* see.

"Well, Smiley kep' the beast in a little lattice box, and he used to fetch him down-town sometimes and lay for a bet. One day a feller — a stranger in the camp, he was — come acrost him with his box, and says:

" 'What might it be that you've got in the box?'

"And Smiley says, sorter indifferent-like, 'It might be a parrot, or it might be a canary, maybe, but it ain't — it's only just a frog.'

"And the feller took it, and looked at it careful, and turned it round this way and that, and says, 'H'm — so 'tis. Well, what's *he* good for?'

" 'Well,' Smiley says, easy and careless, 'he's good enough for *one* thing, I should judge — he can outjump any frog in Calaveras County.'

"The feller took the box again, and took another long, particular look and give it back to Smiley, and says, very deliberate, 'Well,' he says, 'I don't see no p'ints about that frog that's any better'n any other frog.'

" 'Maybe you don't,' Smiley says. 'Maybe you understand frogs and maybe you don't understand 'em; maybe you've had experience, and maybe you ain't only a amature, as it were. Anyways, I've got *my* opinion, and I'll resk forty dollars that he can outjump any frog in Calaveras County.'

"And the feller studied a minute, and then says, kinder sad-like, 'Well, I'm only a stranger here, and I ain't got no frog; but if I had a frog, I'd bet you.'

"And then Smiley says, 'That's all right — that's all right — if you'll hold my box a minute, I'll go and get you a frog.' And so the feller took the box, and put up his forty dollars along with Smiley's, and set down to wait.

"So he set there a good while thinking and thinking to himself, and then he got the frog out and prized his mouth open and took a teaspoon and filled him full of quail-shot — filled him pretty near up to his chin — and set him on the floor. Smiley he went to the swamp and slopped around in the mud for a long time, and finally he ketched a frog, and fetched him in, and give him to this feller, and says:

" 'Now, if you're ready, set him alongside of Dan'l, with his fore paws just even with Dan'l's, and I'll give the word.' Then he says, 'One — two — three — *git!*' and him and the feller touched up the frogs from behind, and the new frog hopped off lively, but Dan'l give a heave, and hysted up his shoulders — so — like a Frenchman, but it warn't no use — he couldn't budge; he was planted as solid as a church, and he couldn't no more stir than if he was anchored out. Smiley was a good deal surprised, and he was disgusted too, but he didn't have no idea what the matter was, of course.

"The feller took the money and started away; and when he was going out at the door, he sorter jerked his thumb over his shoulder — so — at Dan'l, and says again, very deliberate, 'Well,' he says, '*I* don't see no p'ints about that frog that's any better'n any other frog.'

"Smiley he stood scratching his head and looking down at Dan'l a long time, and at last he says, 'I do wonder what in the nation that frog throw'd off for — I wonder if there ain't something the matter with him — he 'pears to look mighty baggy, somehow.' And he ketched Dan'l by the nap of the neck, and hefted him, and says, 'Why blame my cats if he don't weigh five pound!' and turned him upside down and he belched out a double handful of shot. And then he see how it was, and he was the maddest man — he set the frog down and took out after that feller, but he never ketched him. And — "

[Here Simon Wheeler heard his name called from the front yard, and got up to see what was wanted.] And turning to me as he moved away, he said: "Just set where you are, stranger, and rest easy — I ain't going to be gone a second."

But, by your leave, I did not think that a continuation of the history of the enterprising vagabond *Jim* Smiley would be likely to afford me much information concerning the Rev. *Leonidas W.* Smiley, and so I started away.

At the door I met the sociable Wheeler returning, and he buttonholed me and recommenced:

"Well, thish-yer Smiley had a yaller one-eyed cow that didn't have no tail, only just a short stump like a bannanner, and —"

However, lacking both time and inclination, I did not wait to hear about the afflicted cow, but took my leave.

"English as She Is Taught"
(Delivered at West Point 30 April 1887)

This essay was first published in April 1887, the month Mark Twain delivered this speech at West Point. He based it upon actual examples of bloopers by the pupils of Caroline B. LeRow, a Brooklyn schoolteacher, who had shared her manuscript with him. Mark Twain most likely abridged this version in his presentation at West Point.

In the appendix to Croker's Boswell's *Johnson* one finds this anecdote:

Cato's Soliloquy. — One day Mrs. Gastrel set a little girl to repeat to him [Dr. Samuel Johnson] Cato's Soliloquy, which she went through very correctly. The Doctor, after a pause, asked the child:

"What was to bring Cato to an end?"

She said it was a knife.

"No, my dear, it was not so."

"My aunt Polly said it was a knife."

"Why, Aunt Polly's knife *may do*, but it was a *dagger*, my dear."

He then asked her the meaning of "bane and antidote," which she was unable to give. Mrs. Gastrel said:

"You cannot expect so young a child to know the meaning of such words.

He then said:

"My dear, how many pence are there in *sixpence*?"

"I cannot tell, sir," was the half-terrified reply.

On this, addressing himself to Mrs. Gastrel, he said:

"Now, my dear lady, can anything be more ridiculous than to teach a child Cato's Soliloquy, who does not know how many pence there are in sixpence?"

In a lecture before the Royal Geographical Society Professor Ravenstein quoted the following list of frantic questions, and said that they had been asked in an examination:

Mention all the names of places in the world derived from Julius Caesar or Augustus Caesar.

Where are the following rivers: Pisuerga, Sakaria, Guadalete, Jalon, Mulde?

All you know of the following: Machacha, Pilmo, Schebulos, Crivoscia, Basecs, Mancikert, Taxhem, Citeaux, Meloria, Zutphen.

The highest peaks of the Karakorum range.

The number of universities in Prussia.

Why are the tops of mountains continually covered with snow [sic]?

Name the length and breadth of the streams of lava which issued from the Skaptar Jokul in the eruption of 1783.

That list would oversize nearly anybody's geographical knowledge. Isn't it reasonably possible that in our schools many of the questions in all studies are several miles ahead of where the pupil is? — that he is set to struggle with things that are ludicrously beyond his present reach, hopelessly beyond his present strength?

This remark in passing, and by way of text; now I come to what I was going to say.

I have just now fallen upon a darling literary curiosity. It is a little book, a manuscript compilation, and the compiler sent it to me with the request that I say whether I think it ought to be published or not. I said, Yes; but as I slowly grow wise I briskly grow cautious; and so, now that the publication is imminent, it has seemed to me that I should feel more comfortable if I could divide up this responsibility with the public by adding them to the court. Therefore I will print some extracts from the book, in the hope that they may make converts to my judgment that the volume has merit which entitles it to publication.

As to its character. Every one has sampled "English as She Is Spoke" and "English as She Is Wrote"; this little volume furnishes us an instructive array of examples of "English as She Is Taught" — in the public schools of — well, this country. The collection is made by a teacher in those schools, and all the examples in it are genuine; none of them have been tampered with, or doctored in any way. From time to time, during several years, whenever a pupil has delivered himself of anything peculiarly quaint or toothsome in the course of his recitations, this teacher and her associates have privately set that thing down in a memorandum-book; strictly following the original, as to grammar, construction, spelling, and all; and the result is this literary curiosity.

The contents of the book consist mainly of answers given by the boys and girls to questions, said answers being given sometimes verbally, sometimes in writing. The subjects touched upon are fifteen in number: I. Etymology; II. Grammar; III. Mathematics; IV. Geography; V. "Original"; VI. Analysis; VII. History; VIII. "Intellectual"; IX. Philosophy; X. Physiology; XI. Astronomy; XII. Politics; XIII. Music; XIV. Oratory; XV. Metaphysics.

You perceive that the poor little young idea has taken a shot at a good many kinds of game in the course of the book. Now as to results. Here are some quaint definitions of words. It will be noticed that in all of these instances the sound of the word, or the look of it on paper, has misled the child:

Aborigines, a system of mountains.
Alias, a good man in the Bible.
Amenable, anything that is mean.
Ammonia, the food of the gods.
Assiduity, state of being an acid.
Auriferous, pertaining to an orifice.
Capillary, a little caterpillar.
Corniferous, rocks in which fossil corn is found.
Emolument, a headstone to a grave.
Equestrian, one who asks questions.
Eucharist, one who plays euchre.
Franchise, anything belonging to the French.
Idolater, a very idol person.
Ipecac, a man who likes a good dinner.
Irrigate, to make fun of.
Mendacious, what can be mended.
Mercenary, one who feels for another.
Parasite, a kind of umbrella.
Parasite, the murder of an infant.
Publican, a man who does his prayers in public.
Tenacious, ten acres of land.

Here is one where the phrase "publicans and sinners" has got mixed up in the child's mind with politics, and the result is a definition which takes one in a sudden and unexpected way:

Republican, a sinner mentioned in the Bible.

Also in Democratic newspapers now and then. Here are two where the mistake has resulted from sound assisted by remote fact:

Plagiarist, a writer of plays.
Demagogue, a vessel containing beer and other liquids.

I cannot quite make out what it was that misled the pupil in the following instances; it would not seem to have been the sound of the word, nor the look of it in print:

Asphyxia, a grumbling, fussy temper.
Quarternions, a bird with a flat beak and no bill, living in New Zealand.
Quarternions, the name given to a style of art practiced by the Phoenicians.
Quarternions, a religious convention held every hundred years.
Sibilant, the state of being idiotic.
Crosier, a staff carried by the Deity.

In the following sentences the pupil's ear has been deceiving him again:

The marriage was illegible.
He was totally dismasted with the whole performance.
He enjoys riding on a philosopher.
She was very quick at repertoire.
He prayed for the waters to subsidize.
The leopard is watching his sheep.
They had a strawberry vestibule.

Here is one which — well, now, how often we do slam light into the truth without ever suspecting it:

The men employed by the Gas Company go around and speculate the meter.

Indeed they do, dear; and when you grow up, many and many's the time you will notice it in the gas bill. In the following sentences the little people have some information to convey, every time; but in my case they fail to connect: the light always went out on the keystone word:

> The coercion of some things is remarkable; as bread and molasses.
> Her hat is contiguous because she wears it on one side.
> He preached to an egregious congregation.
> The captain eliminated a bullet through the man's heart.
> You should take caution and be precarious.
> The supercilious girl acted with vicissitude when the perennial time came.

That last is a curiously plausible sentence; one seems to know what it means, and yet he knows all the time that he doesn't. Here is an odd (but entirely proper) use of a word, and a most sudden descent from a lofty philosophical altitude to a very practical and homely illustration:

> We should endeavor to avoid extremes — like those of wasps and bees.

And here — with "zoological" and "geological" in his mind, but not ready to his tongue — the small scholar has innocently gone and let out a couple of secrets which ought never to have been divulged in any circumstances:

> There are a good many donkeys in theological gardens.
> Some of the best fossils are found in theological cabinets.

Under the head of "Grammar" the little scholars furnish the following information:

> Gender is the distinguishing nouns without regard to sex.
> A verb is something to eat.
> Adverbs should always be used as adjectives and adjectives as adverbs.

Every sentence and name of God must begin with a caterpillar.

"Caterpillar" is well enough, but capital letter would have been stricter. The following is a brave attempt at a solution, but it failed to liquify:

When they are going to say some prose or poetry before they say the poetry or prose they must put a semicolon just after the introduction of the prose or poetry.

The chapter on "Mathematics" is full of fruit. From it I take a few samples — mainly in an unripe state.

A straight line is any distance between two places.
Parallel lines are lines that can never meet until they run together.
A circle is a round straight line with a hole in the middle.
Things which are equal to each other are equal to anything else.
To find the number of square feet in a room you multiply the room by the number of the feet. The product is the result.

Right you are. In the matter of geography this little book is unspeakably rich. The questions do not appear to have applied the microscope to the subject, as did those quoted by Professor Ravenstein; still, they proved plenty difficult enough without that. These pupils did not hunt with a microscope, they hunted with a shotgun; this is shown by the crippled condition of the game they brought in:

America is divided into the Passiffic slope and the Mississippi valley.
North America is separated by Spain.
America consists from north to south about five hundred miles.

The United States is quite a small country compared with some other countrys, but is about as industrious.

The capital of the United States is Long Island.

The five seaports of the U. S. are Newfunlan and Sanfrancisco.

The principal products of the U.S. is earthquakes and volcanoes.

The Alaginnies are mountains in Philadelphia.

The Rocky Mountains are on the western side of Philadelphia.

Cape Hateras is a vast body of water surrounded by land and flowing into the Gulf of Mexico.

Mason and Dixon's line is the Equater.

One of the leading industries of the United States is molasses, bookcovers, numbers, gas, teaching, lumber, manufacturers, paper-making, publishers, coal.

In Austria the principal occupation is gathering Austrich feathers.

Gibraltar is an island built on a rock.

Russia is very cold and tyrannical.

Sicily is one of the Sandwich Islands.

Hindoostan flows through the Ganges and empties into the Mediterranean Sea.

Ireland is called the Emigrant Isle because it is so beautiful and green.

The width of the different zones Europe lies in depend upon the surrounding country.

The imports of a country are the things that are paid for, the exports are the things that are not.

Climate lasts all the time and weather only a few days.

The two most famous volcanoes of Europe are Sodom and Gomorrah.

The chapter headed "Analysis" shows us that the pupils in our public schools are not merely loaded up with those showy facts about geography, mathematics, and so on, and left in that incomplete state; no, there's machinery for clarifying and expanding their minds. They are required to take poems and analyze them, dig out their common sense, reduce them to statistics, and reproduce them in a luminous prose translation which shall tell you at a glance what the poet was trying to get at. One sample will do. Here is a stanza from "The Lady of the Lake," followed by the pupil's impressive explanation of it:

> Alone, but with unbated zeal,
> The horseman plied with scourge and steel;
> For jaded now and spent with toil,
> Embossed with foam and dark with soil,
> While every gasp with sobs he drew,
> The laboring stag strained full in view.

The man who rode on the horse performed the whip and an instrument made of steel alone with strong ardor not diminishing, for, being tired from the time passed with hard labor overworked with anger and ignorant with weariness, while every breath for labor he drew with cries full of sorrow, the young deer made imperfect who worked hard filtered in sight.

I see, now, that I never understood that poem before. I have had glimpses of its meaning, in moments when I was not as ignorant with weariness as usual, but this is the first time the whole spacious idea of it ever filtered in sight. If I were a public-school pupil I would put those other studies aside and stick to analysis; for, after all, it is the thing to spread your mind.

We come now to historical matters, historical remains, one might say. As one turns the pages he is impressed with the depth to which one date has been driven into the American child's head — 1492. The date is there, and it is there to stay. And it is always at hand, always deliverable at a moment's notice. But the Fact that

belongs with it? That is quite another matter. Only the date itself
is familiar and sure: its vast Fact has failed of lodgment. It would
appear that whenever you ask a public-school pupil when a thing
— anything, no matter what — happened, and he is in doubt, he
always rips out his 1492. He applies it to everything, from the
landing of the ark to the introduction of the horse-car. Well, after
all, it is our first date, and so it is right enough to honor it, and
pay the public schools to teach our children to honor it:

George Washington was born in 1492.

Washington wrote the Declareation of Independence in
1492.

St. Bartholemew was massacred in 1492.

The Brittains were the Saxons who entered England in
1492 under Julius Caesar.

The earth is 1492 miles in circumference.

To proceed with "History"

Christopher Columbus was called the Father of his Country.

Queen Isabella of Spain sold her watch and chain and
other millinery so that Columbus could discover America.

The Indian wars were very desecrating to the country.

The Indians pursued their warfare by hiding in the bushes
and then scalping them.

Captain John Smith has been styled the father of his
country. His life was saved by his daughter Pochahantas.

The Puritans found an insane asylum in the wilds of
America.

The Stamp Act was to make everybody stamp all materials
so they should be null and void.

Washington died in Spain almost broken-hearted. His
remains were taken to the cathedral in Havana.

Gorilla warfare was where men rode on gorillas.

John Brown was a very good insane man who tried to get fugitive slaves into Virginia. He captured all the inhabitants, but was finally conquered and condemned to his death. The Confederasy was formed by the fugitive slaves.

Alfred the Great reigned 872 years. He was distinguished for letting some buckwheat cakes burn, and the lady scolded him.

Henry Eight was famous for being a great widower having lost several wives.

Lady Jane Grey studied Greek and Latin and was beheaded after a few days.

John Bright is noted for an incurable disease.

Lord James Gordon Bennett instigated the Gordon Riots.

The Middle Ages come in between antiquity and posterity.

Luther introduced Christianity into England a good many thousand years ago. His birthday was November 1883. He was once a Pope. He lived at the time of the Rebellion of Worms.

Julius Caesar is noted for his famous telegram dispatch I came I saw I conquered.

Julius Caesar was really a very great man. He was a very great soldier and wrote a book for beginners in the Latin.

Cleopatra was caused by the death of an asp which she dissolved in a wine cup.

The only form of government in Greece was a limited monkey.

The Persian war lasted about 500 years.

Greece had only 7 wise men.

Socrates . . . destroyed some statues and had to drink Shamrock.

Here is a fact correctly stated; and yet it is phrased with such ingenious infelicity that it can be depended upon to convey misinformation every time it is uncarefully read:

By the Salic law no woman or descendant of a woman could occupy the throne.

To show how far a child can travel in history with judicious and diligent boosting in the public school, we select the following mosaic:

Abraham Lincoln was born in Wales in 1599.

In the chapter headed "Intellectual" I find a great number of most interesting statements. A sample or two may be found not amiss:

Bracebridge Hall was written by Henry Irving.
Snow Bound was written by Peter Cooper.
The House of the Seven Gables was written by Lord Bryant.
Edgar A. Poe was a very curdling writer.
Cotton Mather was a writer who invented the cotten gin and wrote histories.
Beowulf wrote the Scriptures.
Ben Johnson survived Shakespeare in some respects.
In the Canterbury Tale it gives account of King Alfred on his way to the shrine of Thomas Bucket.
Chaucer was the father of English pottery.
Chaucer was a bland verse writer of the third century.
Chaucer was succeeded by H. Wads. Longfellow an American Writer. His writings were chiefly prose and nearly one hundred years elapsed.
Shakspeare translated the Scriptures and it was called St. James because he did it.

In the middle of the chapter I find many pages of information concerning Shakespeare's plays, Milton's works, and those of Bacon, Addison, Samuel Johnson, Fielding, Richardson, Sterne, Smollett, De Foe, Locke, Pope, Swift, Goldsmith, Burns, Cowper, Wordsworth, Gibbon, Byron, Coleridge, Hood, Scott,

Macaulay, George Eliot, Dickens, Bulwer, Thackeray, Browning, Mrs. Browning, Tennyson, and Disraeli — a fact which shows that into the restricted stomach of the public-school pupil is shoveled every year the blood, bone, and viscera of a gigantic literature, and the same is there digested and disposed of in a most successful and characteristic and gratifying public-school way. I have space for but a trifling few of the results:

> Lord Byron was the son of an heiress and a drunken man.
>
> Wm. Wordsworth wrote the Barefoot Boy and Imitations on Immortality.
>
> Gibbon wrote a history of his travels in Italy. This was original.
>
> George Eliot left a wife and children who mourned greatly for his genius.
>
> George Eliot Miss Mary Evans Mrs. Cross Mrs. Lewis was the greatest female poet unless George Sands is made an exception of.
>
> Bulwell is considered a good writer.
>
> Sir Walter Scott Charles Bronte Alfred the Great and Johnson were the first great novelists.
>
> Thomas Babington Makorlay graduated at Harvard and then studied law, he was raised to the peerage as baron in 1557 and died in 1776.

Here are two or three miscellaneous facts that may be of value, if taken in moderation:

> Homer's writings are Homer's Essays Virgil the Aneid and Paradise lost some people say that these poems were not written by Homer but by another man of the same name.
>
> A sort of sadness kind of shone in Bryant's poems.
>
> Holmes is a very profligate and amusing writer.

When the public-school pupil wrestles with the political features of the Great Republic, they throw him sometimes:

A bill becomes a law when the President vetoes it.

The three departments of the government is the President rules the world, the governor rules the State, the mayor rules the city.

The first conscientious Congress met in Philadelphia.

The Constitution of the United States was established to ensure domestic hostility.

Truth crushed to earth will rise again. As follows:

The Constitution of the United States is that part of the book at the end which nobody reads.

And here she rises once more and untimely. There should be a limit to public-school instruction; it cannot be wise or well to let the young find out everything:

Congress is divided into civilized half civilized and savage.

Here are some results of study in music and oratory:

An interval in music is the distance on the keyboard from one piano to the next.

A rest means you are not to sing it.

Emphasis is putting more distress on one word than another.

The chapter on "Physiology" contains much that ought not to be lost to science:

Physillogigy is to study about your bones stummick and vertebry.

Occupations which are injurious to health are cabolic acid gas which is impure blood.

We have an upper and a lower skin. The lower skin moves all the time and the upper skin moves when we do.

The body is mostly composed of water and about one half is avaricious tissue.

The stomach is a small pear-shaped bone situated in the body.

The gastric juice keeps the bones from creaking.

The Chyle flows up the middle of the backbone and reaches the heart where it meets the oxygen and is purified.

The salivary glands are used to salivate the body.

In the stomach starch is changed to cane sugar and cane sugar to sugar cane.

The olfactory nerve enters the cavity of the orbit and is developed into the special sense of hearing.

The growth of a tooth begins in the back of the mouth and extends to the stomach.

If we were on a railroad track and a train was coming the train would deafen our ears so that we couldn't see to get off the track.

If, up to this point, none of my quotations have added flavor to the Johnsonian anecdote at the head of this article, let us make another attempt:

The theory that intuitive truths are discovered by the light of nature originated from St. John's interpretation of a passage in the Gospel of Plato.

The weight of the earth is found by comparing a mass of known lead with that of a mass of unknown lead.

To find the weight of the earth take the length of a degree on a meridian and multiply by 62 ½ pounds.

The spheres are to each other as the squares of their homologous sides.

A body will go just as far in the first second as the body will go plus the force of gravity and that's equal to twice what the body will go.

Specific gravity is the weight to be compared weight of an

equal volume of or that is the weight of a body compared with the weight of an equal volume.

The law of fluid pressure divide the different forms of organized bodies by the form of attraction and the number increased will be the form.

Inertia is that property of bodies by virtue of which it cannot change its own condition of rest or motion. In other words it is the negative quality of passiveness either in recoverable latency or incipient latescence.

If a laugh is fair here, not the struggling child, nor the unintelligent teacher — or rather the unintelligent Boards, Committees, and Trustees — are the proper target for it. All through this little book one detects the signs of a certain probable fact — that a large part of the pupil's "instruction" consists in cramming him with obscure and wordy "rules" which he does not understand and has no time to understand. It would be as useful to cram him with brickbats; they would at least stay. In a town in the interior of New York, a few years ago, a gentleman set forth a mathematical problem and proposed to give a prize to every public-school pupil who should furnish the correct solution of it. Twenty-two of the brightest boys in the public schools entered the contest. The problem was not a very difficult one for pupils of their mathematical rank and standing, yet they all failed — by a hair — through one trifling mistake or another. Some searching questions were asked, when it turned out that these lads were as glib as parrots with the "rules," but could not reason out a single rule or explain the principle underlying it. Their memories had been stocked, but not their understandings. It was a case of brickbat culture, pure and simple.

There are several curious "compositions" in the little book, and we must make room for one. It is full of naivete, brutal truth, and unembarrassed directness, and is the funniest (genuine) boy's composition I think I have ever seen:

ON GIRLS

Girls are very stuck up and dignefied in their maner and be have your. They think more of dress than anything and like to play with dowls and rags. They cry if they see a cow in a far distance and are afraid of guns. They stay at home all the time and go to church on Sunday. They are al-ways sick. They are al-ways funy and making fun of boy's hands and they say how dirty. They cant play marbels. I pity them poor things. They make fun of boys and then turn round and love them. I dont beleave they ever kiled a cat or anything. They look out every nite and say oh ant the moon lovely. Thir is one thing I have not told and that is they al-ways now their lessons bettern boys.

From Mr. Edward Channing's recent article in *Science*:

The marked difference between the books now being produced by French, English, and American travelers, on the one hand, and German explorers, on the other, is too great to escape attention. That difference is due entirely to the fact that in school and university the German is taught, in the first place to see, and in the second place to understand what he does see.

Mark Twain and the West Point Superintendents

I

When Mark Twain visited West Point, the superintendents he met there were invariably veterans of the Civil War and of the Plains Indian campaigns. These men, all West Point graduates, had spent a lifetime in uniform serving their country. And while he would have made an impossibly bad soldier had he attempted an extended tour of duty, he admired these senior officers, who had made the military their profession. In some cases he developed close, personal relationships.

John McAllister Schofield (1831–1906), the superintendent during Mark Twain's earliest visits, graduated seventh in his class in 1853, and was stationed with the Second Artillery at Fort Moultrie, South Carolina, where another famous West Pointer, Edgar Allan Poe (1809–49), had served earlier as an enlisted soldier. Unlike Schofield, Poe did not finish at West Point, having cut drill and classes for an entire week in order to get himself dismissed.

Taking a year's leave of absence from the army in 1860, Schofield became a professor of physics at Washington University in St. Louis. When the Civil War began, he served as a recruiter or "mustering officer" for Mark Twain's home state of Missouri. Then he organized the First Missouri Volunteer Infantry Regiment, serving as its major. He fought in several operations throughout Missouri, rising through the ranks in both the "volunteer" and "regular" armies. As a major general he became commander of the Department of the Missouri, a command that was far larger than the state alone.

Schofield took part in Sherman's Atlanta campaign as one of three army commanders. Later he led Union troops in Tennessee and North Carolina. Following the war he served as a confidential agent in France for a year, keeping an eye on French involvement in Mexico. He was secretary of war for a short time, but resigned when Grant became president.

Schofield's name is known in the army today because of Schofield Barracks, Hawaii, where he served as commander of the Division of the Pacific, recommending that Pearl Harbor become the principal naval base in that part of the world.

From 1876 to 1881 he was the superintendent at West Point, but his distinguished career was far from over. In 1888 he became commanding general of the army (known today as army chief of staff); he was promoted to lieutenant general in 1895, retiring later that year after forty-six years in the army.

I I

Oliver Otis Howard (1830–1909) followed Schofield as super-intendent from 1881–82. Graduating in the class of 1854, following Schofield's, Howard held Bible readings and prayer meetings in the barracks when he was a cadet, and later he enjoyed a reputation as a biblical scholar. Because of his firm religious convictions and his outspoken opposition to slavery, Howard suffered a measure of ostracism from other cadets. His classmate and chief rival, both academically and socially, was Custis Lee, son of Colonel Robert E. Lee, who became superintendent at West Point at the start of Howard's third year. At graduation young Lee was first in his class and Howard was fourth (McFeely, *Yankee Stepfather* 33).

Back at West Point teaching mathematics when the Civil War began, he became a colonel in the Third Maine Regiment from his home state. In September 1861 he became brigadier general of volunteers; he became major general the next year. He participated in the first battle of Bull Run and in the peninsular campaign, losing his right arm at Fair Oaks. Years later, in 1893, he was awarded the Congressional Medal of Honor for bravery at Fair Oaks.

Howard was not known as a particularly effective leader or commander, being accused of disobeying an order from General Hooker at Chancellorsville and of being indecisive and insubordinate at Gettysburg, though he was later cleared of these charges. Like Schofield, Howard participated in Sherman's campaign; he was appalled by the looting and violence he observed on the march to the sea.

President Andrew Johnson appointed him to head the Freedmen's Bureau, created at the end of the Civil War to assist former slaves. In this role he reaffirmed his reputation as a kind, benevolent person, but also as an inept leader whose department was hopelessly inefficient and rife with fraud and corruption on the part of his subordinates. A special court appointed by President Grant later exonerated him of personal responsibility for these shortcomings.

Not widely known is the fact that Howard University, perhaps the premier predominantly black university in America, is named after General Howard, who founded it and served as its first president from 1869 to 1874. Howard's championing of black enfranchisement during Reconstruction, his directorship of the Freedmen's Bureau, and his founding of Howard University for the advancement of blacks all led to his assignment as superintendent at West Point following the negative publicity in the hazing case of the black cadet Johnson C. Whittaker in 1880.

III

Of all the superintendents he knew, Mark Twain was closest to Howard's successor, Wesley Merritt (1834–1910), who served as superintendent from 1882 to 1887. Mark Twain made three recorded visits to West Point during Merritt's tenure, April and May 1886 and April 1887. Mark Twain's wife, Olivia, was a personal friend of Merritt's wife, Caroline. Merritt, a handsome and polished officer, enjoyed a reputation in the army as a consistently strong commander who possessed an agreeable nature. Merritt was superintendent during John J. Pershing's four years at West Point, and Pershing adopted Merritt's style and manner throughout his distinguished career, and particularly while he was in command of the American forces in France during World War I (Goldhurst 20).

Entering West Point from Illinois in 1855, Merritt graduated in 1860, just in time for the Civil War, serving as a cavalry officer. As did many others he held various permanent and brevet ranks — captain of regulars, brigadier general of volunteers. At Gettysburg he commanded the reserve cavalry brigade and distinguished himself for bravery. Rising to the rank of major general, he was present at Appomattox for the surrender, reverting to the rank of major in the regular army after the war.

A few years before Mark Twain visited him at West Point, Merritt experienced still more combat, fighting the Plains Indians as part of the larger campaign that took Custer's life at Little Bighorn on 25 June 1876. On 1 July, just days after Custer's defeat at the hands of the Sioux, Merritt took command of the U.S. Cavalry's Fifth Regiment, the "Dandy Fifth" as they were known. He was promoted to colonel the same day.

Merritt's scout was the famed William Frederick "Buffalo Bill" Cody (1846–1917), who, upon hearing of Custer's defeat, joined

Merritt's unit directly from the performing stage back East in his Wild West show. Mark Twain draws upon Cody in chapter 7 of *The American Claimant* (1892), and depicts him as a character in "A Horse's Tale" (1906).

Merritt's Fifth Cavalry faced the Cheyenne, one of the most formidable of the northern Plains Indians of the campaign. It was at Warbonnet Creek that Cody killed a young Cheyenne in hand-to-hand combat, scalping him with his bowie knife and dramatically shouting, "The first scalp for Custer!" Although the fight at the ferocious-sounding site at Warbonnet Creek was hardly more than a skirmish (thirty Indians against over four hundred soldiers), Merritt's success received tremendously favorable press back East, where the public demanded revenge for Custer's defeat.

The *Army and Navy Journal* of 23 May 1887 recounting Mark Twain's visit that month contained other news items from the academy. West Point's unnamed correspondent wrote thrillingly that "the absorbing topic of conversation for several weeks has been the musicale, which we awaited and looked for on tip toes of expectation. It took place on last Thursday evening in Schofield Hall" ("West Point").

On the same page a correspondent from the First Cavalry at Fort Custer, Montana Territory, named for the ill-fated West Point graduate, complained about

> the monotony of our dull garrison life. We have an excellent library and a canteen and billiard room; we also have hops and theatrical performances, but we are denied the great source of amusement of most frontier posts — hunting and fishing, with any prospect of success. A few catfish and eels are caught in the muddy Big Horn, but to secure game we must go a long distance from the post. We should be allowed twenty-four men in our bands. Were such the case in the 1st Cavalry, it is certain that our band leader, Mr. Walker, would in a short time show as fine a military band as could be found in the United States. ("Fort Custer")

A third correspondent, this one from the Indian school at Carlisle Barracks, Pennsylvania, wrote on the same page that sixty-two Apache children had arrived on 1 May 1887 and had been "treated to a good breakfast. When they were done eating they were taken outside and grouped, while a photographer took their picture. They were next taken in charge by the matron and superintendent and walked off to the bathrooms, and they will go into the school room on Monday" ("Carlisle Barracks").

Mark Twain witnessed the army in transition. What must he have thought when he read that a musicale by the officers and ladies of West Point — awaited "on tip toes" — was the most important event of the time? What did General Merritt, a cavalry commander in the Indian wars, think when he read the whining complaint that the Big Horn River near Fort Custer, names summoning images of legendary proportion, was a muddy source of unheroic fish? While some danger to soldiers persisted until the Battle of Wounded Knee in 1890, billiards were replacing bivouacs; rehearsals for theatrical performances and musicales were supplanting cavalry drill. Pershing wrote to his brother Jim that "No one expects to hear a gun fired in anger for one hundred years" (qtd. in Goldhurst 24). Huck and Tom might have wanted to go West for "howling adventures amongst the Injuns" (*Adventures of Huckleberry Finn* 404), but the reality in 1887 was that once-feared Apaches were being led away "back East" to be fed, bathed, and educated.

Following his time as superintendent, Merritt rose through a succession of positions of responsibility in the Department of the Dakota, the Department of the Missouri, and the Department of the East, where he regained his official rank of major general. In 1898 he commanded the first Philippine expedition, where he joined forces with Admiral Dewey against the Spanish. Following the defeat of the Spanish troops, he became military governor in Manila for a brief time. He retired at age sixty-four in 1900.

IV

The final superintendent whom Mark Twain knew was John Moulder Wilson (1837–1909). He served as superintendent from August 1889 until March 1893. Wilson (USMA 1860) participated in the Civil War battles of Gaines's Mills and Malvern Hill, as well as in the capture of Mobile and Fort Blakely, Alabama. An engineer, he was responsible for planning the defenses around Washington in 1861, and later he was the superintending engineer for the defenses at Harper's Ferry, Baltimore, Vicksburg, and New Orleans. In 1897 he received the Congressional Medal of Honor for gallantry in the battle of Malvern Hill.

Most of his career was spent directing engineering projects dealing with river and harbor improvements around the country until June 1885, when he received a posting back to his native Washington, DC, to become the superintendent of public buildings and grounds in the district. There he had responsibility for the completion of the Washington Monument and other highly visible projects. During this time he also acted as master of ceremonies at the White House and supervised all the preparations for state functions. In that capacity he dealt daily with the president and his family as well as visiting heads of state and important visitors to the capital — among them Mark Twain. An 1862 graduate of West Point described Wilson in 1907 as "lately a glowing satellite in the planetary system of Washington life" (Schaff 63).

Twain enjoyed the company of these military men who had fought bravely in the Civil War and had served with well-known Indian fighters such as Nelson A. Miles, George Armstrong Custer, and Buffalo Bill Cody. He could see in the eyes of the young cadets who welcomed his visits their own yearning for adventure. Some of those cadets would go out West and fight the last battles with Indians; some would find combat in Cuba or the Philippines; and others would later rise to high rank and command in World War I.

APPENDIX III

Mark Twain's Correspondence with West Pointers

M ark Twain carried on a prodigious correspondence with admirers, business associates, editors, other writers, and influential politicians. The invaluable *Union Catalog of Clemens Letters* (1986), compiled by Paul Machlis, cites over ten thousand letters from Mark Twain to others. The companion *Union Catalog of Letters to Clemens* (1992), lists more than eighteen thousand letters to or about Mark Twain. Of course letters to and from Mark Twain keep turning up in various collections, libraries, and personal holdings, and the Mark Twain Project catalogs new material as it appears.

For the purposes of this study, I have isolated correspondence between Mark Twain and individuals for whom West Point was the nexus of their relationship, thereby excluding figures such as President Grant and General Sherman, whom Mark Twain knew in other social and political spheres. Some of the letters are official requests for Mark Twain to visit the military academy; some are from cadets who were enchanted with his writings; still others, more personal in nature, reflect friendships that grew out of his visits. These letters help to capture the flavor of the special relationship between Mark Twain and West Point.

The letters appear chronologically. Salutations, return addresses, and closings were matters of individual taste in those days, even for official military correspondence. Letterhead stationery at West Point also varied over the years. Formats for dates were inconsistent. Most of the letters were handwritten, typewriters not being in general use during this time. Insofar as possible I have sought to preserve the original spelling, punctuation, syntax, and format of the writers.

Mark Twain's previously unpublished letters quoted here are © 1996 by Chemical Bank as Trustee of the Mark Twain Foundation, which reserves all reproduction or dramatization rights in every medium. Quotation is made with the permission of the University of California Press and Robert H. Hirst, General Editor, Mark Twain Project. Each quotation is identified by a ©, which represents an extension of the copyright page.

CADET ANDREW G. HAMMOND TO MARK TWAIN, 9 JANUARY 1881, ITEM #40699-A

Three letters from Andrew G. Hammond to Mark Twain and one to the Reverend Joseph Twichell, Mark Twain's good friend and spiritual advisor, have been located. The first letter invited Mark Twain to be the speaker at One Hundredth Night, the celebration (which continues today) marking one hundred nights until graduation. Cadet Hammond was a member of Twichell's congregation in Hartford, Connecticut.

West Point, N.Y.
Jan. 9th 1881

My dear Mr. Clemens,
Undoubtedly it is well known to you that the Military Academy is not an institution that turns out geniuses [Hammond finished

thirty-fourth in a class of fifty-three], nor as a rule men who can even make a second rate speech, still some of us do our best to keep life in what is the one literary society of the institution.

It is the custom to have an open meeting one hundred days before the first of June, and entertainment for the Officers of the post, their friends in the Corps of Cadets, a reminder to us that are burning the midnight oil, that studies for the year will soon be over, that summer festivities are coming, and best of all graduation. It is the only affair of the kind that takes place during the year, is always anticipated with gladness and its arrival heartily welcomed and appreciated. The word appreciated however does not always apply to the entertainments past, for we have heretofore depended on native ability. This is explained by the first sentence of my letter. Our failures have taught us that we must let old rules go and adopt new tactics. I happen to be President of the Society, and with all the members desire that our new departure be a success.

It is needless to tell you that we ourselves and guests would all be delighted and consider ourselves most highly favored to listen to remarks from you, so I will simply pray that no circumstances will prevent your being our honored guest and chief deliverer on the evening of Saturday Feb. 19th, and that you will find it in the kindness of your heart to do so. I have written to Mr. Twichell asking him to join his entreaties to ours, and to accompany you, and I hope to also favor us with some remarks.

I will not, in emulation of Mr. Twichell in his interview with General Grant, forget to hint about the acceptance of a speedy reply, although I cannot make the hint delicate as you did in the letter Mr. T. read to us at your house.

Hoping for a favorable reply
I am
Yours Very Respectfully,
A. G. Hammond
U.S. Corps Cadets

CADET ANDREW G. HAMMOND TO MARK TWAIN,
23 JANUARY 1881, ITEM #40679-A

Cadet Hammond continued to correspond with Mark Twain concerning the One Hundredth Night celebration.

West Point, N.Y
Jan. 23rd, 1881

My dear Mr. Clemens,

We were very glad to know that there is a probability of seeing you here, and I should have written before had it not been for the change in our commanding officers [Oliver O. Howard replaced John M. Schofield as superintendent], which left me nobody to whom I should go to see about the date of the event.

My reason for saying Feb. 19th — Saturday — was not because it was the exact day, but was the nearest Saturday to the one hundredth day, and Saturday is our regular meeting day, and Saturday evening is ordinarily our only "off" night, and so I would have to get a special "dispensation" in order to have it any other than Saturday.

The 21st — Monday — is exactly one hundred days from June and as the next day will probably be a holiday, Gen. Howard says that we can have the meeting on that day — (21st), and as this is, I believe, usually a minister's "play day," I thought that this would be just about the thing for Mr. Twichell, and sincerely trust it will suit you.

Of course any programme that you think would suit you, will suit us, so we will not make any objections to any you may suggest or have suggested.

If by any unlucky chance you should be unable to make it Monday, do not you think Mr. T. could find a substitute for his pulpit on Sunday? I am sure we would export our Chaplain, and be glad to do it, tho' we might feel slightly conscience stricken for imposing him on the people of Hartford.

However it may be about Monday or any other day, I can only

say that we desire very much that you all will come if in any way possible, and will do our best to make the occasion enjoyable to you.

If you will kindly let me know soon as to how this change of date suits you, you will greatly facilitate our arrangements, and render me under great obligations.

Very Truly,
A. G. Hammond
U.S. Corps Cadets

* * *

CADET ANDREW G. HAMMOND TO JOSEPH TWICHELL, 16 FEBRUARY 1881, ITEM # 40701

This letter was sent to Joseph Twichell, not Mark Twain, but it confirms the date of the appearance at One Hundredth Night.

West Point, N.Y.
Feb. 16th 1881

Dear Mr. Twichell,

All right for the 28th unless some unforeseen obstacle intervenes, and I sincerely hope that there will not.

The Fellows are delighted and we hope you both like the idea, if we were only untrammeled by rules & regulations, we would get you up a fine entertainment, but as it is your part of the programme will be by far the most important, the rest consisting of music by our band, and of some Cadet Songs and the publication or rather reading of the Society's annual paper, that is if the "funny men" of the Corps cannot give us the "Squibs" & "Gags" that they are so replete with. If you leave Hartford in the morning you can leave New York about 2 or 3 P.M. (I am not sure of the exact time) and we will meet you at the Dock if possible & I guess Genl. Howard will give us the desired permission. We like our

New Superintendent so far very much, tho' we all loved Genl. Schofield more than students usually love their principal, and unlike the Democrats desired no change.

Hoping your children are all well and Mrs. Twichell and yourself also.

I remain

In great haste

Yours

A. G. Hammond

U.S. Corps Cadets

* * *

LIEUTENANT C.E.S. WOOD TO MARK TWAIN, 2 MARCH 1881, ITEM # 40713-A

Lieutenant Charles Erskine Scott Wood was the adjutant at West Point for several of Mark Twain's early visits, one of which occurred just days before this letter. Wood and Mark Twain became good friends and corresponded for several years. The "Academy publication" referred to in this letter is not 1601; that publication on the West Point press took place in 1882.

Adjutant's Office

U.S. Military Academy

West Point, N.Y.

March 2, 1881

Mr. Saml. L. Clemens

Hartford, Conn.

My dear Mr. Clemens

I send by this mail the Academy publication you desired and also some others which may prove of passing interest.

I remember your prompt apology for your future failure to acknowledge the receipt and you need to give yourself no uneasiness in the matter. Yet as an Academic principle I am bound for example's sake to pronounce your explanation "Disapproved" and award you three extra Sunday morning punishments, which Mr. Twichell will see executed. I had a mind to label your bundle "Knits for the Household" and his "Christian Duty" but I know you will extract much profit from this literature without my assistance.

The mess would be very glad to add your photograph — at your convenience — to the "Visitor's Album."

Trusting you may see fit to allow Mrs. Clemens to accompany you here in June

I am

Very sincerely yours
C.E.S. Wood

* * *

LIEUTENANT C.E.S. WOOD TO MARK TWAIN, 3 FEBRUARY 1882, ITEM #41020-A

United States Military Academy
West Point, N.Y. Feb. 3.

My dear Mr. Clemens,

I take my pen in hand to let you know that one of my unreconstructed friends in Norfolk sent me a boxful of diamondback terrapins, the creeping things, & I suppose I must eat them. So Mr. Blackburn of Kentucky — a reconstructed who says he's not afraid of them, is coming up from Washington on or before the 21st of this month. On the night of the 21st we are to have some cadet foolishness as last year when you were here, after which there will be a ball. I know you dote on balls and on the 22d an Officers Hop. Mrs. Wood has gone to Baltimore to stay till April and I want you and Mr. Twichell and Mr. Blackburn and Mr.

[A.W.] Drake Art Supt of the "Century" [Magazine] and Mr. Jones, a young artist lately from Russian & Parisian wilds to occupy my sanity, destroy the terrapins, play whist and use up that Scotch Whisky you left here.

Please communicate with Twichell and let me know. The invitation stands until supper's announced. Feb. 21. 11 P.M.

    With best regards

          I am Yours Sincerely,

            C.E.S. Wood

P.S. I have moved into a larger house. You need not this time be "Enskied and sainted" but you'll have to take a room in common with Twichell.

*   *   *

LIEUTENANT C.E.S. WOOD TO MARK TWAIN,
11 FEBRUARY 1882, ITEM # 41022-A

UNITED STATES MILITARY ACADEMY
West Point, N.Y., Feb. 11 1882

My dear Clemens

Your letter, postmarked the 10 and dated the 11 (You are living too fast) came just now and I am more than grieved to hear that Twichell is afflicted with any distress extra to the always anxious time of childbirth.

I am in a lesser degree sincerely sorry to know that you have a lesser but nevertheless an unusual care in your household.

Under the circumstances I can only sympathize, and accept fate with regret for what might have been. Miss Terese Blackburn, a charming Kentucky schoolgirl, is looking forward (as only guileless youth can look upon idols) with enthusiasm to a genuine talk with Mark Twain.

It falls to my lot to put the idol a little farther from her and defer the séance. See to it that you yourself are not the iconoclast if ever

226

you chance to meet her. But I have no fear. I myself had anticipated some medieval rambles with you; for until Prince & Pauper
I had no idea you were a student of dead days. Let us hope that
our pleasures are only postponed and that all will end well. I want
to know Twichell better, much better than I do, so when the
chance comes run down without ceremony, both of you.

When my Lass (were the lasses ever feminine?) returns to her
lasslorn worshiper we will set our hearts in order and hope for the
women of the Clemens and Twichell families to brighten it.
Meanwhile remember come at any time and the ball and supper
invitation stands till the supper is eaten. Yours faithfully

C. E. S. Wood

P.S. I have written (as I always do) a wordy frivolous letter but I
hope it will not disguise the fact that I shall be really anxious till
I hear good news from Twichell's family.

* * *

MARK TWAIN TO LIEUTENANT C.E.S. WOOD,
21 FEBRUARY 1882, © ITEM # 02161

*Mark Twain's reply to the letter above is important because it
broaches the subject of 1601, his bawdy Elizabethan burlesque.
It also responds to Wood's inducement of "a charming Kentucky
schoolgirl." In his old age Mark Twain was uncommonly
attracted to young girls. He formed an organization called The
Aquarium, consisting of pretty young girls whom he called his
"Angelfish." (For more on this intriguing subject, see Cooley;
Lanier; and Twain,* Mark Twain's Aquarium.*)*

Hartford, Conn. Feb'y 21st 1882

My dear Wood

Twichell's Tribe and mine are still in the doctor's hands. The
circumstances remain in both cases about as they were before.
Do not let the charming Kentucky school girl get away from

there: put her under martial restraint until we come, for Joe and I are certainly coming, just as soon as things will permit.

We bear your proffered hospitality in mind, and propose to take advantage of it as early as we can. Speaking of dead days: Have you seen my 1601? Did not Gen. Sherman or Gen. Van Vliet have it when I was at the Point? It's [sic] circulation is quietly enlarging: A copy of it has just gone to Japan. I shall get into trouble with it yet before I die. With warmest regards to yourself and Mrs. Wood.

Yours faithfully,
S. L. Clemens

P.S. Excuse haste and a bad pen.

* * *

MARK TWAIN TO LIEUTENANT C.E.S. WOOD,
3 APRIL 1882, © ITEM # 02196

Mark Twain conferred with Wood about a private printing of 1601, and Wood agreed to use West Point's printing press to run off about sixty copies.

Hartford, Conn. April 3, 1882

My dear Wood—

I enclose the original of 1603 [sic] as you suggest. I am afraid there are errors in it, also, heedlessness in antiquated spelling — e's stuck on often at end of words where they are not strickly necessary, etc. . . . I would go through the manuscript but I am too much driven just now, and it is not important anyway. I wish you would do me the kindness to make any and all corrections that suggest themselves to you.

Sincerely yours,
SL Clemens

LIEUTENANT ANDREW G. HAMMOND TO MARK TWAIN, 10 JUNE 1882, ITEM # 41295-A

Hammond graduated from West Point in 1881 and was posted to Texas as a lieutenant. This letter acknowledges receipt of a photograph of Mark Twain. Hammond expresses some opinions regarding the Indians and the Chinese who were laborers on the Southern Pacific Railroad. Mark Twain wrote a satire in 1870, not published until 1948, condemning a proposal to tax the citizens of San Francisco to supply a one-million-dollar bond to the Southern Pacific Railroad, with the proviso that no Chinese labor be employed in its construction. (See Wecter; for more about Mark Twain's sympathetic views toward the Chinese, see Stark.)

Mayer's Spring, Texas
10th June 1882.

My dear Mr. Clemens,

Please accept my heartfelt thanks for your photograph which has just been forwarded me from Lt. Clark. There has long been a vacant space in my Class Album alongside of "Rev. Joe's" picture that I have been keeping for yours.

We have been in camp here for six weeks looking out for Indians, but I think the Mexican troops have spared us the trouble & killed them all, for we have seen or heard of none here. It was a rare thing to see a stranger, but now the Southern Pacific Railway has progressed so far that we are overrun with tramps & that usual scum of humanity that follow the line of a new railway. We have them of all nationalities, even China is represented from thousands of them being employed on the western end of the [rail]road. But of all tramps we find the "ornery" free American Citizen is the worst, he thinks that because we belong to the Government, we are bound to feed, clothe & lodge him, and feels insulted when he is run off.

The gentle "Coyote" is pretty scarce now, though we have killed several, our stronghold now is the Tarantula, and Tarantula fights are our principal amusement, we have one now — under glass — who has killed all his opponents, but we hope to find one to match with him, pools are now open.

Please remember me to Mrs. Clemens & Mr. T. and believe me
Very Truly Yours
A. G. Hammond

* * *

LIEUTENANT C.E.S. WOOD TO MARK TWAIN, 14 JULY 1882, ITEM # 41128-A

As a courtesy to Wood for printing 1601, *Mark Twain sent him a copy of his recently published collection of stories,* The Stolen White Elephant, Etc. *(1882). This letter from Wood thanks him for the gift.*

HEADQUARTERS, DEPARTMENT OF WEST POINT
United States Military Academy
West Point, N.Y. July 14, 1882

My dear Mr. Clemens,

I received your letter yesterday or the day before — I forget which — and the White Elephant came today. It is far from being a White Elephant on my hands and I have already very much enjoyed looking over it. I note some old friends between its covers and one at least which I heard you relate but had never seen in print. I have not yet sent the "1601" to the gentlemen named by you because I think you are under a misapprehension due to a blindness in my letter or your hasty perusal. I have more than 20 copies — 6 on antique cream paper — the balance on white bookpaper — all of which are yours. They are as yet <u>unstitched</u>. I wrote asking whether you desired them sent to you in loose leaves or stitched. If you prefer the latter, one printer who has done the whole business for me will return about the 20th of this month and I will have him sew them and will then send <u>all</u> to you for your disposal or will mail the copies mentioned by you and express the remainder to you. You pays your stamps and you takes your chances. We go to Omaha in Sept. which pleases the general and all the staff but me. I attended the law lectures and school of Political Science in N.Y. last winter taking my degree of Ph.B. [Bachelor of Philosophy] and should like to continue two years more taking the Doctorate. Besides I am Librarian here with funds at my command — so buy what books I like — and I hate to give up my little Printing Office which is a sort of pet. It's [sic] capacity for fine artistic modern work you don't know. I fear my visit to Hartford to [you] and yours to me will be still longer in embryo. Unless you will imitate the old farmer who was going to come help his neighbor thrash on Wednesday and would come Thursday <u>anyhow</u>. Kind regards to your family.

Hoping to know them some day.

I am sincerely yours,

C.E.S. Wood

*   *   *

MARK TWAIN TO LIEUTENANT C.E.S. WOOD,
AUGUST 1882, © ITEM # 02243

This brief note on the reverse of a crossed-out message on a postcard thanks Wood in advance for a picture of Mark Twain. Wood's note at the Mark Twain Project at Berkeley reads, "I sent Mark to be autographed a proof of Timothy Cole's wood engraving after Abbot Thayer's black and white portrait of Mark done for The Century Co. to accompany as I remember it an essay on Mark Twain, but it may have been some article by him. I asked him if he would like a proof for himself." Here is Mark Twain's reply:

I'd like it first-rate, Wood, & so would Twichell. The one you sent here for signature is the only one I've seen.

Raining here, now; & cold as Greenland!

Yrs sincerely,

S. L. Clemens

* * *

MARK TWAIN TO C.E.S. WOOD,
24 JULY 1884, © ITEM # 01297

In May 1884 Mark Twain took bicycle lessons, a painful experience recorded in "Taming the Bicycle," written at this time but published after Mark Twain's death in What Is Man? and Other Essays. *Mark Twain's friendship with Wood continued after Wood left West Point and the army to take up his career as a lawyer. The first sentence refers to an investment opportunity with a railroad.*

Elmira, July 24/84

My Dear Mr. Wood—

Oh, the devil! why didn't you get into the Pacific & be done with it? I tried to get to West Point in June but made a failure of it; so I can't tell you any news from there. But I've brought a bicycle here to this mountain-top, & if you will wait a while, <u>that</u> can be made to furnish you some [news].

I'll enclose the introduction with great pleasure.

Begging to be kindly remembered to Mrs. Wood, I am

Truly Yours

SL Clemens

* * *

GENERAL WESLEY MERRITT TO MARK TWAIN,
17 MARCH 1886, ITEM # 42900-A

This is the first in a series of letters arranging Mark Twain's visit of 3 April 1886.

United States Military Academy
West Point, New York
March 17, 1886

Mr. Samuel Clemens:
Hartford Conn.

My dear Sir:

There is a great desire on the part of the Corps of Cadets and the Army people stationed at this Post to hear you lecture at West Point.

Can you gratify the wish?

The cadets are occupied every evening of the week except Saturday evenings. If you could aim for the 20 or 27 or the 3rd of April it would be satisfactory.

There are many pleasant recollections of a visit you made here some few years since.

Hoping to hear favorably from you I am

Very respectfully,
W. Merritt
B't [Brevet] Maj Genl U.S.A.
Supt.

* * *

GENERAL WESLEY MERRITT TO MARK TWAIN,
22 MARCH 1886, ITEM # 42906

U.S. MILITARY ACADEMY
West Point, N.Y.
March 22 '86

Mr. S. L. Clemens
Hartford, Conn:
  My dear Sir: I am delighted that the prospects of your coming
are good. You will find many friends and admirers here. Mrs.
Merritt and I would be very glad to have you and the Chaplain
[Joseph Twichell] lodge with us while you remain at West Point.
However, we can arrange that later. I write in haste just as I leave
for the city for a day or two.
                    Very Truly Yours
                    W. Merritt

* * *

GENERAL WESLEY MERRITT TO MARK TWAIN,
30 MARCH 1886, ITEM # 42911-A

United States Military Academy
West Point, New York
March 30, 1886

Mr. S. L. Clemens:
Hartford Conn.
  My dear Sir:
    Your note is just received. I am very glad you are coming. Mrs.
Merritt and I will be delighted to have you and the Rev. Mr.
Twitchell [sic] as our guests during your stay, and will let you do
as you please as to hours of "coming in" and returning. Our
quarters are always open.

There are stages at the stations for all trains and you can drive at once to my quarters. In haste

Very Truly Yours

W. Merritt

* * *

GENERAL WESLEY MERRITT TO MARK TWAIN,
22 APRIL 1886, ITEM # 42926

United States Military Academy
West Point, New York
April 22, 1886

My dear Mr. Clemens:

Your visit to West Point and the honor we had of entertaining you in one sense, and being entertained by you in another and better sense is among the pleasantest recollections of our lives. Mrs. Merritt's and mine and the rest of West Point including the Corps of Cadets.

I hope your promise to visit West Point in May will not constitute a patch of pavement for a nameless place. I am delighted to say our "weather" promises to be all that even you could desire for outdoor work.

Joining Mrs. Merritt in most pleasant rememberances to you and Dr. Twichell I am

Sincerely Your Friend

W. Merritt

* * *

GENERAL WESLEY MERRITT TO MARK TWAIN,
17 APRIL 1887, ITEM # 43270-A

One year after Mark Twain's 3 April 1886 visit, General Merritt sent the following letter to arrange another visit, this one occurring 30 April 1887 (see fig. 21).

West Point, N.Y.
April 17th 1887

Dear Mr. Clemens:

I hope you have not forgotten your promises to visit us this Spring. Now is the time. We hope for Spring and the artillery drill which was another important specification in your visit is at its full. I want to express to you that you will favor us with a visit bringing Mrs. Clemens with you, say Thursday the 21st or the 28th and remain over until the following Monday. Of course you must lecture on the Saturday evening of your stay and you must be here Thursday and Friday to see the dress drills. In other words

Figure 21. Mark Twain enjoyed watching the cadets conduct artillery drill on the plain. These guns are 12-pounder Napoleons.
SOURCE: USMA Archives

we can't have drill on Saturday and can't have a lecture any other evening than Saturday. Mrs. Merritt will write Mrs. Clemens seconding this invitation. I hope to hear from you that you will come. Also, won't Dr. Twichell come? He will have a warm welcome and be cared for by friends here. Everybody, including the Cadets, is wild to have you here again.

Hoping to hear from you favorably, I am with Great Respect
Very Truly Yours
W. Merritt

* * *

GENERAL JOHN M. WILSON TO MARK TWAIN, 1 NOVEMBER 1889, ITEM # 44740-A

Wilson succeeded John G. Parke as superintendent at West Point. Shortly after his assignment to the military academy, he wrote to Mark Twain.

U.S. Military Academy
West Point, N.Y.
Nov. 1. 1889

Mr. Saml. Clemens
Hartford Conn.
My dear Sir:

Since I had the pleasure of meeting you in Washington, I have been assigned to the command of this post, and I am anxious to do something this winter for the entertainment of the Cadets.

The only time that can be devoted to amusement is on Saturday evening between seven and nine P.M. and I write to ask whether your engagements will admit your devoting one Saturday evening during the winter to the entertainment of the Cadets.

If you can do so, will you kindly inform me of your terms for such entertainments.

Should you visit our post I trust that I may have the pleasure of your company as my guest when you are at the post.

Yours very truly
John M. Wilson
Col. of Engineers
Superintendent

* * *

GENERAL JOHN M. WILSON TO MARK TWAIN,
11 NOVEMBER 1889, ITEM # 44762

U.S. Military Academy
West Point, N.Y.
Nov. 11th/89

Mr. S. L. Clemens
Hartford Conn.
My dear Sir:

Your very kind note of the 8th inst. reached me this A.M. and I am greatly indebted for your kindness in agreeing to address the Cadets.

I will arrange for the evening of Saturday December 7th and will look forward with pleasure to having you as our guest at home at that time.

If you will kindly telegraph me in advance of your hour of arrival, I will meet you at the dock.

Yours very truly
John M. Wilson
Colonel of Engineers

* * *

GENERAL JOHN M. WILSON TO MARK TWAIN,
22 NOVEMBER 1889, ITEM # 44779

U.S. Military Academy
West Point, N. Y.
Nov. 22/89

My dear Mr. Clemens:

Your kind note is just at hand and it will give us great pleasure to have you with us at the time you indicate and unless something occurs to prevent you from coming, we will look for and welcome you on Dec. 14th.

Please let me know the time of your arrival, so that I may meet you at the dock.

Yours very sincerely,
John M. Wilson
Col. of Engrs.

Mr. Saml. L. Clemens
Hartford Conn.

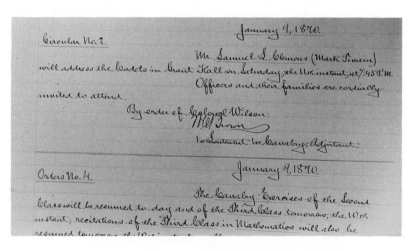

Figure 22. Announcement of Mark Twain's
lecture in Grant Hall, 11 January 1890.
SOURCE: USMA Archives

GENERAL JOHN M. WILSON TO MARK TWAIN,
12 DECEMBER 1889, ITEM # 44821

HEADQUARTERS
UNITED STATES MILITARY ACADEMY
WEST POINT, N.Y.
Dec. 12/89

My dear Mr. Clemens:

Mrs. C's letter is just received and I regret that you are ill.

I trust that you will soon be yourself once more, and that the pleasure of hearing you address the Cadets will be only temporarily postponed.

> Yrs. very truly
> John M. Wilson
> Col. of Engrs

Mr. Saml. L. Clemens
Hartford Conn.

* * *

MARK TWAIN TO C.E.S. WOOD,
21 MARCH 1900, © ITEM # 05779

From England Mark Twain wrote to Wood requesting copies of 1601, but by now the original copies had all been dispersed, and Wood had no others.

London, March 21/00

My dear Wood:

I greatly need a couple of copies of "1601" to fulfill promises with. Can you help me? I've been out of the humble classic for many years.

With my kindest regards & best wishes to you & the family.
Sincerely yours,
SL Clemens

*　*　*

WILLISTON FISH TO MARK TWAIN,
26 AUGUST 1900, ITEM # 37788

Fish was a member of the USMA *class of 1881 and heard Mark Twain speak at the One Hundredth Night celebration that year. Years later Fish felt compelled to write a letter of gratitude to him. In this letter Fish errs in saying that Mark Twain spoke at the 1880 One Hundredth Night.*

Chicago
August 26th, 1900

Samuel L. Clemens, Esq.,
London, Engl.

My dear Mark Twain:
In the spring of 1880 [sic] you came to West Point, and aided the celebration of our One Hundred Nights to June. The next day you came over to barracks, and told us stories. I do not mention this as a great event in your life, but simply to go back to old times and get on a proper basis. This letter now is just to thank you a million times for the pleasure I have had out of your existence. Countless times when I have been reading something of yours, or recalling something of yours or talking about something of yours, I have felt a strong hunch to write you and let you know that I was listening to what you said. I am a hopeless insolvent in the debt I owe you. I began to run in debt to you 34 years ago back in Ohio when one day I lingered in the village post office to hear read aloud an article of yours in the New York Tribune, which was

received as being full of merry jests [Fish probably refers to some travel letters that Mark Twain published in the *Tribune* in 1867, appearing in *Innocents Abroad* in 1869]. As long ago as that you were perfectly well established in the high opinion of that little bunch of men that you never heard of. They didn't have any hesitation in laughing at your jokes. They knew they were all right, and they laughed out boldly and loud. After that I borrowed the Innocents Abroad of my aunt. From this beginning I have gone along reading everything I could beg or borrow — even buying something when pushed to it — and I am head over heels in debt to you. To think that I have not had the usual debtor's manliness to write you an occasional letter and dun myself, or tell you that I was expecting a turn in my affairs, and would straighten things out.

I want at least to acknowledge my debt, and to say that time cannot outlaw it. The world would not have been the same world without you. Mark Twain is just like the sun and the skies and the apple-orchards. His books are just the same as living. All good people would like to do something to give you pleasure, such as you give the rest of us, but I don't know how we can do it unless we send you a set of your own works. If we could print them out in some shape so that you would not know you wrote them — say, but you would enjoy them in your idle hours, or your busy hours or any hours. When you go to bed, and everybody thinks you are going to sleep, as you should, you take one of those books, and get the light right, and bunch your two pillows — and there you are. You ought to read the Yankee at King Arthur's Court. Wasn't that dinner they gave the rich blacksmith great? And wasn't it great when the king and the yankee were being smoked out of the tree, and the king said they would go down, and take each a side of the tree, and draw their swords, and each pile his dead after his own taste and fancy. And the king's irritation over the low figure put on him by the slave-dealer, and the yankee's advice to his lady to put local color in her tales of knights, be jabbers. And in Following the Equator (a book which ought to be as long as the Equator itself, and equally without an end) that story of the bashful lover. It would certainly pay you to read it.

Well, the world would be a barren promontory without such files as Mark Twain. I wish you would come back to this country and go about so that people could see you. If you would, I can say about you as W[illiam] S[hakespeare] said about Opportunity:
"One poor returning moment in an age
Would win for thee a thousand thousand friends."
With many thanks to you I beg to be, affectionately yours.
Williston Fish

* * *

MARK TWAIN TO WILLISTON FISH,
12 SEPTEMBER 1900, © ITEM # 06217

Mark Twain replied to Fish's paean from Dollis Hill House, the English estate where he lived from early July until early October 1900.

Dollis Hill House
NW
London, Sept 12/00

Dear Mr. Fish:
You make me feel very proud; and if there was a debt, you have most liberally paid it, interest & all, & now we stand a little more than square, with the advantage in my favor. And so I thank you very cordially for your letter.

I am coming home now in a month, after an exile of nine years; & if I were as young as I was in 1880, I would take the hint & raid the country & sack it from the platform, & foregather with the old friends & do my best to make some new ones — but that is a dream; & dreams do not come true.

With my best thanks to you for remembering me, I am
Sincerely Yours
SL Clemens

* * *

MARK TWAIN TO GENERAL OLIVER O. HOWARD, 8 JANUARY 1901, © ITEM # 05961

Oliver Otis Howard was the superintendent at West Point during three of Mark Twain's visits in 1881 and 1882. Howard frequently wrote to Mark Twain asking him for personal or financial support for various social causes. Mark Twain warns Howard about an article that would appear in the February 1901 issue of the North American Review. *This distinguished publication, founded in Boston in 1815, published the social and political views of influential leaders of the day. He had written against American policy in the Philippines in his classic article "To the Person Sitting in Darkness."*

14 West 10th Street [New York City]
Jan. 8. 1901

Dear General:

I'm venturing to accept — on condition that you will be frank & disinvite me if you find you don't want a person of my stripe after you read my article in next North American Review. I give you my word I shall not take offense.

With the love of
S. L. Clemens

* * *

MARK TWAIN TO OLIVER O. HOWARD, 7 FEBRUARY 1901, © ITEM # 05991

This letter from Mark Twain requests that Howard obtain three seats for Mark Twain's wife and daughters for the celebration of Lincoln's birthday at Carnegie Hall on 11 February 1901. Curiously Mark Twain was chairman of the event; announced the choral songs; read a letter from President McKinley, who was unable to attend; and introduced the main speaker, Henry Watterson, an influential journalist of Louisville, Kentucky. Present in the audience were Generals Miles, Dodge, Wheeler, Howard, Greene, Sickles, McCook, and others from both sides in the Civil War. Mark Twain's remarks were conciliatory: "The old wounds are healed, and you of the North and we of the South are brothers again" (Mark Twain Speaking 383).

14 W. 10th, Feb. 7.

Dear General:

My wife and 2 daughters require me to secure good seats for them for the Lincoln night, and I do not know where to apply. So I throw myself upon your indulgence and beg you to forward this note to the ticket department, with the request that the tickets and the bill for them be sent to me at above address—and I shall remain

Your obliged servant and friend
S. L. Clemens

* * *

MARK TWAIN TO GENERAL OLIVER O. HOWARD,
13 FEBRUARY 1901, © ITEM # 05993

O.O. Howard,
Major General U.S.A. Retired,
    30 West 59th Street, City.

Dear General:
  You are a busy man, and I thank you cordially for taking the
time to say those pleasant and welcome words.
            Sincerely yours,
              S. L. Clemens

* * *

MARK TWAIN TO C.E.S. WOOD,
23 FEBRUARY 1901, © ITEM # 06009

*Mark Twain very likely is responding to a letter from Wood
complimenting him on his participation in Lincoln's birthday
event, which received widespread newspaper coverage.*

            14 West 10th Street,
          New York, February 23, 1901.

My dear Wood:
  I am glad you like it. By and by I mean to do it again. You must
not fail to come and see me when you reach town. My address is
as above, and I am always at home at 10:30 in the morning, the
rest of the family at 5:00 in the afternoon.
  With warm regards to you and yours,
            Sincerely
            SL Clemens

* * *

MARK TWAIN TO C.E.S. WOOD,
7 JUNE 1901, © ITEM # 06071

Mark Twain wrote to Wood complimenting him on the publication of his poem "Destiny" in Louis F. Post's anti-imperialist magazine the Public *(12 January 1901: 634–35) in Chicago. Wood's handwritten note on the copy of this letter at the Mark Twain Project says that the poem was "inspired by our imperialism of the war with Spain" and that it was "not propaganda, rather an ode to Freedom." Wood's poem reads in part: "Gone are the sons of Freedom with the trumpet voice of God. / Blind in the stony mill of shame, treads the giant of the west." Mark Twain often spoke out against American involvement in the Philippines and elsewhere. The "Hundred Year Book" was an autobiography that he said he would write, with the stipulation that it would not be published until one hundred years after his death so that his children might not be hurt or embarrassed by what they read. He regrets in this letter that Wood had not sent his poem to the more widely read* North American Review. *During the 1890s that magazine published a dozen of Mark Twain's essays, including his strongest writing on anti-imperialism (Rasmussen 381).*

New York, June 7, 1901

My dear Wood:

I am so sorry you interred that noble poem in an obscure publication. It should have been sent to the North American, whence it would have been copied into even hostile publications purely on account of its merit as a poem.

No, the Hundred Year Book is not a secret and there is no indiscretion.

We have broken up the house and are packing to leave for the Adirondacks for the summer. We are negotiating for another house in this neighborhood and shall not occupy this one again. Just as you enter New York at one end we shall be going out the other end on a summer flight; which is too bad, I wish I could have another talk with you and make you well acquainted with Mrs. Clemens. We shall return early in October and then we must be sure and get together and set this world right once more.

Sincerely yours,
SL Clemens

* * *

MARK TWAIN TO C.E.S. WOOD,
24 JUNE 1901, © ITEM # 06079

As indicated in the letter above, Mark Twain had relocated to the Adirondacks. Once again he and Wood discuss financial matters. At this time Henry Huttleston Rogers of Standard Oil Company was helping Mark Twain to make more judicious investments.

Saranac Lake, N.Y.
June 24. [1901]

Dear Wood—

Good—I shall be glad to have a copy when it issues; & I am thanking you in advance.

Very well, I will wait for the [price of] Steel to fall. I did place an order when it was at 90—intending to sell when it went up 8 or 9 points—but I was a day late & didn't get it. Up here I don't trade at all, nor look at the stock-list, nor subscribe for any daily paper. I have retired from the world for 3 months, or 4.

We live on the lake, 2½ miles from the above village, & haven't a neighbor any where near. It is as reposeful as the cemetery.

Sincerely Yours
SL Clemens

* * *

MARK TWAIN TO C.E.S. WOOD,
29 JANUARY 1902, © ITEM # 06258

Wood had asked Mark Twain for his support in obtaining an endowment from philanthropist Andrew Carnegie (1835–1919) for a "School of the Theatre," an idea Wood subsequently abandoned. Mark Twain knew Carnegie well, and tried to obtain investment capital from him in the 1890s for the Paige compositor, an enterprise that bankrupted Mark Twain. Perhaps his prior failure in this investment caused him to demur about approaching Carnegie on Wood's behalf.

Riverdale
on the Hudson
Jan. 29 /02

Dear Wood—

Think it over, then ask me again if you like, & I will give you a letter to Carnegie, the which I have never done before, because I think I know him. I believe I know him well enough to know that he would not take any interest in it.

But it's for you to say; if you sound the call, I'll answer.

I've been away since Jan. 20 & have just returned.

Sincerely yours
SL Clemens

* * *

MARK TWAIN TO C.E.S. WOOD,
31 OCTOBER 1904, © ITEM # 06941

Wood sent Mark Twain a copy of his poem "A Masque of Love," and the latter acknowledged its receipt and complimented Wood. This is the last known letter from Mark Twain to his old friend.

S.L. Clemens

Oct 31/04

Dear Wood:

I have read "A Masque of Love" with strong pleasure. It is a beautiful poem & wise & deep. What Alp shall you subdue next? You were an able instructor of West Point lads in the science of war; then you took up the law & distinguished yourself in that profession; & now you have proven that you are a poet.

Well, go on, old time friend; the more triumphs you achieve the better [I] will be pleased.

> Yours as always,
> Mark

* * *

COLONEL ALBERT L. MILLS TO MARK TWAIN,
28 FEBRUARY 1906, ITEM # 35276

Colonel Mills (USMA 1879), who wrote this letter in his capacity as superintendent, heard Mark Twain speak at West Point during his earliest visits. This letter thanked him for a photograph he had recently sent to the Officers Mess. Searches by West Point archivists failed to reveal the present whereabouts of Mark Twain's autographed picture. Colonel Mills addresses Mark Twain as "Dr. Clemens" because Yale University conferred on him the Litt.D. degree in October 1901; he received the same honorary degree from the University of Missouri in June 1902 and from Oxford University in June 1907.

HEADQUARTERS
UNITED STATES MILITARY ACADEMY
WEST POINT, NEW YORK
February 28, 1906

Samuel L. Clemens, LL.D.,
21 Fifth Avenue, New York City.

My dear Dr. Clemens:

The Military Academy is greatly pleased at receiving from your own hands your excellent photograph with its most happy epigram. For the Academy and all connected with it I thank you for this testimony of your regard, and I venture to hope when the spring blossoms are fully out and it is more comfortable to move about than at present, you may feel inclined to again honor West Point with a visit. I believe you will find much here to interest and entertain you in the changes that have taken place and are under way, and I certainly can assure you a hearty welcome from many friends who recollect and often speak of your former pleasant visits.

Very sincerely yours,
A. L. Mills

* * *

CAPTAIN S.F. BATTARNS TO MARK TWAIN,
22 JANUARY 1907, ITEM # 38886-E

Captain Battarns wrote to Mark Twain in the old army tradition of extending "the privileges of the mess," a customary way of honoring high-ranking officers and civilians who had rendered a favor to the officers and soldiers of a unit.

West Point Army Mess
West Point, N.Y.

Sir:

It gives me pleasure to inform you that the priveleges [sic] of the West Point Army Mess are extended to you for the ensuing year.

Yours very truly,
S. F. Battarns
Captain Comsy [Commissary]
Secretary-Treasurer

* * *

MARK TWAIN TO CAPTAIN S.F. BATTARNS,
C. 24 JANUARY 1907, © ITEM # 10965

Sir:

I thank you very much for the honor you confer in extending to me the privileges of the West Point Army Mess for the coming year. I accept them with pleasure, & hope that I may be able to use them.

Sincerely Yours
[signature cut from note]

* * *

MARK TWAIN TO GENERAL OLIVER O. HOWARD, 12 JANUARY 1909, © ITEM # 08312

The final known letter relating Mark Twain and West Point is one to his old friend and former superintendent General Howard. This letter expresses Mark Twain's regret at not being able to participate in a fund-raiser for one of Howard's endeavors, Lincoln Memorial University in Cumberland Gap, Tennessee (Carpenter 297). This area of Tennessee had largely remained loyal to the Union, and was thus receptive to having in its midst a university honoring Abraham Lincoln. Howard was instrumental in the founding of this university, just as he had been with Howard University in Washington, DC. Mark Twain expresses warm feelings for Howard, teasing him about not appreciating his military prowess during the Civil War. He admitted many times in public that he served as a volunteer in the Confederacy for only about two weeks, finding a separate peace in the West. He hyperbolically equates himself with Xenophon (c. 428–354 BC), the famous Greek general.

STORMFIELD

REDDING

CONNECTICUT

Jan 12/09

Dear General Howard:

You pay me a most gratifying compliment in asking me to preside, & it causes me very much regret that I am obliged to decline, for the object of the meeting appeals strongly to me, since that object is to aid in raising the $500,000 Endowment Fund for Lincoln Memorial University. The Endowment Fund will be the most fitting of all the memorials the country will dedicate to the memory of Lincoln, serving, as it will, to uplift his very own people.

I hope you will meet with complete success, & I am sorry I cannot be there to witness it & help you rejoice. But I am older than people think, nearly twice as old as I used to be; & besides I live away out in the country & never stir from home, except at geological intervals to fill left-over engagements made in Meso-zoic times when I was younger & indiscreeter.

You ought not to say sarcastic things about my "fighting on the other side." General Grant did not act like that. General Grant paid me compliments. He bracketed me with Zenophon — it is there in his Memoires [sic] for anybody to read. He said if all the Confederate Soldiers had followed my example & adopted my military arts he could never have caught enough of them in a bunch to inconvenience the Rebellion. General Grant was a fair man & recognized my worth; but you are prejudiced & you have hurt my feelings.

But I have an affection for you, anyway.

Mark Twain

WORKS CITED

Abbott, Frederic V. *History of the Class of 'Seventy-Nine*. New York: Putnam's, 1884.

(Members of the class of 1879 recall their cadet days and give accounts of their activities since graduation.)

Agnew, James B. *The Eggnog Riot: The Christmas Mutiny at West Point*. San Rafael, CA: Presidio, 1979.

(A historical novel about the cadet mutiny of 1826. Contains an excellent introduction.)

Albion, Robert G. "George M. Robeson." *American Secretaries of the Navy*. Ed. Paolo E. Coletta. Vol. 1. Annapolis: Naval Institute P, 1980. 369–84. 2 vols.

(Mark Twain corresponded with Robeson concerning corruption in government.)

"Appreciably Serious." Editorial. *New York Times* 17 Jan. 1901: 8, col. 4.

(Laments the practice of fighting between upper- and lowerclassmen.)

"The Army of the Potomac." *Army and Navy Journal* 11 June 1881: 944–46.

(Mark Twain's speech to the Society of the Army of the Potomac the night before his visit to West Point.)

Arnold, Matthew. *General Grant*. Ed. John Y. Simon. Carbondale: Southern Illinois UP, 1966.

(Contains a "Rejoinder by Mark Twain" defending Grant's grammar in his *Personal Memoirs*.)

Barber, Henry E., and Allen R. Gann. *A History of the Savannah District U.S. Army Corps of Engineers*. Savannah: Savannah District U.S. Army Corps of Engineers, 1989.

(Contains evidence that Captain Carter retained the support of many in Savannah following his conviction for fraud.)

Bingham, Edwin R. *Charles Erskine Scott Wood.* Western Writers Series. Boise: Boise State UP, 1990.

(Bingham's literary biography discusses the life and writings of Mark Twain's friend, the adjutant at West Point who arranged for the printing of Mark Twain's *1601.*)

Biographical Directory of the United States Congress, 1774–1989. Washington: GPO, 1989.

(Contains information about Congressmen Whittemore and Butler, who sold their cadetships to West Point for personal gain.)

"Booz's West Point Fight." *New York Times* 22 Dec. 1900: 2, col. 3.

(An account of the fight between Cadets Booz and Keller.)

Boynton, Edward C. *History of West Point.* New York: Van Nostrand, 1863.

(Boynton was the adjutant at West Point when he wrote this discussion of the early history.)

Breter, Carl. "West Point Discipline." *New York Times* 19 Nov. 1887: 2, col. 3.

(Enumerates the various offenses by which a cadet might incur demerits.)

Brownell, George Hiram. "January Meeting." *Twainian* 2 (1940): 1–3.

(This newsletter of the Mark Twain Society of Chicago contains an account by Captain Oberlin M. Carter, then eighty-four years old, who recalled seeing Mark Twain at West Point at least three times during his cadet years.)

"Cadet Dying from Hazing." *New York Times* 1 Dec. 1900: 3, col. 1.

(The first newspaper article about the controversial Booz hazing case.)

"Cadets Abolish Hazing." *New York Times* 20 Jan. 1901: 1, col. 2.

(Representatives of each class sign a letter pledging to eliminate fistfights.)

"Cadets Describe Hazing." *New York Times* 20 Dec. 1900: 6, col. 1.

(Cadets testify during the court of inquiry about various hazing practices, including the use of "hell sauce.")

"Careful Reading of the Testimony." Editorial. *New York Times* 21 Dec. 1900: 8, col. 5.

(Supports West Point against charges of hazing in the Booz case.)

"Carlisle Barracks." *Army and Navy Journal* 23 May 1887: 815.

(An account of efforts to "civilize" the Apaches brought to the Indian school in Carlisle, Pennsylvania.)

Carpenter, John A. *Sword and Olive Branch*. Pittsburgh: U of Pittsburgh P, 1964.

(This is the best biography of General Howard.)

"The Case of Capt. Carter." *New York Times* 6 Oct. 1898: 5, col. 1.

(Captain Carter's conviction for fraud was upheld by the secretary of war.)

The Centennial Report of the United States Military Academy. Washington: GPO, 1904. 2 vols.

(An extensive account of West Point's first century, containing official reports, curricula, and essays by famous graduates.)

Chapman, Guy. *The Dreyfus Case: A Reassessment*. New York: Reynal, 1955.

(A detailed account of the case of Captain Dreyfus, a cause of great interest to Mark Twain.)

Chittenden, Hiram. Letter to his mother. 6 Mar. 1881. Hiram Chittenden Papers. West Point Archives.

(A brief account of Mark Twain's visit of 28 February 1881.)

Coffman, Edward M. *The Hilt of the Sword: The Career of Peyton C. March*. Madison: U of Wisconsin P, 1966.

(March, who would become a major general and army chief of staff, was a member of the class of 1888, and recalled Mark Twain's visits to Pershing's room to entertain cadets.)

——. *The Old Army: A Portrait of the American Army in Peacetime, 1784–1898*. New York: Oxford UP, 1986.

(Deals extensively with the role West Pointers played in shaping the army before and after the Civil War.)

"Col. B.T. Clayton Killed." *New York Times* 5 June 1918: 11, col. 3.

(Colonel Clayton, a classmate of Pershing's, heard Mark Twain speak at West Point.)

"The Congressional Investigation." *New York Times* 10 Jan. 1901: 1, col. 6.

(The congressional committee investigating the Booz case arrives at West Point.)

"Congressional Booz Inquiry." *New York Times* 5 Jan. 1901: 2, col. 7.
(Recounts the first day of testimony in the Booz hazing case.)

Cook, Nancy. "Charles L. Webster." *Mark Twain Encyclopedia* 780.
(Biographical sketch of Mark Twain's partner in a publishing firm that went bankrupt.)

Cooley, John R. "Mark Twain's Aquarium." *Mark Twain Journal* 27 (1989): 18–24.
(Mark Twain became inordinately fond of young girls in his old age.)

Davis, Jefferson. *The Rise and Fall of the Confederate Government*. New York: Appleton, 1881. 2 vols.
(The president of the Confederacy and a West Point graduate, Davis defends the Southern secession.)

Davis, John H. "Which Was the Dream?" *Mark Twain Encyclopedia* 788–89.
(Discusses Mark Twain's unfinished story, which uses West Point as a symbol of honor and integrity.)

"Death Ends Fight of Oberlin Carter." *New York Times* 20 July 1944: 19, col. 2.
(Obituary of Captain Carter, who died at age eighty-eight after years of unsuccessfully trying to clear his name.)

"Editor Moffett Dies, Struggling in Surf." *New York Times* 2 Aug. 1908, sec. 2: 1, col. 3.
(An account of the death of Mark Twain's nephew, Samuel E. Moffett.)

Fish, Williston. "Memories of West Point, 1877–1881." Typescript, 1957, West Point Archives.
(An entertaining eyewitness account of several of Mark Twain's visits by a member of the class of 1881.)

"Former Cadet Booz Dead." *New York Times* 4 Dec. 1900: 1, col. 3.
(Describes family members' grief and cites specific hazing charges.)

"Fort Custer." *Army and Navy Journal* 23 May 1887: 815.
(Soldiers at the army post named for Custer lament their boredom.)

Friedman, Lee M. *Zola and the Dreyfus Case*. Boston: Beacon, 1937.
(Zola wrote the famous "J'accuse" open letter in support of Dreyfus.)

Frost, Richard H. *The Mooney Case*. Stanford: Stanford UP, 1968.
(Describes C.E.S. Wood's defense of labor activist Tom Mooney in the 1916 San Francisco bombing case.)

Gamble, Thomas. "Carter's Death Revives Memories of Noted Case." *Morning News* [Savannah] 24 July 1944: 34.
(A former mayor of Savannah recalls divided opinions in the Carter case.)

Gold, Charles H. "Grant and Mark Twain in Chicago: The 1879 Reunion of the Army of the Tennessee." *Chicago History* 7 (1978): 151–60.
(Contains an interesting discussion of the parallels of the lives of Mark Twain and Grant.)

Goldhurst, Richard. *Pipe Clay and Drill; John J. Pershing: The Classic American Soldier*. New York: Crowell, 1977.
(Devotes attention to Pershing's formative West Point years and their impact on his career.)

Gribben, Alan, and Nick Karonovich, eds. *Overland with Mark Twain*. Elmira, NY: Center for Mark Twain Studies at Quarry Farm, 1992.
(Recounts Mark Twain's visit with C.E.S. Wood in Portland, Oregon, in 1895.)

Guttman, Jon. "Personality: Henry O. Flipper." *Wild West* Feb. 1994: 20–32.
(A synopsis of the controversial life of the first African American graduate of West Point.)

Hancock, H. Irving. *Life at West Point*. New York: Putnam's, 1902.
(Describes the daily routine and course of instruction at West Point at the turn of the century.)

Hersey, Mark Leslie. "Recollections of West Point." Typescript, 21 Mar. 1929, West Point Archives.
(Hersey, a member of the class of 1887, discusses Mark Twain's visit in 1886.)

Hesseltine, William B. *Ulysses S. Grant: Politician*. New York: Dodd, 1935.

(Discusses Grant's financial problems following his two terms as president.)

"House Looks into Hazing." *New York Times* 12 Dec. 1900: 7, col. 1.
(Members of Congress want to conduct their own inquiry into the Booz hazing case.)

Howells, William Dean. *My Mark Twain: Reminiscences and Criticisms.* New York: Harper, 1910.
(One of Mark Twain's closest friends recalls their discussion of the Cadet Whittaker case.)

Inge, M. Thomas. "Daniel Carter Beard." *Mark Twain Encyclopedia* 64.
(An account of the life of the illustrator of *A Connecticut Yankee.*)

Johnson, Virginia Weisel. *The Unregimented General: A Biography of Nelson A. Miles.* New York: Houghton, 1962.
(The famous Indian fighter General Miles, who held a long-standing mistrust of West Pointers, was a friend of Mark Twain's for over thirty years.)

Joughin, Louis, and Edmund M. Morgan. *The Legacy of Sacco and Vanzetti.* 1948. Chicago: Quadrangle, 1964.
(Describes C.E.S. Wood's defense of the famous anarchists.)

King, Charles. "Cadet Life at West Point." *Harper's Magazine* 75 (1887): 196–219.
(King participated in the campaign against the northern Plains Indians with Generals Custer and Merritt.)

Kleeblatt, Norman L., ed. *The Dreyfus Affair.* Berkeley: U of California P, 1987.
(Contains a detailed chronology of events of the Dreyfus case.)

Kruz, Danny. "The 'Spirit Lights' of General Nelson Miles." *Wild West* June 1994: 86–88.
(Miles demonstrated the heliograph communication system to persuade Geronimo and the Apaches to surrender.)

Lanier, Doris. "Mark Twain's Georgia Angel-Fish." *Mark Twain Journal* 24 (1986): 4–16.
(Discusses Mark Twain's attraction to young girls in his later years.)

Long, E. Hudson, and J.R. LeMaster. *The New Mark Twain Handbook.* New York: Garland, 1985.

(Lists critical works on Mark Twain, most of them published before 1957.)

Lorch, Fred W. *The Trouble Begins at Eight: Mark Twain's Lecture Tours.* Ames: Iowa State UP, 1968.

(Reliable version of standard stories such as those in the *Roughing It* lecture.)

Lowell, James Russell. *Letters of James Russell Lowell.* Ed. Charles Eliot Norton. New York: Harper, 1893. 2 vols.

(Mark Twain entered a marginal comment in his copy of Lowell's letters concerning his efforts to obtain a cadetship for his nephew Sammy Moffett.)

MacDonnell, Kevin. Letter to the author. 4 Dec. 1995.

(MacDonnell's copy of Lowell's *Letters* contains marginalia by Mark Twain about West Point.)

McDonough, James L. *Schofield: Union General in the Civil War and Reconstruction.* Tallahassee: Florida State UP, 1972.

(Focuses on Schofield's "reasonably important and competent" execution of his duties as a Union officer.)

McFeely, William S. *Grant: A Biography.* New York: Norton, 1981.

(A good account of Grant's West Point years.)

——. *Yankee Stepfather: General O.O. Howard and the Freedmen.* New Haven: Yale UP, 1968.

(An excellent monograph of Howard's work with the Freedmen's Bureau following the Civil War.)

Machlis, Paul, ed. *Union Catalog of Clemens Letters.* Berkeley: U of California P, 1986.

(The catalog of letters from Mark Twain at the Mark Twain Project.)

——, ed. *Union Catalog of Letters to Clemens.* Berkeley: U of California P, 1992.

(Holdings of letters at the Mark Twain Project, Berkeley.)

Mark Twain Encyclopedia. Ed. J.R. LeMaster and James D. Wilson. New York: Garland, 1993.

(A collection of entries on Mark Twain, his writings, acquaintances, and criticism.)

"Mark Twain on Hazing." *New York Times* 20 Jan. 1901: 1, col. 3.
(Mark Twain speaks out on the Booz hazing case.)

Marszalek, John F. Jr. *Court-Martial: A Black Man in America*. New York: Scribner's, 1972.
(An account of the hazing incident involving Cadet Whittaker and of his subsequent court-martial and dismissal from West Point.)

"Methods at West Point." *New York Times* 13 Jan. 1901: 5, col. 1.
(Superintendent Albert L. Mills testifies before the Booz Congressional Committee.)

"The Military Academy." *Army and Navy Journal* 11 June 1881: 943.
(Recounts the June Week festivities in which Mark Twain participated.)

"The Military Academy." *Army and Navy Journal* 18 June 1881: 955.
(Describes the graduation of the class of 1881 with Mark Twain in attendance.)

Morison, Samuel Eliot, and Henry Steele Commager. *The Growth of the American Republic*. Vol. 2. New York: Oxford UP, 1962. 2 vols.
(Contains an excellent account of corruption at high levels in the Grant administration.)

"National Capital Topics." *New York Times* 23 Mar. 1882: 2, col. 3.
(The charges against Cadet Whittaker at court-martial were dismissed because of the improper introduction of evidence.)

"The Needs of West Point." *New York Times* 8 June 1890: 16, col. 1.
(Discusses the need for the competitive examination of candidates.)

Nevins, Allan. *Frémont: Pathmarker of the West*. New York: Appleton, 1939.
(Frémont was one of Mark Twain's models for General X. in "Which Was the Dream?")

"No Censure in Booz Report." *New York Times* 10 Jan. 1901: 1, col. 6.
(The military court of inquiry finds that Booz's death was not due to hazing.)

Nolan, Charles J. Jr., and David O. Tomlinson. "Mark Twain's Visit to Annapolis." *Mark Twain Journal* 25 (1987): 2–8.

(Mark Twain visited the capital of Maryland as a guest of Governor Warfield and toured the naval academy, where he violated the prohibition against smoking.)

"Oberlin Carter Dies in Chicago." *Morning News* [Savannah] 20 July 1944: 34.

(Obituary recalls events of the Carter case.)

Ooms, Casper W. "Carter: An American Dreyfus." *Illinois Law Review* 43 (1948): 23–39.

(Like Dreyfus, Carter battled the forces of government in an attempt to clear his name.)

Piacente, Steve. "Black Cadet Posthumously Commissioned." *Post and Courier* [Charleston] 13 Mar. 1996: 3-B.

(President Bill Clinton approved a commission as second lieutenant for James Webster Smith, the first black cadet at West Point.)

"A Plebe at West Point." *New York Times* 7 June 1891: 17, col. 5.

(Offers examples of the humorous aspects of hazing.)

"President Upsets His Own Hazing Law." *New York Times* 2 Aug. 1908, sec. 2: 1, col. 7.

(President Theodore Roosevelt reinstated eight upperclassmen at West Point who had severely hazed and hospitalized a fourth classman.)

Purdum, Todd S. "Black Cadet Gets a Posthumous Commission." *New York Times* 25 July 1995: A10.

(Cadet Whittaker received a posthumous commission as a second lieutenant from President Bill Clinton.)

"Put through Their Paces." *New York Times* 14 June 1890: 1, col. 3.

(Describes the medical examination and some humorous hazing of new cadets.)

Rasmussen, R. Kent. *Mark Twain A to Z*. Detroit: Facts on File, 1995.

(A thorough and useful reference to Mark Twain's life and detailed synopses of his major works.)

Reeder, Russell P. Jr. *Heroes and Leaders of West Point*. New York: Nelson, 1970.

(Discusses Mark Twain's 1886 visit to Cadet Pershing's barracks room for informal stories with cadets.)

Rhodes, Charles Dudley. "Intimate Letters of a West Point Cadet." Typescript, 10 June 1935, West Point Archives.

(A member of the class of 1889 recalls Mark Twain's visit of 30 April 1887.)

Riché, Charles Swift. *A Brief History of the Class.* West Point, 1911.

(This commemorative volume is a souvenir of the twenty-fifth anniversary of the graduation of the class of 1886, which enjoyed Mark Twain's visit in April of that year.)

Rorison, Brainard. Letter to C.E.S. Wood. 26 Apr. 1907. Mark Twain Project. The Huntington Library, U of California, Berkeley.

(Rorison requests a copy of *1601* from Wood.)

"The Sale of Cadetships." Editorial. *New York Times* 23 Feb. 1870: 4, col. 2.

(Calls for the expulsion of Congressman Whittemore from Congress for selling his cadetships for money to pay off his campaign debts.)

Schaff, Morris. *The Spirit of Old West Point.* Boston: Houghton, 1907.

(A member of the class of 1862 presents an informative account of the men who left West Point to fight on both sides in the Civil War.)

Schofield, John M. *Forty-Six Years in the Army.* New York: Century, 1897.

(General Schofield complained that his reputation was damaged by the Whittaker hazing scandal.)

"Small Politicians." Editorial. *New York Times* 23 Dec. 1900: 18, col. 4.

(An editorial in support of West Point against the clamor to close the institution.)

Smith, Gordon B. Letter to the author. 18 Jan. 1995.

(Colonel Smith, an attorney at law in Savannah, Georgia, has made a study of the fraud and conspiracy case of Captain Carter.)

Smith, Henry Nash, and William M. Gibson, eds. *Mark Twain– Howells Letters: The Correspondence of Samuel L. Clemens and William D. Howells, 1869–1910.* Cambridge: Harvard UP, 1960. 2 vols.

(William Dean Howells, the "dean of American letters," was the influential editor of *Atlantic Monthly* and Mark Twain's close friend.)

Stark, John D. "Mark Twain and the Chinese." *Mark Twain Journal* 24 (1986): 36.

(A letter from Mark Twain to General Grant reveals his respect and concern for Chinese immigrants in America.)

Tenney, Thomas A. *Mark Twain: A Reference Guide*. Boston: Hall, 1977. (This is an indispensable source for anyone attempting serious scholarship on Mark Twain.)

Turner, Martha Anne. "Mark Twain's *1601* through Fifty Editions." *Mark Twain Journal* 12 (1965): 10–15, 21. (A good account of the publication history of Mark Twain's naughty Elizabethan burlesque.)

Twain, Mark. *Adventures of Huckleberry Finn*. New York: Harper, 1912.

———. *The Adventures of Tom Sawyer*. Berkeley: U of California P, 1980.

———. *Autobiography*. Ed. Albert Bigelow Paine. New York: Harper, 1924. 2 vols.

———. *Collected Tales, Sketches, Speeches, and Essays*. Vol. 1. Ed. Louis J. Budd. New York: Library of America, 1992. 2 vols.

———. *A Connecticut Yankee in King Arthur's Court*. Ed. Barnard L. Stein. Berkeley: U of California P, 1979. (This is the authoritative edition, complete with 221 illustrations by Dan Beard, and explanatory and textual notes.)

———. *Complete Humorous Sketches and Tales*. Ed. Charles Neider. Garden City, NY: Hanover, 1961.

———. *Complete Short Stories*. Ed. Charles Neider. Garden City, NY: Hanover, 1957.

———. *[Date, 1601.] Conversation, as it was by the Social Fireside, in the Time of the Tudors*. Ed. Franklin J. Meine. Mattituck, NY: Amereon House, 1938. (Contains a facsimile of the West Point edition of *1601*.)

———. *The Innocents Abroad*. Vol. 1. New York: Harper, 1911. 2 vols.

———. Letter to William W. Belknap. 28 Aug. 1874. Mark Twain Project. The Huntington Library, U of California, Berkeley.

———. Letter to William W. Belknap. 5 Sept. 1874. Mark Twain Project. The Huntington Library, U of California, Berkeley.

———. Letter to William W. Belknap. 24 Sept. 1874. Mark Twain Project. The Huntington Library, U of California, Berkeley.

———. Letter to G.W. McCrary. 27 Feb. 1877. Mark Twain Project. The Huntington Library, U of California, Berkeley.

———. *Life on the Mississippi*. New York: Harper, 1911.

———. *Literary Essays*. New York: Harper, 1899.

———. *Mark Twain, Business Man*. Ed. Samuel Charles Webster. Boston: Little, 1946.

(Charles L. Webster's son seeks to exonerate his father for Mark Twain's business failures.)

———. *Mark Twain's Aquarium: The Samuel Clemens–Angelfish Correspondence, 1905–1910*. Ed. John R. Cooley. Athens: U of Georgia P, 1991.

(Discusses Mark Twain's attraction to young girls in his later years.)

———. *Mark Twain's Letters*. Ed. Albert Bigelow Paine. New York: Harper, 1917. 2 vols.

———. *Mark Twain's Letters*. Ed. Edgar Marquess Branch et. al. Vol. 1. Berkeley: U of California P, 1988. 4 vols.

———. *Mark Twain's Library of Humor*. New York: Bonanza, 1964.

(Reprint of the 1888 edition published by Charles L. Webster.)

———. *Mark Twain's Notebooks and Journals*. Ed. Frederick Anderson, Lin Salamo, and Bernard L. Stein. Vol. 2. Berkeley: U of California P, 1975. 3 vols.

———. *Mark Twain's Speeches*. Ed. Albert Bigelow Paine. New York: Harper, 1923.

———. *Mark Twain Speaking*. Ed. Paul Fatout. Iowa City: U of Iowa P, 1976.

(A collection of Mark Twain's speeches, lectures, and interviews from 1864 to 1909.)

———. *Pudd'nhead Wilson* and *"Those Extraordinary Twins."* Ed. Sidney E. Berger. New York: Norton, 1980.

———. *The Science Fiction of Mark Twain*. Ed. David Ketterer. Hamden, CT: Archon, 1984.

(Contains the short story "From the 'London Times,' 1904.")

———. *Sketches New and Old*. New York: Harper, 1917.

———. *Susy and Mark Twain: Family Dialogues*. Ed. Edith Colgate Salsbury. New York: Harper, 1965.

(A sampling of letters capturing the affection between Mark Twain in midcareer and his favorite daughter, Susy.)

———. *A Tramp Abroad.* New York: Harper, 1907. 2 vols.

———. *What Is Man? and Other Essays* Ed. Paul Baender. Berkeley: U of California P, 1973.

———. "Which Was the Dream?" *Which Was the Dream? and Other Symbolic Writings of the Later Years.* Ed. John S. Tuckey. Berkeley: U of California P, 1967. 31–73.

("Which Was the Dream?" uses General Grant and West Point as metaphors for noble behavior.)

United States Military Academy. *Post Orders.* West Point Archives. 16 vols. 1838–1904.

Wecter, Dixon. *Mark Twain in Three Moods.* San Marino: Friends of the Huntington Library, 1948.

(Contains a story of Mark Twain as a guest in the home of C.E.S. Wood at West Point.)

"West Point." *Army and Navy Journal* 7 Apr. 1886: 75.

(An account of Mark Twain's visit of 3 April 1886.)

"West Point." *Army and Navy Journal* 23 May 1887: 815.

(An account of Mark Twain's visit of 30 April 1887.)

"The West Point Cadets." *New York Times* 27 Jan. 1887: 2, col. 4.

(Discusses the need for competitive examination for entrance.)

"The West Point Inquiry." *New York Times* 23 Dec. 1900: 6, col. 1.

(Cadets who were sons of the rich and famous were likely to receive more intensive hazing than cadets of more humble birth.)

"The Whittaker Court-Martial." *Army and Navy Journal* 11 June 1881: 935.

(Recounts the prosecution's closing argument in the court-martial of Cadet Whittaker.)

Wood, Charles Erskine Scott. *The Collected Poems of Charles Erskine Scott Wood.* New York: Vanguard, 1949.

(A collection of Wood's best works, including "The Poet in the Desert.")

———. *Heavenly Discourse.* New York: Vanguard, 1927.

(A collection of satiric dialogues in which Mark Twain is a participant along with other historic figures.)

——. Letter to Brainard Rorison. c. 26 Apr. 1907. Mark Twain Project. The Huntington Library, U of California, Berkeley.

(Wood penned a brief reply to Rorison's letter to him of 26 April 1907).

——. Letter to Lieutenant Colonel E.E. Farman. 31 Dec. 1939. West Point Archives.

(Wood discusses his role in the printing of *1601*.)

——. "The Surrender of Joseph." *Harper's Weekly* 17 Nov. 1877: 906.

(Wood's eyewitness account inflates General Howard's role in Chief Joseph's surrender.)

INDEX

imprimerie gagné ltée